FIRE from the FLINT

FIRE from the FLINT

The Amazing Careers of THOMAS DIXON

BY RAYMOND ALLEN COOK

JOHN F. BLAIR, *Publisher*
Winston-Salem, North Carolina

Library of Congress Catalog Card Number: 67-30728

Printed in the United States of America
by HERITAGE PRINTERS, Inc.
Charlotte, North Carolina

To Katrina, whose little hands smeared many a page

Foreword

PROUD, HUMBLE; CONTENTIOUS, CONCILIATORY; ABUSIVE, charming; grasping, generous; vindictive, forgiving; liberal, reactionary; versatile, narrow—these are but a few of the contradictory terms that may be applied to one of the most controversial and paradoxical figures in American culture. Born in obscurity, this man became familiar to millions of people, but by the time of his death he was virtually forgotten. Reared in poverty, he rose to great wealth, only to die bankrupt. He was a prolific and famous novelist of the Civil War and Reconstruction periods, who said his aim was to reconcile the North and South, but his books and the plays and motion pictures made from them created bitter controversy and dissension. The praise of the original Ku Klux Klan in his works may have had a strong influence on the growth of the resurrected Klans of the 1920's, yet he was the bitter and uncompromising foe of the "renegade Klans," as he called them. Strongly biased against the Negro, he ironically became one of the forces that drove the Negro to militant demands for equality. Phenomenally successful in almost everything to which he gave his attention, he was relentlessly pursued by the incubus of inadequacy and dissatisfaction. He was a man who talked and wrote of the virtues of stability and tradition, yet he was always trying to project himself over new and untried horizons. Beginning his career as an agnostic, he became one of the most famous preachers of his day, only to withdraw later from the ministry. In his books and lectures he denounced the evils of urban life, yet he lived the major portion of his adult life in New York City. A strong Democrat for fifty years, he was an ardent supporter of, and speaker for, Roosevelt's New Deal; but he later opposed the Roosevelt administration and campaigned vigorously against it. Called almost every name imaginable by his enemies, he was known as the soul of charm by his supporters. Denounced in the twenties by many critics as a prophet of doom in his denunciations of Communism, he left some remarkably prophetic statements about the dangers of that growing social order. Laughed at by the agents, who considered his scenarios so much "historical beeswax," he finally was instrumental in convincing the world that the motion picture was an art form more compelling than anything previously known in the history of mankind.

He was a full-fledged plowhand at ten years of age, and though he had almost no schooling before he was thirteen, he applied himself so closely to his books that by his fifteenth year he was well grounded in mathematics, geometry, Latin, and Greek and was ready to enter college. After a school career in which he won the highest awards ever achieved at his institution and earned both a bachelor's degree and a master's degree in four years, he went on to be elected to the state legislature before he was old enough to vote.

Sometimes vain and dogmatic, he pushed everything aside to achieve his ambitions, yet when he had been dealt fortune's heaviest blows, he rapidly recovered without bitterness or despair and accepted his situation with equanimity and the determination to make his loss serve as a step to higher achievement. He is hardly listed in current biographical references, and with one or two minor exceptions, writers of American history ignore him completely. Yet he was one of the most colorful, influential, dynamic, and amazing figures of his time. He is today unknown to 99 per cent of our present population, but in his famous careers as lawyer, legislator, preacher, lecturer, playwright, actor, novelist, motion picture producer, and real estate entrepreneur, he has had a pervasive influence upon several major aspects of our culture.

His name is Thomas Dixon.

How is this remarkable man to be accounted for? From what matrix was he formed? What implications for society does a man like Thomas Dixon provide? As an extraordinary instance of human nature, what made him tick? To trace the development of his careers and to seek the answers to these questions is the purpose of this book.

I should like to acknowledge the aid and facilities provided for the research going into this book by the staffs of the Widener Library, Harvard University; the departments of the Library of Congress; Johns Hopkins University; Duke University; the University of North Carolina; Wake Forest University; Gardner-Webb College; and Emory University. I also wish to thank the numerous persons who have directed to me incidental bits of information in their possession. To Professors Kenneth M. England and Paul G. Blount of Georgia State College and Professor Robert W. Hays of Southern Technical Institute I want to express my indebtedness for their excellent suggestions and help in the preparation of the manuscript. Mrs. Clara Dixon Richardson, niece of Thomas Dixon, by making available the voluminous records of the Dixon family, made possible the inclusion of many pieces of human interest in Dixon's life.

RAYMOND A. COOK

Valdosta State College
September 12, 1968

Contents

Illustrations

At length I feel my head to ache,
My fingers itch, and burn to take
Some new employment; I begin
To swell and foam and fret within.

HENRY VAUGHAN ("the Silurist"),
Silex Scintillans [often called *Fire from the Flint*], Newton-by-Usk, 1650

~

"A hell of restlessness
I have drained, drained."

THOMAS DIXON, in a poem to
Harriet Bussey, July 22, 1885

FIRE from the FLINT

I

Antecedents

The late spring of 1863 saw the whole Confederacy breaking at the seams. Admiral Farragut had captured New Orleans and Memphis, clearing the Mississippi to its source, and Grant was laying siege to the last Confederate stronghold at Vicksburg. With the Confederacy cut in half, the state of Arkansas was in immediate danger of occupation by Union forces. Realizing the precarious position of himself and his family, Thomas Dixon, Sr., a well-to-do planter and Baptist preacher who had moved from North Carolina to Arkansas at the outbreak of the war, knew that if he were to save his old home and his wife's inheritance, he must return to North Carolina with all possible haste.

Thomas Dixon, Sr., had always been a serious man of independent thought. He had been only eighteen years old when his father, David Dixon, died, apparently from complications brought on by heavy drinking. The son attributed his lack of formal schooling to the fact that he had had to assume the burden of supporting the family left by his father. Throughout adult life Thomas Dixon, Sr., had two great passions—an undying hatred of liquor and a pathetic worship of higher education.

During the first half of his life in Cleveland County, North Carolina, Mr. Dixon had been a student of three books only—the Bible, *Pilgrim's Progress*, and *Spurgeon's Sermons*; and his conviction that a minister should get down immediately to the basic truths of the Scripture is well revealed in his ordination charge to an aspiring young preacher. Mr. Dixon was preceded by two rather long-winded ministers. When they had finally finished, he arose and charged the young man in these words: "My brother, preach the Word, the whole Word, and nothing but the Word";[1] whereupon he returned to his seat and sat down.

As a young preacher, Mr. Dixon was invited into many of the homes of the surrounding area. Among them was the home of Abner McAfee, a prosperous planter of York County, South Carolina. In the family of three girls and two boys Mr. Dixon's serious attention was taken by Amanda Elvira, a full-blown girl of thirteen. Soon a romance blossomed, and after considerable persuasion on the part of the young preacher, Abner McAfee consented to the marriage of his daughter, barely in her teens, to the determined suitor, now twenty-seven years of age.

At the time of his marriage, Mr. Dixon, a pastor of four churches, drew crowds large for his rural area whenever he preached. Completely devoted to the matter of soul-winning, it was his custom to start singing a hymn in a loud voice the moment he alighted from his horse in the churchyard. Bearing the refrain in deep, rich tones as he entered the door of the church, he would motion to his congregation to join him, until the little church was resounding in song. The effect of his sermons was profound, even devastating, upon his hearers, for on many occasions people known in the community as "hardened sinners" would groan and cry aloud for salvation.

During the foreboding period that preceded the outbreak of the War Between the States, Mr. Dixon passionately urged his congregations to do everything in their power to maintain the union of the states, for he realized that the South's salvation lay only in the direction of careful, temperate reasoning in the dark days ahead. But when hostilities broke out in Charleston Harbor on January 9, 1861, Mr. Dixon's appeals, along with those of many other sane, far-sighted men, were swept aside like chaff in the whirlwind of war.

In the turbulent months preceding the formal declarations of war, Mr. Dixon decided to move westward to comparatively safer regions. One morning before daylight, in the spring of 1861, with his wife, two children, thirty-two slaves, and a cavalcade of covered wagons, he left his home at Shelby for a settlement near Little Rock, in the state of Arkansas.

The peace and further prosperity that he had expected in his new home, however, were not forthcoming. The earth was hard and unyielding; every few days brought news of the darkening picture of the war. Amanda, though she said little, could scarcely conceal her homesickness and fear. By 1863 she had already lost three children in their infancy, and she dwelt upon the possibility of losing her eight-year-old son Clarence.[2] The settlement near Little

Rock was remote, and professional medical care was not to be found. Most of all, Amanda held a nameless dread of giving birth to a newly-expected child so far from relatives in North Carolina. As the weeks progressed, Mr. Dixon learned that General Grant was now in possession of Tennessee and the Mississippi River and that General Sherman was in command of all the troops at Memphis. Added to these disquieting facts was the news that General Steele had just been appointed commander of the Department of Arkansas and was planning to take up immediate quarters in Little Rock. It at last became obvious to Mr. Dixon that it would be impossible to remain longer in safety, so he began preparations for the long journey homeward.

The move back to his native state, however, presented many difficulties. The region through which the Dixon family would have to travel lay between the opposing armies, through a land now swarming with thieves and deserters from both sides of the conflict. There was also the problem of moving such a large family group for so great a distance. Though the Dixons had thirty-two slaves, whose number would hamper greatly the speed of the return journey, Mr. Dixon refused an offer of one hundred thousand dollars in gold, stating that he would never sell a slave. Never an advocate of slavery, he felt embarrassment at owning the slaves, whom his wife Amanda had recently inherited from her father. The idea of selling them to be possibly mistreated by other masters was unthinkable to him.

The road upon which the Dixons had traveled to Arkansas was now closed by the Union armies, but, winding slowly to the southeast, the group moved into Alabama, then into Georgia and South Carolina. Early in September, nearly three and a half months after leaving Arkansas and after traversing nearly a thousand miles of byways and back roads away from enemy forces, the wagon train drew up at Mr. Dixon's birthplace, the Hambright home at King's Mountain, North Carolina. Inquiring among the neighboring families, Mr. Dixon learned that about nine miles from Shelby, on the road to Marion, a substantial old house called the "Allen Place" was for sale. Here, late in September, 1863, he settled his family after the long journey. By this time, General Sherman's army had swept over the wagon trails that the Dixons had left behind, Chattanooga and Knoxville had fallen, and the savage battle of Chickamauga had been fought.

On January 11, 1864, Montgomery Blair, a member of President Lincoln's cabinet, secretly entered Richmond, Virginia, in an effort to open tentative peace negotiations with the South. The end of the long, bitter struggle was now definitely in the making. That same night, during the last throes of the war, Amanda Dixon gave birth to a son, Thomas Dixon, Jr., in the farmhouse near Shelby.

II

"This Strange World of Poisoned Air"

The old Allen Place was on the main road from Virginia to the deep South, and when the war was over, thousands of weary, hungry soldiers, by day and by night, trudged the powdery road by the farm on their way homeward. The last months of the war had brought the South to her knees, and many families were confronted by the specter of famine. Coffee was now selling at forty dollars a pound, flour at five hundred dollars a barrel, and potatoes at thirty dollars a bushel.[1] The Dixon family was no exception to the poverty now in the land, and as the soldiers came by, day after day, begging for food, the situation for the Dixons became desperate indeed. Sometimes well over a hundred soldiers in a day would be welcomed to whatever poor fare the family could provide.

Until the end of the war the slaves had remained with

the Dixons, planting and working the crops, but with the return of peace, the elder Thomas Dixon was forced to give up nearly all of his laborers, for cash payment in wages was now impossible. "Aunt Barbara," an old slave who had been with the family for several decades, remained, however, until her death a few years afterward. Aunt Barbara had been taught to read and was a close student of the Scriptures. So thoroughly had she assimilated the idiom of the King James Bible that her speech possessed a remarkable flavor of the early seventeenth century, and she spoke with no trace of the Negro dialect common to her fellow slaves. Her influence had a great part in bringing about the spiritual awakening of young Thomas Dixon some years afterward.

The freeing of the slaves left a strong impression upon Clarence, Thomas' older brother, who said many years later:

> I shall never forget the day when father called the slaves about him, and with the Emancipation Proclamation of Abraham Lincoln in his hand, read it, and told them they were free; they could now go where they pleased. There was no hilarity; they smiled, but they did not shout. There was a sense of newness and responsibility that bewildered them.
>
> . . . .
>
> It was a pathetic occasion when father told the slaves they were free. But the most pathetic part was nearly a year afterwards when they sent a committee to beg father to take them back on to the plantation on the old terms, and look after them as he had done before.[2]

Of course, the poverty-stricken Mr. Dixon could not see means of supporting his own family, to say nothing of the numerous Negro families now asking aid.

In the fall of 1865, the Dixons, now stripped of all their possessions, not knowing how or where to find the necessities of life from day to day, and faced with the prospect of no harvest because of a lack of laborers to till the soil, gave up the farm and moved to an old-fashioned white house facing the public square in Shelby. When the elder Dixon had first moved from Arkansas to the Allen Place, he had secretly buried one hundred dollars in gold in a secluded spot near the farmhouse against the day when he knew he would have nothing else. That day had now arrived, and he dug up the money and opened a little general store adjoining the house in Shelby. By hard work and very close budgeting, he managed somehow to hold the family together. Although he had resumed preaching, he now received little or nothing from his charges, for his parishioners were as destitute as he.

Then came the terrors of Reconstruction. The young Thomas Dixon was never to forget the impressions he received during this chaotic period, for he was to say over three quarters of a century later: "The dawn of my conscious life begins in this strange world of poisoned air. My first memories still vibrate with its tense excitement."[3]

When Lincoln was assassinated, the most powerful political figure among the Northern leaders was Thaddeus Stevens, whose complex character has puzzled later critics of the Reconstruction period. Previous to the war, Stevens had held little regard for the South, and when Lee's forces burned his ironworks in Pennsylvania, Stevens' determination to subjugate the South became almost an obsession. After the war, he envisioned the South as a conquered land with no rights, and he was determined to subject the defeated white population to his demands for Negro privilege and suffrage. To a people who had recently thought of the Negro as a slave only, the plan of Stevens was utterly repugnant. The two main instruments by which Stevens hoped to bring about the subjugation were the "Union League" and the "Freedmen's Bureau." The official title of the "Freedmen's Bureau" was the "Bureau of Freedmen, Refugees and Abandoned Lands." Signs bearing this title hung in thousands of towns and hamlets throughout the desolated land. Stevens planned to confiscate the farms of the South and give them to the Negroes. By offering food, clothing, and free land, the agents hoped to induce the poverty-stricken Negro to cease working for the white man.

In the fall of 1866 and throughout the next year, many men from the Union Leagues of Philadelphia and New York filtered through the Negro population, sowing discontent. The Leagues had become bitterly divided in their loyalties and goals by the end of the war. Now, in an effort to consolidate their party, they were seeking the Negro vote in the South. The agents of the Leagues wandered about the plantations, seeking the Negro in field and cabin, promising him preposterous wealth and privilege if he would turn against his white neighbor and vote himself free of the white man's restraint. Unscrupulous agents took advantage of the ignorant, illiterate Negro populace, often inciting it to acts of treachery and violence. The enmity, fear, and distrust thus aroused between the white and Negro populations resulted in a reign of terror that is still remembered as one of the darkest periods in American history. Deeds of violence became common, and no one slept easily in a land that might at any moment break into complete revolution. Laws and courts were contemptuously disregarded by a people who lived in constant fear.

Out of these terrible conditions arose the dreaded secret society called the Ku Klux Klan, which spread rapidly over the South and inspired terror in the heart of the black man and the "carpetbagger." Playing upon the superstitious beliefs of the ignorant Negroes, the Ku Klux Klan, by secret signs, symbols, and hooded masks, wrought its retributive measures under cover of darkness and intimidated its terrified victims into a docility that finally enabled the white Southerners to regain control of the governments of their respective states.

During the turmoil of Reconstruction, Thomas Dixon as a young boy accompanied his uncle, Colonel Lee Roy McAfee,[4] to a session of the state legislature in Columbia, South Carolina. Dixon, in later years, spoke of the lasting effect upon him of the desolation of the city. Remembering the vivid impressions of those days, he said:

> Columbia was a mass of ruins. Intellectuals of the college faculty, in rags, were supplied with clothing by a charity organization. Women and children who had been used to luxury were begging from door to door.[5]

This same session of the legislature was recorded by Dixon as being composed of "ninety-four Negroes, seven native scalawags [Republicans], and twenty-three white men,"[6] a description amusingly significant of Dixon's Southern cast of mind.

The turbulent air was so filled with such words as "carpetbaggers," "scalawags," and "radicals" that little Thomas, listening to his elders with childish half-understanding, sometimes delivered his own views in terms that horrified his parents. On one occasion, when asked by an adult what he planned to be when he grew up, he promptly answered: "I'm going to be a Gawddam Pussecuter"[7] [prosecuting attorney], a term he had evidently overheard in the town square. Oddly enough, there was an element of prophecy in the childish remark, for all of Dixon's later legal cases were for the prosecution.

Through all the dark, uncertain days of the period, young Thomas Dixon was profoundly impressed by the violence he saw about him. His first experience with the Ku Klux Klan was one he never forgot. Upon being awakened by horses' hooves pounding outside the bedroom walls, he jumped from his bed and ran to the window:

> I looked and my heart stopped beating for a moment in amazement that deepened into a panic of terror. A procession of horsemen were passing within twenty feet of our windows, both horse and rider clothed in flowing white robes. . . . Not a sound came from the white ghostly lines save the steady thump of horses' hooves on the hard ground. The men all wore white spiked helmets, some of them with silver spangles and tassels glittering weirdly in the moonlight. It was a strange, terrifying spectacle.[8]

The corruption of the Reconstruction period can scarcely be exaggerated. Dixon said in his old age, "We are too close to realize the tragedy. The scholar and historian must have the perspective of more than a hundred years in which to tell this story to make it credible."[9] Unscrupulous political leaders, interested only in the wealth they could obtain from the disrupted government of the South, aroused antagonisms that never died among those who experienced the terrible years after the Civil War. Instead of following the conciliatory measures for remolding the nation as laid down by President Lincoln, many corrupt leaders sought means to give vent to the hatreds that had been aroused by the war. William G. Brownlow, better known as "Parson

Brownlow," a preacher who became Governor of Tennessee during the Reconstruction era, had declared in a speech to a convention in New York in 1862:

> If I had the power, I would arm every wolf, panther, catamount and bear in the mountains of America, every crocodile in the swamps of Florida, every Negro in the South, every fiend in hell, clothe them in the uniforms of the Federal army and turn them loose on the rebels of the South and exterminate every man, woman and child south of the Mason Dixon line. I would like to see especially the Negro troops, marching under Ben Butler, crowd the last rebel into the Gulf of Mexico and drown them as the Devil did the hogs in the Sea of Galilee.[10]

Such fanaticism from influential leaders was not conducive to soothing the wounds of the war. In Dixon's native state, North Carolina, as a result of proceedings brought by Dixon's uncle, Colonel McAfee, William W. Holden became the first governor to be impeached in an American commonwealth when his corrupt practices could no longer be borne by the people.

Many sane, responsible men, such as Dixon's father and Colonel McAfee, took part in the Ku Klux Klan in an effort to bring some sort of order out of the tragedy of Reconstruction. These men did not tolerate injustice, and when they saw that the Klan had served its purpose, they immediately wanted to disband it. However, the secret nature of the society's actions made it possible for irresponsible and disreputable persons to commit unjust acts under the apparent aegis of the original Ku Klux Klan, and eventually it came under the leadership of men who have made it a trademark of evil to later generations. These men planted the seeds of violence and brutality that saw the terrible blossoming of the "resurrected Klans" of the twentieth century.

In later years, Dixon wondered how any person could have lived through Reconstruction and still have retained his sanity. Lawlessness was, for a period of many months, the rule rather than the exception. On one occasion young Thomas accompanied his father and his older brother Clarence to a trial involving the Adairs, a family of criminal desperadoes. The Adairs had become angered at Silas Weston, a farmer, because he had said that he was going to inform the authorities of their illicit whiskey dealings. They planned to kill Weston, his mulatto wife, and all his family and place the blame on the Ku Klux Klan, which they knew forbade miscegenation. They killed Weston and the rest of his family except his wife, who miraculously survived terrible injuries and dragged herself to the home of friends. In a period when both the opposing forces of Reconstruction frequently winked at injustice in their ranks, this crime was so shockingly brutal that it could not be overlooked. The Adairs were held without bail, quickly tried, and executed.

The tragedies of Reconstruction left many vivid impressions upon the mind of young Dixon. Tragedy, however, can be only a wavering, uncertain sentiment to a young boy when Christmas is coming on. Though Santa Claus was almost in rags in those days, the romance of his visit vastly excited young Dixon, and the two weeks before Christmas, 1870, were filled with visions of stuffed stockings and hidden sweets.

But Dixon's eager expectation of Christmas Day was saddened by an accident encountered by his four-year-old brother Frank. While riding in a wagon, Frank lost his footing and fell to the ground, dislocating his hip.[11] His leg and hip became greatly swollen, and he tossed in agony as the family tried to comfort him. The sight of so much pain awed and frightened Thomas, and when he went into the room where Frank lay, he seemed scarcely to recognize the brother who only a short time before had been laughing and playing about the house. Gradually the swelling subsided, but permanent injury had been done, and Frank was to walk upon crutches for the rest of his life.

By 1872 the Dixon family was living upon the verge of poverty. Eight-year-old Thomas longingly gazed at the candies in the store windows, but the luxury of a sweetmeat was reserved for rare occasions. The miracle "ice cream" had just been introduced to Shelby through the medium of an old hand freezer operated by "John the Barber." Whenever John's loud, clear voice rang through the town square announcing the delicacy, Thomas could hardly suppress the memory of the dish of ice cream he had enjoyed weeks before. Finally, he decided that he had a right to take fifty cents from the cash drawer of the store as "wages" for sweeping the floor and digging the slimy salt mackerel out of the fish barrel. Awaiting the opportunity, he slipped a fifty-cent piece of paper money, called a "shinplaster," from the drawer and triumphantly ran out to seek the ice cream wheelbarrow of John the Barber. Since the price of the cream was ten cents a dish, young Dixon had dreams of filling himself with five delicious helpings. To his great disappointment, the ice cream man had been unable to get any ice that day. Not wanting to waste the fifty-cent piece, Thomas spent all his wealth on cookies, which he stuffed into his shirt and pockets. The bulges in his clothing made it impossible for him to escape undetected by his mother. After being forced to return every cookie to the store, he was lectured at length on the evils of theft. He

The Birthplace of Thomas Dixon near Shelby, North Carolina

New Prospect Church near Shelby, North Carolina
Obelisk in background marks grave of Thomas and Amanda Dixon

Thomas Dixon, Sr., Age 86

came to the evening meal chastened by his recent slip from virtue, only to find that his mother had baked for him a delicious cake with hard sauce. Even more impressed by the sacrifice his mother had made in using their slender resources of food than he had been by the lecture, Thomas resolved never again to beg for things that he knew his family could not afford.

But all was not poverty and terror in young Dixon's life. The town was alive with activities dear to a boy's heart. Frequently, great droves of mules were driven through Shelby on their way to farmers throughout the state. Thomas eagerly looked forward to the arrival of the mules, and he considered it a great honor to be allowed to water and "guard" them while the drivers were resting or eating. From this early association he acquired a lifelong love for the much maligned animals, which he praised extravagantly in later years:

> I wish to enter a defense of mules. The mule is the most patient and efficient work animal that walks the earth today or has ever walked its roads. And their love and loyalty to a master who treats them well is as great as their patience and common sense.[12]

One of the brightest periods in Thomas' childhood began on the day when a little Negro boy, bloody, unconscious, and almost dead, was brought to the home of the Dixons. The boy's father, in a drunken fit, had tried to kill him with an axe. Several days later, when the little fellow was conscious enough to speak again, he looked long at young Thomas with big, questioning eyes; then he spoke: "I wants ya Pa ter keep me. De Bureau kin bind me. Dey do dat fer a lot o' little niggers now. Will ya ax him to?"[13] Thomas spoke to his father about the matter, the papers were drawn up, and from that day forward young Dixon and little Dick were inseparable companions. Thomas loved his playmate devotedly. Dick was a sprightly, effervescent child, a veritable Puck in ebony, who enthusiastically followed the leadership of his friend. Together they climbed the hills, ran after bees and butterflies, climbed into the dark lofts of barns and peered into birds' nests, and lost themselves in a make-believe world far removed from the tragedy about them.

Thomas admired the proud, fiery spirit of little Dick, who vowed that he would run away if anyone ever whipped him. Thomas fully believed his playmate and dreaded the day when Dick's impishness would involve him in trouble. That day finally arrived. One steaming Sunday afternoon Dick accompanied several of the Negro families to a local church where "Uncle Josh" was preaching a fiery sermon on the fate of sinners. Frequently shouting in a loud voice for the Lord to send his fires of destruction upon those who would not heed the call, Uncle Josh became more and more enthusiastic in his oratory. As the sermon progressed, Dick, who had found a seat near the window of the gallery, proceeded to amuse himself by focusing the hot sun's rays upon the straw on the seats with a magnifying glass which Thomas had given him the day before. At a particularly dramatic moment, when Uncle Josh seemed to be significantly awaiting the fiery destruction which he had been calling from above, the straw burst into flame. The first person to see the fire shouted that destruction was at hand; the congregation rose screaming, knocking over benches and chairs in frantic efforts to leave the church by window or door, whichever proved to be the nearer exit. Once outside, several members of the congregation regained enough presence of mind to rush back into the church and extinguish the flames. Fortunately, little harm was done, but Uncle Josh vowed that he would punish Dick, who had made himself conspicuously absent by this time. The next day, after catching Dick in an unguarded moment, Uncle Josh made good his word by thrashing the boy with considerable energy. When Uncle Josh had completed the punishment, the defiant boy forced a laugh and retorted: "I think a flea musta bit me. Mebbe hit wuz a chigger."[14] The day after the whipping, Dick drooped about the house, dejected in spirit. The next morning he was nowhere to be found, nor the next. As the days lengthened into weeks, Thomas began to face the saddening reality that his friend would not return. Often at dusk, Thomas, with a lump in his throat, would watch from the hill on the road that led into South Carolina for the sprightly little figure, but the boy never came back. Years later Dixon heard that Dick had been hanged, but he could not believe that the unquenchable spirit of little Dick was stilled. Nearly three quarters of a century later, Dixon recalled the playmate of his childhood with nostalgic tenderness.

The idol of Dixon's boyhood was his mother's brother, Colonel McAfee. Colonel McAfee had been wounded several times in the war; he had risen to the rank of colonel at twenty-five years of age and had distinguished himself for many acts of bravery. He had been graduated with first honors from the University of North Carolina in 1859 in the commencement at which James Buchanan, President of the United States at the time, delivered the principal address. After the war was over, Colonel McAfee had established a law office in Shelby. Young Thomas Dixon asked no greater glory than to have the job of sweeping out his uncle's office, running errands for him, and basking in the warmth of his renown. A tall, handsome man with flowing beard, Lee Roy McAfee was the Southern ideal of chivalry and bravery, which endeared him to his friends. When he died at twenty-nine from tuberculosis, probably contracted during the war, hundreds of people, some walking as far as twenty-five miles, came to his funeral.

The disrupted economy of the South made it more and more difficult for Dixon's father to support the family by storekeeping and preaching. To complicate the situation further, the house burned shortly after Amanda had given birth to a daughter, Delia. Faced by the possibility of starving, the elder Dixon gathered up his few belongings, and on Christmas Eve, 1872—doubly cold and bleak for a family who had little to look forward to for Christmas—the Dixons moved to a farm on Buffalo Creek, about six miles from Shelby. The move to Buffalo Farm was only a desperate remedy, for the land was heavily burdened by taxes that the elder Dixon had little hope of paying. The family now numbered six, and only one son was available for heavy work. Clarence, or A. C. as he was sometimes called, was now at Wake Forest College, for the elder Dixon was determined that his children should go to college whatever the sacrifice. Frank, two years younger than Thomas, was unable to help because of the leg injury he had received. Thus, at the age of nine, Thomas found much responsibility thrust upon him, and the following year he became a full-time plowhand. But the "honor" of handling the plow soon palled as the long half-mile rows of bottom land stretched endlessly before him. "Often," he said in later years, "I'd . . . think of the long days and weeks and months of it with a sickening sense of doom."[15] Month after month he arose before daylight in constant disbelief that nights could pass so quickly or that days could be so long. Dixon in maturity frequently repeated a conviction he had acquired in childhood that a heavy routine of unremitting farm labor dehumanizes mankind.

A gregarious and communicative boy, young Dixon was most affected by the isolation of his daily labors. During this period on the farm, the Dixon family received little mail, and so foreign was an occasional newspaper to their grim world that the paper usually lay unread. The elder Dixon's nightly reading from the family Bible was the only continuing source of inspiration from the written word.

On rare occasions Thomas was permitted to escape from the monotony of his labors to accompany Hosea Norman, a powerful, strapping young animal of a man, on coon-hunting expeditions. "Hose" had a remarkable dog named Napoleon Bonaparte. According to Hose, the intelligence and courage of "Old Boney" far exceeded that of his famous namesake. Old Boney would bark, dig, and bite his way into a den full of raccoons that the ordinary dog would not dare enter. But even the excitement of following Old Boney ended when young Dixon became sickened at the sight of four beautiful gray raccoons and a dog torn to death in a desperate battle that lasted several hours.

Hosea Norman was also to be young Dixon's instructor in undertakings other than raccoon hunting. In the second year of the family's stay at Buffalo Creek Farm, when Thomas was eleven years old, Hose asked him early one evening if he didn't want to go "gallin' " with him that night. Not fully understanding the invitation but eager to escape for a little while the monotony of farm work, Thomas answered "yes" without hesitation. On the Dixon farm there were three sharecropping tenants, one of whom had three sons and two plump, comely daughters, who seemed to be able to stand the back-breaking farm labor even better than did the boys. The girls slept in one end of the house, and the father and mother in the other. The boys had a room in the attic, which they reached by ladder. When night came and the Dixon family had gone to bed, young Thomas slipped out the back door and followed Hosea to the end of the tenant's house where the two girls slept. Dixon's experience is best told in his own words as he recalled the evening years later:

I drew myself erect in spite of a long day's work, squared my shoulders and passed into the house after Hose. They greeted us with giggles. We sat down before the open fireplace, Hose between the two girls, while I edged off into the corner.

Hose hugged and kissed first one and then the other, and I watched with as much dignity as I could command. We heard the old folks drop their shoes and crawl into bed. Pretty soon one of them began to snore and the moment the sound was heard, Hose led one of the girls into the far shadows of the room where a bed stood.

The other one held out both arms to me and said: "Come over here and talk to me."

I was scared but made up my mind I wouldn't be a coward, so I walked over and she drew me into her lap. She had pretty blue eyes and blonde hair. When she kissed me I didn't object. She was a jolly bundle of soft flesh, and I rather enjoyed my seat as she squeezed me and told me what a fine big boy I was getting to be.

She asked me to kiss her and I did as a matter of accommodation and good fellowship purely. She was content and let it go at that. She talked with me in a quiet, nice way, and I asked her how her crops were getting on and if she thought the grass in the cotton would give them much trouble.

I finally became conscious that she was glancing over her

shoulder in the direction taken by Hose and her sister, and I slipped out of her lap and got back into my chair. I had hardly taken my seat when her sister appeared in the firelight smiling at me, and the one I had been talking to slipped back into the shadows.

The other girl did not honor me with any attentions except polite conversation, and I was considerably relieved.

In half an hour Hose and the other girl drew up to the fire and all four of us passed a few polite remarks and the party broke up.[16]

Thus young Thomas, who, at the age of ten, had had thrust upon him the responsibilities of a full-time plowhand, now found himself at eleven introduced to the mysteries of "gallin'." Later in the year, even before the crops were "laid by," Thomas heard that the tenant with the two buxom daughters had been given notice by the elder Dixon to find another place. Mr. Dixon, who did not tolerate moral laxity among his tenants and who had heard rumors floating about the neighborhood, lectured Hose severely and gave him fair warning of what would happen to him in the future if he did not live up to what was expected of him.

A spirited counterpart to the intrepid Hose was Wash Hogue, a Negro workman, who was remarkably addicted to profanity, the use of which in his presence the elder Dixon sternly forbade. One afternoon, when the wagon had been loaded in the field with fodder for the barn, the horse rebelled at what he considered to be too large a burden. A heavy thunderstorm was in the making, and despite the frantic efforts of Mr. Dixon, the animal would not budge. Several other workers in the field tried to threaten, cajole, or whip the horse into motion, but to no avail. Finally, Wash told the elder Dixon that he believed he could make the horse move but that first Mr. Dixon must promise not to scold him for his method. As the thunder rumbled ominously overhead, Mr. Dixon, in some desperation, consented; whereupon Wash let loose a stream of colorful epithets that fairly staggered the horse. A tremor went over the animal's frame; he stiffened convulsively, laid his ears back, and plunged forward. Taking the hill at a gallop, he swept into the barn in time to save the fodder from the cloudburst which followed a few moments later. The next week Mr. Dixon sold the horse, saying that he would not keep a beast that could be moved only by profanity.

As the days wore on, the deadly monotony of the heavy farm labor, month after month, provoked Thomas to cudgel his brain for ways to get some fun out of the brutalizing tasks, but he had little success. He and the other two plowmen spent two weeks breaking up an enormous piece of new ground exasperatingly filled with roots, rocks, and stumps. Before the crop was laid by, the field would have to receive five such plowings. As the young boy wearily reached the end of one row and turned his mule around, he seemed to see in the half-mile rows still ahead his whole future existence leading down an apparently endless pathway of depressing, hideous, soul-destroying toil. Wearied beyond expression at the end of the day, he fell into bed heavily, unconsciously, grotesquely, like a stalled ox. Days and weeks went by without making young Dixon aware of their passage. He took little interest in his surroundings, and in his deep-set eyes could be seen a distant, irreconcilable bitterness at the trick life had played upon him. Moroseness and belligerency contended in his nature, and the examples of hard labor set by those around him had little effect in relieving the feeling that he lived under a special kind of injustice.

Then a wonderful thing happened. Clarence came home for the summer vacation from Wake Forest College and brought with him his college friend, a remarkable young man named Dick Vann. Thomas had never seen such a happy, spirited boy as Vann and within a few days was captivated by his charm. What most impressed Thomas was that, in spite of having lost both hands as a little boy while feeding a cane mill, Vann could do almost anything a normal boy could do except dress and undress himself completely. By an ingenious system of holding his knife and fork in the crook of his elbow and applying the proper leverage, he could feed himself with hardly any trouble. Vann had developed a way of pulling the trigger of a gun and was an expert marksman. As Thomas in amazement watched the handicapped Vann going about his daily routine, happy and laughing, his own troubles seemed small and selfish ones indeed. He felt ashamed of himself at having been so concerned with his own interests that he could not see the problems of others. He determined that henceforth he would try to follow the example set by young Vann. In looking back, Dixon in old age commented that Dick Vann was one of the great influences of his life:

> When I thought of his tragedy, my own seemed a small thing. I wondered at his unfailing cheerfulness, his wit, his brilliant mind. He helped me over a dark and dangerous crisis of spirit. He radiated tenderness, good fellowship, faith and a boundless joy of living. And he graduated from Wake Forest College, became a great preacher and college president, after marrying happily and raising a family of children.
>
> In dark hours this man has always been an inspiration to me as he has been to thousands.[17]

On Sundays Dixon's father preached at one or more of

the several churches in the area, often spending a great part of the day in his buggy, traveling the country roads in order to reach a distant charge. A natural trader, the elder Dixon owned at various times a variety of horses and buggies, sometimes changing two or three times a month. The buggy that he most prized, however, was bought from Stonewall Jackson's widow after the death of her husband. So fond of buying and selling was Mr. Dixon that one of his daughters in later years was heard to remark jokingly: "I should think [that] at one time or another father had owned every house and every horse in Cleveland County!"[18] The elder Dixon was a favorite among the young couples of the region, for he remembered his own courtship and often listened sympathetically to their requests for his blessing. Many runaway couples, knowing that he would pass a certain large tree near the North Carolina–South Carolina line on his way to church, would await him to ask if he would marry them. So popular did the place become as a marriage site that it came to be called the "Gretna Green" of North Carolina, after the famous hamlet in Dumfriesshire, Scotland, where so many clandestine marriages took place in the eighteenth and nineteenth centuries.

Thomas Dixon's father was a just man to whom many people turned in their troubles, yet he could be severe and inflexible on occasion. He strictly forbade his children to fight, and one of the worst whippings that Thomas ever received came as a result of a fight with Collier Cobb, another minister's son. One Sunday, in the yard of New Prospect Church, while awaiting the beginning of services, Thomas and Collier became involved in a heated argument over Governor Holden. The Cobb boy argued that Holden had a right to send his militia anywhere in the state to quell any opposition to the Reconstruction government, and Thomas as energetically insisted that the low creatures sent by Holden could not truly be called militia. The argument was probably occasioned by the fact that Holden had recently appointed George W. Kirk, an adventurer from Tennessee, to lead a band of released criminals to put down the work of the Ku Klux Klan in Cleveland County. As the argument between the small boys grew hotter, Thomas called Collier a liar; whereupon Collier spat in Thomas' face. A rousing fight ensued between the two boys. When Thomas' father heard of the matter, he immediately punished him. The indomitable and uncompromising will that characterized Thomas' mature years is foreshadowed in his refusal to weep at a whipping that he thought humiliating and unjust:

> He struck me blow after blow that cut my back with pain so awful, so strangling that it sent me into suppressed convulsions. About to scream I thrust my fist . . . into my mouth and danced first on one foot and then on the other in paroxysm after paroxysm of rage and pain.[19]

Though Dixon loved his father and spoke of him in later years with reverence, the inflexibility of their natures was a source at times of misunderstanding and unhappiness between them. Surely father and son came by their personalities naturally. Suzannah Hambright Dixon, Thomas' paternal grandmother, who had come to live with the Dixons for a time, was the youngest of a family of twenty-two children and a woman of unusual force of mind and character. Although she knew that her minister son strongly disapproved of her habits, she was openly devoted to her jug of whiskey and her corncob pipe. Her jolly good nature and ready store of tales about the Revolutionary War made her a favorite with young Thomas, and she, in turn, loved the boy devotedly. "Grandma" Dixon, like her son and grandson, never relinquished an idea or an opinion that she felt to be right.

On one occasion, in the winter of 1874, when the elder Dixon planned to send Thomas and Frank to a Mrs. Barnard at Sulphur Springs, three miles away, for a few weeks of school, Grandma Dixon slyly took young Thomas' side in objecting to "learning" which would interfere with his short vacation from farm work, saying:

> If I were just as young as you, boy, I wouldn't care if school kept or not. For that matter, I can still climb a mountain with the best of them—at eighty-six, too. Hand me my whiskey, Son. I like my toddy on Christmas Day. You let it alone, but it's never hurt me and never will.[20]

In referring to her earlier life, she added:

> We didn't make the hullabaloo over whiskey some folks do now. I'm not saying it's good for boys. It's not. And don't you drink it, Son. But fill up my glass again. That's awfully good liquor. Polly got it on the mountain for me before I left. Don't you touch it, now or ever. I'll do all the drinking for the family, and it won't hurt me either.[21]

In spite of Grandma Dixon's sympathy, however, Thomas was unable to avoid the "learning."

One morning, as Thomas was hitching up the buggy to go to school, his grandmother called him aside and gave him a dollar with which to get her some whiskey at Aaron Mooney's barroom, or "doggery," located at the crossroads not far from the farmhouse. The elder Dixon, who had often warned Thomas about the dangers of drink, was furious when he learned of the disobedience:

> I've told you again and again never to enter a "doggery." Whiskey killed your grandfather, took me from school and sent

me a slave into the fields to work for a living for the family. I never got to college for that reason. I've promised God to fight liquor with every ounce of strength he has given me.[22]

And with these words Dixon's father proceeded to keep his promise, but the spirit of defiance in Thomas would not let him whimper, and some sixty years later Thomas recalled that "he could have beaten me into unconsciousness before I'd have uttered a cry."[23] Grandma Dixon's reaction to the whipping was swift and final. Without uttering a word, she put a few clothes in her black bag, threw the bag over her shoulders, and started walking down the sandy country road to the home of Thomas' Aunt Polly, eighteen miles away at King's Mountain. In spite of her eighty-six years, Suzannah Dixon made the journey with no ill effects. Thomas never saw his dear Grandma Dixon again, though she lived twenty more years, to die at one hundred and six years of age, the last survivor in North Carolina of Revolutionary War days.[24]

Amanda Dixon was so angered over the whipping her son had received that she determined to have the family move back to Shelby into her mother's house. The elder Dixon had already started building a house next to Amanda's mother on Washington Street so that the children could be near the local school, and he urged Amanda to wait until the house was completed, but she would not be dissuaded. The emotional reaction to the whipping of Thomas was a by-product of a far more imperious consideration that caused Amanda to look with dread toward the coming months in a farmhouse distant from medical care. At forty-three years of age, Amanda Dixon realized that she was to have another child. The heavy responsibilities following her marriage at thirteen years of age, the hardships she had endured during the sojourn in Arkansas, the loss of three of her first four children, and the terrible experiences of Reconstruction had taken their toll of her. Now, physically ill and upset by the thrashing Tom had received, she insisted upon moving immediately.

Early in 1876, the elder Dixon leased out Buffalo Farm and moved his family into the home of Amanda's mother, Mrs. Webber, who had remarried after the death of her first husband, Abner McAfee, and was again a widow. Before her first marriage, "Grandma" Webber had been a Ferguson, a member of a family that claimed direct descent from Fergus, a king of ancient Scotland. She was a dark, thin, nervously constituted woman of sharp and sometimes bitter speech. Her bright, penetrating eyes reflected much of the tragedy she had seen about her. In her presence the children spoke in whispers, and Thomas walked on tiptoe whenever he entered her house. Young Dixon was with her on one occasion that remained vivid in his memory. An agent of the Freedmen's Bureau drove up to tell Mrs. Webber that old Nelse, the Negro man who had been with the family for thirty years, must be "freed." Her eyes snapping, Grandma Webber retorted that she would be "glad" to inform Nelse of it. Nelse, who had a room over the kitchen, was called down, and the agent told him that he was free to go anywhere he pleased. Seeing that Nelse was apparently not understanding his message, the agent pressed his point by saying "free" a number of times, very loudly. When the agent had finished, Nelse threw up his arms, turned around, and proceeded to climb back to his room. Upon reaching the top of the stairs, he sat down and began mending his clothes. The agent, believing that he still had not made Nelse understand, came to the foot of the stairs and called up in a loud voice: "I tell you that you're free!"[25] Nelse's reaction to these words was immediate and startling. Grabbing behind him, he turned and swiftly hurled a hatchet, which whistled by the agent's head and buried itself in the far wall of the kitchen. The next few moments were ones of vast confusion as the agent, Grandma Webber, and young Thomas frantically vied to be the first through the door!

During March and April, Amanda Dixon experienced an increasing sense of anxiety and physical premonition of the trying time ahead. Taking care of her daily tasks aggravated a condition already dangerous. On May 4, after a long period of anxiety for the family, Amanda gave birth to a daughter, named Addie May. On several occasions during the hours following the birth of the child, the elder Dixon despaired of Amanda's life. Sitting by her bedside, he listened to the wandering, incoherent mutterings of his wife as her vitality ebbed and flowed. Within a few weeks, she seemed to be a little stronger physically, but her utterances reflected only the tortured, aimless gropings of a mind incapable of reason. The doctors advised that she be removed to a sanatorium for treatment, but the elder Dixon insisted that his wife be kept at home, for he was convinced that nothing could be wrong with her that loving care would not cure.

Fearing lest Amanda attempt to leave her bed or need them at any moment, the family agreed to watch by her bedside every minute of the day and night. Clarence, now at the Southern Baptist Theological Seminary in Greenville, South Carolina, was called home to help the family. To young Tom fell the task of watching by his mother's side each night from two in the morning until breakfast.

Through the long night hours, the twelve-year-old boy sat in the dark room, listening to the occasional hooting of an owl, jumping fearfully when a board creaked, or leaning forward anxiously when his mother's breathing became irregular. Time dragged on at an agonizing pace. The long watches were to Thomas like an eternity on some strange, faraway planet devoid of life and light. Dark phantoms from a dream world flickered through his dozing consciousness as he fought to stay awake so that he could give his mother medicine at the proper intervals. Finally, after three trying, watchful months, Amanda one morning looked about her with recognition of her surroundings. The crisis was over; Amanda Dixon was going to get well.

By the summer of 1876, Thomas had become a tall, spindling boy with abundant black hair and deep-set, compelling eyes. His height and demeanor gave the impression that he was older than his twelve years. Though he had a pulse rate far below normal, which made it difficult for him in later years to obtain life insurance, his lungs were strong and threw off colds easily. His senses of sight and hearing were exceptionally acute, and he impressed, and at times awed, the persons around him by the keenness of his wit and by the ease with which he grasped the meaning of matters that met his boyhood fancy. Fond of argument, he began early to reveal those characteristics that were to mark him in manhood as a complex, controversial personality.

Clarence, the eldest son, having been graduated from Wake Forest College two years before with highest honors, was now studying for the ministry. With the burden of helping Clarence through college lifted, the elder Dixon and Amanda turned their serious attention to the educa-

Amanda Dixon

THOMAS DIXON, AGE 15

tion of the other children. At a time when the people of the region opposed higher education, the elder Mr. Dixon strongly advocated it, and Amanda was no less concerned than her husband about the children's schooling. Herself an avid reader of magazines, histories, and novels, she had named the eldest child Amzi Clarence after a fictional character whom she admired, in spite of the objections her husband had offered to a name he considered too fanciful. In Thomas she recognized another enthusiastic reader, and she held special hopes for his future.

The idea of regular schooling fascinated young Dixon. Of inquisitive mind, he was eager to study mathematics, Latin, and Greek. It was not until the following year, however, in the fall of 1877, that he was able to begin his schooling at the Shelby Academy. The drudgery of the past several years now faded and became only an indistinct blur before the keen pleasure he found in study. In an era in which he was not constantly beset on all sides by influences diverting to the teen-age mind, Dixon became an interested student. The world of the intellect was constantly new, constantly fresh. How far removed he now seemed from the soul-destroying months on Buffalo Farm. J. A. White and Henry Sharp had organized the Shelby Academy as a private school, and their influence had a great effect upon Dixon.

It was at the Academy that Thomas had the experience of "first love." In the schoolroom the boys sat on the right side, the girls on the left. Thomas became aware of a remarkably pretty girl across the aisle. When she recited, her voice sounded like exquisite music to him. This girl grew to be almost an obsession with Thomas, and although he made up his mind that he would speak to her, his courage failed each time he met her in the hallway. His worship of the girl remained painfully static until one day he noticed a schoolmate, Charlie Blanton, looking at her also. Thomas knew that he had a powerful rival, for Charlie was the handsomest and best-dressed boy in the class, and unlike Thomas and most of the other boys, he wore shoes throughout the summer. Realizing that he must act, Thomas wrote the girl a note meticulously copied from a book of etiquette, asking the pleasure of her company at the evening church services. He sent the note by a friend, Bob Ryburn, and a little while later the messenger returned with the wonderful answer also copied from the book of etiquette: "Miss Mollie Durham returns the compliments of Mr. Thomas Dixon and accepts his invitation to accompany him to the Baptist Church tonight."[26]

Mollie Durham was a charming girl, and Thomas Dixon was not the only boy in Shelby who recognized her qualities. But his dreams were short-lived, for one day, after the school session was over, his mother met him at the door with the news that Mollie, victim of an unknown disease, had suddenly died. For several days Thomas was so stunned that he could only walk aimlessly about the woods, and it was quite a while before he could again apply himself wholeheartedly to his work.

Two short years at the Shelby Academy wrought a remarkable change in the callow boy who before had known little beyond unremitting daily toil. In May, 1879, at the end of his second school year, Dixon had finished the course in geometry, had read in Latin Caesar's *Gallic Wars*, much of Ovid's *Metamorphoses*, and Cicero's *Orations*, and in Greek Xenophon's *Anabasis*. So rapid had been his progress that his teachers pronounced him ready for college.

III

The Beckoning World

In September, 1879, the fifteen-year-old Dixon left home to enter Wake Forest College in the east-central portion of the state. Poor roads and Dixon's youth made the distance from Shelby to Wake Forest seem much farther than two hundred miles. Clarence had painted such glowing colors of life at college that Thomas eagerly thought of the new life ahead.

Wake Forest College was the Baptist institution of higher learning in North Carolina, having been organized some forty-five years earlier after many Baptists had received unfavorable reports of the University of North Carolina at Chapel Hill. In its early days, the University was popularly regarded in many church circles as catering to the wealthy and prominent families of the state. A sense of materialism and worldliness was created by the gay social events, at which drinking and cockfighting were common. The churches of the state met the challenge and established colleges of their own. During the same decade in which Wake Forest had been established, the Presbyterians had founded Davidson College, and the Methodists had opened Trinity College, later to become Duke University.[1] The trials of Reconstruction had sorely taxed the existence of the University at Chapel Hill, and Governor Holden, before his impeachment, had so weakened the administration of the institution that it closed its doors entirely for a time. The denominational colleges, not hampered by political corruption, struggled through the trying period despite a great reduction in students and little money. These colleges profited to some degree when the state university was closed, for some of the faculty members from Chapel Hill accepted positions in the denominational colleges.

The postwar atmosphere at Wake Forest was one of "plain living and high thinking." The terrible rigors of war and Reconstruction had left students and faculty alike with a profound sense of responsibility for bringing order to a land that had long known only turmoil. The students, like young men of all times and places, were enthusiastic and sometimes a bit reckless in their expression of the zest for living, but the general attitude was one of seriousness toward the studies made possible by the sacrifices of their parents' slender resources. Into such an environment Dixon was plunged early in September, homesick before he had been on the campus an hour. He was at first shocked at the sight of the old, dilapidated buildings, far different from what he had expected. The main building, standing in the center of the campus, was a dull gray structure, four stories high. Dixon had heard his brother Clarence speak of this building, and he had visualized it as much larger than it was. At the north end of the campus was a small, two-story, red brick building, housing on the first floor the library and two classrooms and on the second floor the halls of the Euzelian and Philomathesian literary and debating societies. A new building at the south quadrant of the campus was being erected to provide for an auditorium and four classrooms.

Dixon's disappointment at the physical appearance of the college was soon forgotten, however, as he became acquainted with the students and faculty. Inspired by the enthusiasm of his teachers, he entered upon his college career determined to earn a Master of Arts degree before he left. Though he had started his schooling late and had had only two full years of regular training before arriving at Wake Forest, he passed the entrance examinations without great difficulty.

Among Dixon's favorite teachers at Wake Forest were William Royall and William L. Poteat. Dr. Royall was professor of Greek, and his enthusiastic and learned discussions of the Greek classics tremendously impressed Dixon. A man of remarkable vigor, Royall continued to hold his Greek classes at Wake Forest until he was well over eighty years of age. At the time of Dixon's matriculation, Dr. Royall was a young man of thirty-five, handsome and compelling in personality. Dixon's attitude toward his teacher was little short of idolatry. Dixon's other favorite, William Poteat, was the youngest member of the faculty when Dixon enrolled. A friendship developed between teacher and student that lasted all their lives. Poteat was later to be president of the college for twenty years.

The favorite recreation of the students at Wake Forest was debating. Before Dixon left home, he had already heard from Clarence of the college's two debating societies. The societies, known as the Euzelian and the Philomathesian, contended strenuously for the membership of new students who they thought would make the best debaters. To be an official debater for the societies was quite an honor among the young men, and Dixon determined to try hard to win the Orator's Medal, which was awarded at the end of each year to the best debater. In October he was initiated into the Euzelian Society, the organization to which his brother Clarence had belonged. Having loved argumentation from childhood, Dixon was happy in the hot debates conducted with all the enthusiasm of youth. His first efforts at formally trying to match wits with his opponents on the platform were among the most memorable occasions in the life of the young student. The hours spent in the "old Eu," as the meeting hall was affectionately called, frequently came to mind in later life:

> As soon as I found myself settled in this Literary Society I felt at home in the new world the College had created. I reveled in the long hours of passionate debate, in which were discussed with the vigor and daring of youth, every question under the sun, religious, political, social and scientific.[2]

Tom Dixon's first year at Wake Forest inspired ambitions of which he had only dreamed before. He saw himself variously in the professional world as a future lawyer, minister, scientist, or writer. The competition offered by some of his classmates was rigid and at times discouraging. The fact that both his uncle Lee Roy McAfee and his brother

Clarence had been graduated with highest honors placed an additional responsibility upon Dixon to succeed.

During the academic year, Dixon spent much time over his books, having developed particularly strong interests in history, language, and oratory. In an age that still considered public speaking one of the fine arts, Dixon was particularly eager to excel in the debating hall. His fire, dramatic flair, and strong convictions commanded the attention of his fellow students as soon as he began to speak. Though he was at first untutored in the art of oratory, the force of his argumentation drew complimentary reports soon after he had joined the debating society. Nearly thirty years later, an old college mate recalled the fiery vigor of the young college freshman:

> I remember the first time Tom Dixon, as we shall always call him, took part in a debate in the Euzelian Society. The subject was Napoleon. No; I remember nothing that he said—only the zest with which he took hold. . . . From the tip of his bony finger to his toe [he] appeared to be fully eight feet [tall]![3]

Toward the end of the school year, with a sense of recklessness and possible disaster, Dixon made bold to list himself as a candidate for the Orator's Medal, the forensic prize most coveted among the student body. He felt particularly rash in that his brother Clarence, who still was Dixon's idol, had won the prize only at the end of his senior year. During the few weeks that remained, Dixon worked upon his speech at every opportunity, frequently roaming the woods and declaiming to the trees as though they were his judges. Finally the great night arrived. As he stood before the audience, he tried to think of all he had studied about effective oratory; he remembered and avoided repeating the weak points of the speakers who had preceded him on the stage. When he sat down, the enthusiastic response of the audience told him that he had won. What a prize to take home to the family in Shelby!

Within a few days the good news had reached Clarence, who now held a pastorate at the First Baptist Church in Asheville, North Carolina. In a letter dated June 21, 1880, to his fiancée, Mollie Faison, whom he was to marry a few days later, Clarence wrote:

A young man from Wake Forest stayed with me last night, and gave me a very favourable account of Tom's progress. From what he told me, I see he is far ahead of his big brother, when he was in college, as an orator. I have never heard Tom speak and never thought he had anything much of the Orator about him, and his getting the Orator's Medal has raised my curiosity to hear him. He is very anxious to come to the mountains [for the summer vacation] with us, but I hardly think Ma and Pa will consent.[4]

Apparently Clarence now began to look upon his younger brother with a new interest. The winning of the Orator's Medal showed him that Tom was not the fumbling adolescent who had left for school the previous fall. Here was a young man who was to be reckoned with. Only a short time before, in a letter of June 10, Clarence had intimated to Mollie that Tom was hardly more than a child:

The idea of your dreading to meet Tom is simply funny to me. Why, he is nothing but an awkward boy of sixteen years old, about the age I suppose, of Leonidas [Mollie's younger brother], a perfect bookworm with nothing of the awe inspiring about him at all. I suspect he will be half frightened to death when he meets you, for I have not heard of his forming a lady's acquaintance since he has been at Wake Forest.[5]

At Wake Forest Dixon was eager to get home and bask in the renown of his newly-acquired laurels, but Clarence had written that he would stop by for him on his way from a preaching assignment at Salisbury. The assignment was changed to a later date, and Dixon found himself with the prospect of having to stay on the deserted campus for two weeks after the other students had left. For the first few days he roamed the grounds and buildings fretfully but finally decided to make the best of his time and set himself a course of reading to occupy the hours. At last Clarence arrived, and they set off together for "Wood Lawn," the home of Mollie Faison, in Duplin County near Warsaw.

The wedding of Clarence Dixon and Mollie Faison was the event of the season in that area. Dr. T. H. Pritchard, president of Wake Forest, was on hand to perform the ceremony. Mollie, popularly known to the young suitors of the section as "The Rose of Duplin," had excited much interest in finally giving her heart to the poor young preacher from the mountains. A degree of social antipathy existed between the wealthy planters of the plains region of North Carolina and the more rugged, simple folk of the western highlands. It was with considerable interest, not to say curiosity, therefore, that friends in great numbers flocked to Wood Lawn on the first day of July, 1880. Wood Lawn was quite enough to awe and impress young Tom Dixon. Colonel Abner Faison, Mollie's father, after spending a great sum of money and five years in constructing Wood Lawn, had sent to Philadelphia for a noted landscape gardener to lay out the grounds. Dixon had seen nothing so splendid in all his life.

At the wedding Tom met Eliza Faison, a pretty seventeen-year-old cousin of Mollie's. After much mutual teasing and playful badinage, they promised faithfully to write to each other. But this incipient romance was ended almost before it began, for although Thomas kept his side of the bargain, he never received a reply to his first effusion, learning a short time later that Eliza had married in the meantime.

The day after the wedding, Dixon left for home, his eagerness to see his family and tell them of his successes at college making the journey seem endless. His triumph on arriving home was short-lived, however, for his father announced that it would hardly be possible to send Dixon back to college in the fall. Dixon's hopes sank as his father explained his financial plight:

> Last year I didn't get quite a hundred dollars from all four churches where I preached a hundred and four sermons at the regular services besides fifty or sixty more at our revivals.[6]

The elder Thomas Dixon had earned less than a dollar a sermon, far from sufficient to support a family and keep a boy in college. The end of Tom's dreams had come, only a few months after his new resolutions to accomplish great things in the world.

As the summer wore on, Dixon tried to think of possible ways to earn money to get back into college someday, but there were few means by which adults could earn money, to say nothing of a sixteen-year-old boy. Concerned as he was about his future, he did not worry more about the matter than did his father. The elder Dixon had made a vow that his children should go to college, but with only one of five children through school, he now saw no way of maintaining his vow. Finally, in a move of desperation that was strictly against his principles, the elder Dixon went to see one of the deacons of New Prospect Church. When Mr. Dixon had told his situation, Deacon Hoyle gravely arose from his chair and stepped over to a deposit box in the corner of the room. Counting out two hundred dollars, piece by piece, he said that the money was to be repaid in exactly the same denominations. The economy of the time was so unstable that the only sure way of getting back money of the same value was to demand repayment in the same denominations of gold and silver. Though the elder Dixon did not know just how he would be able to repay Deacon Hoyle, he would be able to send his son back to college for another year. When he returned with the good news, Thomas was jubilant and could hardly await the beginning of the fall term.

The young Thomas Dixon who returned to Wake Forest in the fall of 1880 was far removed from the awkward, uncertain youth of the previous year. Now known to all the student body as the winner of the Orator's Medal and as one of the best students in his class, Dixon began his sophomore year with confidence. His keen mind and his attractive personality, in and out of class, marked him as one of the most promising students at the college. As the school year wore on, Dixon gained more and more facility in meeting the requirements of his courses. Making the highest marks of his class on examinations was now the rule. But success, too easily won, lulled him into a false sense of security. His attitude became cavalier, both toward his courses and toward his instructors. In his pride he forgot that the goals he had set for himself when he first entered college could be reached only by great effort. Dixon was rapidly advancing toward a precipice to which his sophomoric pride had blinded him.

The most coveted prize of the sophomore year was the Latin Medal, given to the student who demonstrated the greatest facility in translating Latin into English and vice versa. In class, Dixon appeared to have little real competition. His only serious rival was Charlie Smith, a brilliant older student, but the ease with which Dixon had made high grades in the preceding months caused him to look upon Smith's rivalry with little real concern. In the weeks before the examination for the Latin Medal, Dixon spent much time in pleasant, leisurely dreaming of the prize he was sure would be his.

When the examination was held early in June, Dixon walked into the examination hall with a feeling of disdain for his opponents and the judges. The prize was so surely his that the formality of the examination seemed to him a little silly. With a feeling of secret triumph, he proceeded to the desk pointed out to him and opened his examination folder. Here was a surprise. Something was wrong. The Latin sentences, culled from some of the more obscure passages of classical authors, were more difficult than the assignments to which he had been accustomed. After recovering from the initial shock, he regained some of his former confidence, consoled in the knowledge that the other candidates were confronted with the same difficulty that he was. After both the written and the oral phases of the examination were over, Dixon returned to his seat to await the decision of the judges. After nearly an hour, the chairman of the judging committee arose and announced that Charlie Smith had received the unanimous vote of the judges. Almost incredulous at what he had heard, Dixon arose and somehow managed to congratulate Smith. The whole structure of the fool's paradise that Dixon had been erecting in the past months had collapsed in a moment. In a stupor of pain and humiliation, he pushed through the crowd, ashamed at the memory of the boasts he had made to his friends. The lesson he learned from his experience often reminded him in later times of the danger of expecting reward without labor:

> God had given me brains and I hadn't used them. He had given me long rich hours in which to study, and I had wandered through fields and woods in idle day dreaming.[7]
>
> Instead of hard work, I mused and dreamed and consulted the Sybilline books. All was propitious. Success was sure. I saw the new moon a hand's breadth above the eastern horizon unobscured by leaf or twig. The zephyrs whispered to the leaves and told of success—the stars all proclaimed it. Shall I ever forget that night in June, when with fallen crest, I walked out of the brilliantly lighted hall, with that awful decision of the judges ringing in my ears! I found that the stars had been talking about another man, and the zephyrs had whispered about another fellow entirely, and the moon had proven false to all her vows! I lay down on the grass beneath the kindly shadow of a spreading oak, and cooled off for an hour. That night all the idiocy of fate and fatalism, signs and wonders, oozed out of my body. . . .[8]

Dixon's humiliating defeat caused him to do some thinking in the weeks that followed. The fact that he had ranked at the top of his class for the year no longer blinded him as to the possible limits of his abilities. He could not gain any measure of composure until he had taken complete stock of his false impulses. With a fierce, almost frenetic determination, he resolved to start upon a Spartan program of study the following fall.

Throughout the summer of 1881, during every available moment, Dixon read, preparing himself for the coming school year. The biggest goal immediately ahead of him was the French Medal, and his desire to win this prize was such that he was willing to go to any lengths in studying for it. Upon re-entering college in the fall, he set for himself an almost impossible regimen of study. By budgeting his time mercilessly, he found that he could devote about thirteen or more hours a day to his studies, in addition to the four hours spent in class. He obtained a quiet room on the top floor at the end of the hall of his dormitory so that he could study undisturbed. His meals and the conversation accompanying them he limited strictly to thirty minutes. This amount of time might be shortened, but it was never to be lengthened. By adhering to the letter of his program of study, he found that he could devote six full hours a day to French.

Charlie Smith was his rival for the French prize also, and Charlie had already taken two years of the language. Dixon, as a newcomer to French, realized that only by the most determined efforts could he overcome the disparity in their facility in the language during the months ahead. Within three weeks Dixon had mastered his text in French grammar; in three more weeks he had completed all the exercises in his textbook on composition. He felt that he was now ready to begin translating French authors.

To develop a facility in French, Dixon carefully translated into English Voltaire's complete *Histoire de Charles XII, roi de Suède* and Madame de Staël's *Corinne*. While continuing to read other French authors, he laid his translations aside for three months so that he would have time to forget the original idioms. He then retranslated his English versions into French, comparing his own work, line by line, with the authors' language. Having heard Dr. Royall on one occasion refer to the difficult French idioms of Madame de Sévigné's letters, full of woman's gossip, Dixon obtained a volume of the letters and translated three hundred pages to gain facility with the piquant style of the French authoress.

In spite of the months of intense preparation, Dixon entered the examination room with many misgivings. The humiliation of the previous year had taught him to look suspiciously on every feeling of confidence. When the examinations were distributed, however, Dixon saw with ill-concealed delight that the major portion of the French passages were from the volume of Madame de Sévigné's letters. The language and style were by this time as familiar to Dixon as his native English, and he translated with a sense of sureness and precision. When the judges announced that the decision would have to be withheld until the following day, the old doubts began once more to assail Dixon. He remembered that Charlie Smith had also been present on the occasion when Dr. Royall had referred to Madame de Sévigné's writings. The next day, upon meeting Dr. Royall on the campus, Dixon asked in an unsteady voice if the decision had been made. Professor Royall for a moment smiled enigmatically and then broke into a hearty laugh. The exactness with which Dixon had followed the intricate style of the letters amused Royall greatly, for he had been aware of the fact that young Dixon had become a near hermit in his determination to master French. With surging heart, Dixon heard the wonderful news that he had demonstrated an ability considerably beyond that of the other contestants—even beyond that of Charlie Smith.

Dixon had now found his stride as a student. The school year closed with his having won two other medals and the highest marks in his class. In addition, he had been chosen by his debating society as the principal speaker at the yearly anniversary banquet. Here was a boy now filled with a zest for living and an enthusiasm for accomplishment. The whole world lay before him, waiting to be conquered.

A mind with as much curiosity as Dixon's is bound to range widely through the great heritage of man's writings, and if that mind is eighteen years old, vast, even cataclysmic changes may be wrought in a short time. Much reading in the then-seeming heretical writers—Darwin, Huxley, and Spencer—worked powerfully upon the imagination and logic of Dixon. The new concept of man's evolution, though almost universally accepted in our own age, was to Dixon's time a bombshell that brutally tore apart the anthropomorphic view of the Old Testament. One may well imagine Dixon's confusion as he turned from the traditional view of man's genesis to the apparently contradictory logic of the new scientists who had brought doubt and bitter controversy to the nineteenth century. Further reading shook the very foundation of Dixon's religious faith, and by the end of his last year in college Dixon found that he was an agnostic. Finally, in the spring of 1882, he went to Professor Royall with a pronouncement of his views. Expecting Dr. Royall to be profoundly shocked at his heretical sentiments, Dixon was nonplused to see his teacher listening with a smile and finally replying: "It's a phase, my son. I passed through it. You will."[9]

Frank, who had entered Wake Forest the previous fall, discussed the problem at length with his older brother. In spite of his handicap, Frank was a boy of gay, humorous spirit who was distressed to see Dixon becoming rather cynical of the beliefs and simple virtues that had been taught at home. Through the summer of 1882, Dixon felt out of place at home, and though he did not openly confront his father with his views, the family sensed his moodiness and volatile temperament. When the fall term of 1882 came, Dixon returned to Wake Forest still an inwardly troubled and confused young man, though to most outward appearances a person determined and self-assured.

During his last year at Wake Forest, Dixon thought of taking up writing as his ultimate profession, but fearing that he had not "lived enough" to make a convincing writer, he thought perhaps the fulfillment of such a career must be left to some distant, undetermined time.

Dixon was now the acknowledged leader of the school both in and out of class. His personal charm, his great facility at debates and conversational repartee, and his high scholastic standing made him the natural recipient of many student honors. When graduation day arrived in June, 1883, Dixon had won the highest honors ever achieved by a student at Wake Forest. In addition to having earned the Master of Arts degree in four years, rather than five or more, and to having won many medals in extracurricular activities, he was given a scholarship to The Johns Hopkins University for the purpose of furthering his study in history and political theory. Dixon's mother and father had cause to be proud indeed, for, in addition to the honors won by Thomas, a reward for their sacrifices had also come from another quarter. Upon the retirement of Dr. T. H. Pritchard in the spring from the presidency of Wake Forest, the college trustees had earnestly urged Clarence, now well known as a dynamic religious leader, to become the new president. Such an offer was quite an honor for a young man only twenty-eight years old. At the same time that the presidency was being offered to him, Clarence was being sought as the pastor of a large church in Baltimore. Clarence had a period of doubt before he could reach a decision. The opportunity of influencing hundreds of young men like Thomas and Frank and Leonidas Faison (Mollie's brother) appealed to him tremendously. In addition, the offer of the presidency was very flattering to a person of his age. Finally, the prospect of being settled in the general area of both his family and Mollie's was indeed a pleasant one. Yet he at last decided that he had been called to the ministry by divine providence and that nothing must deter him from his life's mission. He wrote the college trustees, announcing his decision, and then notified the church committee in Baltimore that he was ready to fill the charge.

Clarence Dixon's decision concerning the presidency of Wake Forest was characteristic of his later sincerity. Three years later, Washington and Lee University decided to confer upon him the honorary degree of Doctor of Divinity in recognition of his outstanding religious work, but he promptly declined the honor, replying in part: "I am convinced that the whole D.D. business is out of harmony with the spirit of the New Testament, and partakes of 'the pride of life,' which needs to be crucified rather than fostered."[10] The committee of the University insisted, however, that its action could not be withdrawn, and Clarence Dixon, realizing that his open refusal of the honorary degree might appear to many people as a bid for notoriety, was finally persuaded to accept the degree. He maintained that he did not possess the learning that he felt such a title indicated, and neither he nor his family ever made use of the title.

In 1883 The Johns Hopkins University already held a considerable reputation among scholars, and young Dixon was proud to become a member of the student body at the beginning of the fall term. The atmosphere at Johns Hopkins was considerably more sophisticated than that at Wake Forest, and Dixon soon found himself enjoying the companionship and influence of a number of graduate students of wide educational background. At his first seminar, he met on his left Albert Shaw of Ohio, and on his right sat a young graduate student named Woodrow Wilson.

When the two students met, Wilson was eight years Dixon's senior. The twenty-seven-year-old Wilson was immediately attracted to the dynamic, zestful, nineteen-year-old student from North Carolina, and Dixon in turn was awed by the wide historical knowledge of his new friend. They soon were close companions, and Dixon became a frequent visitor at Wilson's quarters at Mount Vernon Place. Here the two young men spent long hours in eager discussion. Besides their interest in political theory, they shared a passion for the theater. The more conservative Wilson was sometimes amused at his friend's political vagaries, but when the discussion fell upon acting and actors, everything else was forgotten in the enthusiasm. As the months wore on, Dixon found the stage more and more appealing, and he gave every moment he could spare to the study of dramatics. By the end of his first year at Johns Hopkins, he was "bubbling over with a desire to fire the world in Shakespearian roles."[11]

Through Wilson, Dixon met the editor of the Baltimore *Mirror*, who was impressed by the enthusiasm of the young student. As a result of the meeting, the editor offered Dixon a job as dramatic critic for the paper. For the next four months Dixon filled this highly interesting extracurricular position while continuing his heavy schedule of work at Johns Hopkins. The study of history and political theory now grew pale before the brilliance of footlights.

Dixon saw every play in the city for which he could possibly spare the time; the more he saw, the more he felt that he must go to New York, the Mecca of the dramatic world, and devote all his energies to a dramatic career. Wilson finally became alarmed at his friend's determination, for though he knew of Dixon's great interest in the theater, he had not realized that this interest was more than academic. He urged Dixon to remain at Johns Hopkins at least two years, but the young would-be actor was not to be dissuaded. During the last week in December, 1883, Dixon busily made arrangements to leave the University. During his stay in Baltimore, he had been living with Clarence, who had come the previous September to fill the pulpit of the Immanuel Baptist Church. The church committee had urged Clarence to accept a four months' trip abroad for rest and travel before he assumed his new charge, but Clarence had refused and was, therefore, in Baltimore when Thomas arrived for the fall term at Johns Hopkins. Clarence was very much disturbed by Dixon's enthusiasm for the stage; a career in dramatics seemed to Clarence to be not altogether respectable. He pleaded with Thomas to give up this foolish notion of becoming an actor, but to no avail.

Without money, there would be no way of getting established in New York. But money or no money, Dixon was determined to carry out his plan. With many misgivings, he wrote to his father, asking for sufficient funds to enroll in one of the dramatic schools in New York. Dixon fully expected to receive an answer showing disappointment in a son who would give up a promising career in politics for the uncertainties of the theater. He was very much surprised, therefore, when he soon received from his father a letter enclosing the desired money. There was only a hint of reproach, and, deeply moved, Dixon read his father's closing words: "Of course, I know that you will come home one of these days and enter the ministry as your brother has. I can wait the Master's time. God bless you."[12]

On the morning of January 11, 1884, his twentieth birthday, Dixon said good-bye to his friend at Mount Vernon Place and boarded the train for New York, now the focal point of his dreams. Upon his arrival, he immediately put his plans into motion by attending a matinee performance of Edwin Booth, whose portrayal of the musing, introspective Hamlet revolutionized that role and made the actor famous. After the performance and a hasty meal, Dixon proceeded to the Academy of Music to hear his idol, Adelina Patti, sing. When his first day in New York had ended, Dixon felt that his twentieth birthday had been suitably celebrated and that at last he had found himself.

The great city was exciting to Dixon. The variety of experiences that the city offered would require, it seemed, several lifetimes of study and enjoyment. Life here was far removed from that of the lonely, isolated days at Buffalo Farm. A few nights after his arrival, Dixon attended a lecture by Colonel Robert Ingersoll, the eloquent agnostic about whom he had heard much. The logic and force of Ingersoll's speech were powerfully persuasive to young Dixon, who had only two years before expressed his own agnostic views to Dr. Royall at Wake Forest. The Sunday following the lecture by Ingersoll, Dixon listened with close attention to Henry Ward Beecher, the great abolitionist, at Plymouth Church in Brooklyn. Though he had gone to the sermon strongly prejudiced by Southern comments he had overheard as a boy, Dixon came away from the church convinced that he had heard "the greatest preacher in the world."[13]

Dixon began his dramatic career by becoming a student in the Frobisher School. He applied himself eagerly to his studies and saw every important play in the city. At this time New York had seventeen first-class theaters in operation, and the wide variety of dramatic fare provided Dixon with endless study. A. M. Palmer was successfully producing Shakespearean plays with Booth and Barrett in the leading roles; Augustin Daly, the brilliant young man from North Carolina, had just opened his theater with a play by Bronson Howard; and Kate Clayton was playing the leading role in *The Two Orphans*. In addition, such notables as Joseph Jefferson, Tommaso Salvini, Helena Modjeska, and Maggie Mitchell kept the drama student enthralled.

At last, several weeks after his arrival in New York, Dixon thought that he had reached the verge of a great career when a theatrical manager, Richard Foote, offered him the role of the Duke of Richmond in a traveling production of *Richard III*. To finance the company, the actors were required to place sums of money in trust with the manager, the amount depending upon the importance of the role. Dixon's share was three hundred dollars, which he raised by applying again to his father and to Clarence. The loans would be only temporary, Dixon thought, for he hoped soon to have the amount returned to him many times over.

Soon after Dixon took the part, Clarence, becoming more disturbed, made a trip to New York in order to try to dissuade Thomas from the uncertain future of the stage. Finding Dixon in rehearsal, Clarence then and there pleaded with his brother before the other actors not to continue his plans for a stage career. Dixon was now, however, more confident than ever. With great enthusiasm he told Clarence of the success that was sure to come his way if he could make good use of the role that had been assigned him. But Dixon's high hopes lasted hardly beyond the mastery of his lines. At Herkimer, New York, where the cast was to offer a one-night stand, the manager of the company disappeared during the performance with all the funds. The cast, made up mostly of young, inexperienced actors like Dixon, were greatly disillusioned at such a cruel turn in their efforts to become great actors. The near-penniless group paid their bills as best they could and dispersed, some of them convinced that they had had enough of the theater.

With dampened spirits, Dixon made his way back to New York City. He was to spend several anxious weeks before he again found a possible opening. Finally he discovered on Twenty-fourth Street a very small company, headed by several ambitious young men—Daniel and Charles Frohman, Steele MacKaye, Charles Hoyt, and David Belasco—who were to revolutionize the theater during the next twenty-five years. Dixon later recalled his interview with the company:

> I applied to the director, Mr. Franklin Sargent, for a position and he gave me a reading from the script of "Hazel Kirk." When I finished he looked at me in a friendly way.
>
> "You read well. With sympathy and understanding. But you are six feet, three and a half inches, and how much do you weigh?"
>
> "One hundred and fifty pounds. I know, I am a little thin."
>
> "Your physique will make success as an actor a very difficult if not impossible thing. You are a man of university training.

We have plenty of actors. Great actors. We need plays by American authors. That's the big need of the theatre. Forget acting and write."[14]

At twenty years of age, Dixon looked like a latter-day Ichabod Crane. Bitterly disappointed at Sargent's words, but still determined to become an actor someday, however distant that time might be, he went back to his quarters and started packing for the trip home.

How different this homecoming was to be from the one after he had won the Orator's Medal at Wake Forest. He felt that his family could now well say, "We told you so." How could he face his father, his mother, Frank, and Clarence again? A letter from Mollie, Clarence's wife, to her parents is indicative of the general feeling of Dixon's family toward his venture in acting:

> Tom wrote us that he would be here the first of next week on his way to Shelby. He said his father and mother seemed so distressed about him, he would go home and study and write awhile. He is writing a play. The truth is his acting is quite a failure. I saw a notice from a dramatic paper which stated that Foote, the man Tom was acting with, was a perfect burlesque on acting and his company was still worse. Tom has spent a great deal of money and his father refused to send him any more. He has written Mr. Dixon [Clarence] for money twice. Mr. Dixon sent him sixty dollars, but did not send him any the second time. I never was so disappointed in anyone in my life, as I have been in him.[15]

The hope of becoming an actor now became secondary to the pressing realities of home life in Shelby, where Dixon's family and friends were far removed, both temperamentally and geographically, from the theatrical world. Once more Dixon's interest turned to politics, and he decided to enter the law school at Greensboro, North Carolina. While he was studying law, his father, still disturbed by his interest in the theater and hoping that his attention would be diverted toward politics, suggested that he run for the state legislature. Thomas was at first reluctant to enter the race, believing that his extreme youth would cause the voters to look upon him as a joke. The more he thought of the matter, however, the more enthusiastic he became. He recalled his success as a student orator at Wake Forest College; now he would again put that oratory to the test in ascertaining whether or not he could persuade people to vote for him.

Dixon's opponents from his home district were Captain John W. Gidney and Major Dameron, a cousin of Dixon's, who was the mayor of Shelby at the time. Captain Gidney was a man of considerable political experience, having already served two terms in the legislature, and Dixon recognized him as a formidable opponent. But Dixon had already acquired the power of saying the proper word or phrase at the right moment. Speaking before a large gathering of farmers, Dixon put Captain Gidney beyond consideration by remarking that he would read the entire political record of his opponent's two terms in the legislature. Taking a tiny pair of tweezers, and working with infinite care, he at last produced from his billfold a piece of paper about the size of a postage stamp. From this small piece of paper, he read with squinting eyes the very small words concerning the few bills Captain Gidney had introduced. This action had just the sort of broad appeal to attract his audience, and Dixon realized from their laughter and shouts of derision that he was on the right track to win votes.

Major Dameron seemed, however, to be a harder opponent to deal with than Captain Gidney. Dameron made telling remarks about Dixon's "infancy" and his lack of experience, both as a legislator and as a person who had missed struggling through the throes of war. But Dixon was also getting in remarks about Dameron's record and qualifications, much to the resentment of the latter. Dameron finally warned Dixon that any further remarks about him in future speeches would be dangerous, and he ended his threat by saying, "I'll lick the stuffing out of you."[16] Dixon politely agreed to drop Dameron's name from his speeches, and Dameron went away satisfied that he would have no more trouble with the young candidate. But Dameron had underestimated the fiery orator. At his next speaking engagement Dixon introduced his speech by telling the people what Dameron had said. Dixon remarked that he was glad of an opportunity to drop Dameron's name in future speeches because he now realized that Dameron did not have a chance to win anyway. The fighting spirit that Dixon displayed and his humorous twist of a serious threat appealed to the crowd immensely, and they roared their approval. When election day had come and gone, Dixon learned that he had won over his opponents two to one and found himself elected as a legislator of his state before he was old enough to vote.[17]

Dixon had hardly been elected as a legislator when he was urged to run for Speaker of the House. His dynamic oratory had convinced many people that Dixon could prove himself both an interesting and a worthy leader in the House of Representatives. Dixon waged a strong campaign and was becoming a serious contender against his leading opponent, Colonel Thomas M. Holt, when Colonel Holt learned that Dixon was not yet twenty-one. Holt insisted that his young opponent would not be seated even if he were elected, so Dixon finally withdrew from the race.

Dixon's maiden speech in the legislature was a proposal to change the name of Whitaker, a small town in Cleveland County. Since there was a Whitakers in Nash County, the similarity of names frequently caused confusion in mail deliveries. As a great admirer of the President of the United States at this time, Dixon proposed that the name of the town in Cleveland County be changed from Whitaker to Grover. The bill was passed and Dixon sent a copy of it to President Cleveland, telling him that his name was now immortalized in Grover, Cleveland County, North Carolina. Cleveland replied promptly and urged Dixon to visit him soon at the White House. Within a few days after the legislative session was over, Dixon went to Washington and formed a lasting friendship with the President.

Dixon's first legislative speech was reported by a young man, Walter Hines Page, who was then editor of the Raleigh *State Chronicle*. Page, who later was to become a great publisher and Ambassador to the Court of St. James, was very much impressed by the force and persuasion of the twenty-year-old legislator. Page reported Dixon's speech in glowing terms, and the two young men soon became close friends. A few days after seeing his first proposal pass through legislative channels into law, Dixon successfully introduced the first bill in the South to pension Confederate veterans, an example soon followed by other states. His speech in support of the bill drew high praise and was published in many important newspapers throughout the South.

In February, 1885, Dixon, who was an enthusiastic advocate of industrial education, introduced a bill for the establishment of a state industrial school. He had already helped to organize the "Watauga Club," whose object was "to encourage free discussion and to promote the educational, agricultural, and industrial interests of the state."[18] Among the first members of this club were such prominent North Carolinians as Arthur Winslow, Josephus Daniels, Walter Hines Page, William S. Primrose, and Charles W. Dabney. A few days after Dixon introduced his bill, the Committee on Education approved a plan for studying the matter, and Dixon's bill was dropped for the current session. Two years later an expanded bill was passed, establishing the North Carolina College of Agriculture and Mechanic Arts, now North Carolina State University.

After unsuccessfully introducing a bill for raising state funds by certain taxes on gifts and inheritances, Dixon became very much interested in a petition for the establishment of schools for Croatan Indians in the region. These Indians claimed to be direct descendants of early English settlers and Indians. Their pronunciation of the English language had a strong Elizabethan flavor, and forty-five of their family names were identical with those of Captain White's lost colony. Dixon gave serious thought to the riddle of the colony which has puzzled many other people, but he could never find the clue that would settle the matter.

Becoming more and more disillusioned at the corruption he saw in the political circles of the capitol, Dixon left Raleigh at the end of the legislative session with a determination never to return as a legislator. He was not to enter politics again as an active participant for nearly fifty years, though he continued to speak openly and militantly concerning the political issues of the day. His short career as a legislator left him with outspoken contempt for the politician, referring to him as "the prostitute of the masses."[19] The politician, Dixon said, cannot rise above the masses because of the very nature of his profession:

> He may make his tones ring from the halls of Legislation and resound through the world, but he must also beat a tambourine from the street corner. He may rise at times to be a despot. He is at all times a beggar rattling his cup in every crowd. He must court the populace or die. He must give himself to the masses, not to great ideals. He cannot do what he wishes. The public is his master.[20]

In March, 1885, Dixon decided to go to New Orleans to witness the festivities of the Mardi gras season. At the St. Charles Hotel, where he was staying, Dixon met Dr. J. W. Bussey and his family, who had come from Columbus, Georgia, to take part in the celebration. Dr. Bussey was impressed by the brilliant, though at times somewhat jolting, conversation of the young man. Dixon in turn found Dr. Bussey's daughter Harriet a most attractive young lady. A romance appeared to be in the making when Dr. Bussey put a stop to its progress. Dixon might be acceptable as a companion, but not at all acceptable as a son-in-law, especially since Dr. Bussey knew little about him beyond his engaging qualities as a conversationalist. But Dixon was not to forget Harriet Bussey in the months that followed.

In the spring of 1885, Dixon completed his law training in Greensboro. A few weeks later Frank came home from Wake Forest College with the news that he, like his two older brothers, had won the Orator's Medal. During the following term, Frank was to leave Wake Forest. In his freshman year he had been elected to membership in the Kappa Fraternity, and later, after becoming president of the chapter, he was antagonized by a resolution of the administration forbidding students to form or join fraternities. Frank resolutely refused to accept the new ruling and, in protest, withdrew from Wake Forest, taking with him to the University of North Carolina the entire membership of the fraternity.

At home in Shelby, Dixon was busy setting up a law practice and organizing a little theater group. After producing and directing the cantata *Hayman,* he found at the last minute that he would have to fill a vacancy in the cast and take one of the leading singing roles, in spite of the fact that he had never sung publicly before. His efforts were not an overwhelming success, though he did acquit himself creditably. During the time that he was working with the little theater group, he became acquainted with Mamie Crow, a young student at the Baptist Female College, which Dixon's sister Delia was also attending. Dixon courted Mamie half in earnest, half in jest, for he had not forgotten his New Orleans meeting with Harriet Bussey. The acquaintance with Mamie Crow ended when she had to withdraw from school because of illness.

Dixon's first case in court proved to be very disappointing. After speaking forcefully to the jury, he felt assured that a favorable verdict would be returned. One juror, however, sitting in the second row, refused to look at him, even though the attention of the rest of the jury was fixed on Dixon's every gesture and word. Retiring to a large tree in the courtyard, the jury deliberated the case, while Dixon, with a pair of binoculars, watched the proceedings from his office window. Sure enough, the man who would not look at Dixon seemed to be hanging the verdict of the jury. Sitting down at the foot of the tree and lighting his pipe, the man waved the other jurors away as if to say that he would have none of their persuasion. When the jury reported the next morning that, after an all-night discussion, a verdict still had not been reached, Dixon stared in anger at the man who had caused the disagreement and demanded that the jury be polled. Great was Dixon's astonishment and consternation when the poll revealed eleven people *against* his case and only one *for* it. The one juror who had been convinced by Dixon's speech was the man who had refused to look at Dixon. Only later did Dixon learn that the man was badly cross-eyed, and while he had seemed to be looking out the window during Dixon's speech, he had in reality been looking at the speaker.

Taken considerably aback by such an unexpected conclusion to his first trial, Dixon proceeded in future cases with more deliberation and less self-assurance. Though his law career was brief, it was distinguished by an originality rarely found in the profession. His actions following the conviction of a defendant on trial for arson reveal a devotion to principle altogether refreshing. The defendant was charged with burning a mill, and Dixon's forceful and eloquent prosecution served to convict the man and to secure a sentence of twenty years' imprisonment. Dixon, however, somehow could not rejoice that evening in the conviction which his eloquence had brought about. There was a lurking feeling that the man was innocent. So seriously did Dixon consider his position in the case and his career as a lawyer that he lay awake far into the night pondering what action he should take. Later, recalling that troubled night, he said:

> The whole system of law trials, the more I thought of it, seemed little short of a crime. Why should a lawyer be allowed to use his powers of eloquence to befog the minds of a jury? The sole purpose of his speech is to sway their feelings, not to do justice, according to the evidence, but to force the acceptance of his view of the issue, the view of his client who has paid him a fee to make the appeal.[21]

Dixon reviewed the whole case, and in a short time publicly acknowledged the error of his prosecution. He petitioned the governor for the man's release as energetically as he had worked to secure his conviction, and within a few weeks the governor had pardoned the man.

During the fall of 1885, Dixon's thoughts turned more and more frequently to the girl he had met at New Orleans. Though he and Harriet Bussey had kept up a correspondence since parting, her father sternly forbade a marriage. Finally, after spending a restless night at Wrightsville Beach, where he had gone for a short holiday, Dixon decided that he must go immediately to see Harriet at her home in Columbus, Georgia. "Late one afternoon at the falls of the Chattahoochee River, I declared my love, she accepted me and we drove home in the twilight."[22]

The marriage was not to be an easy matter, however, in view of the opposition offered by Harriet's father. At last they took the course of determined lovers and eloped to Montgomery, Alabama.

> On March 3rd, 1886, we stood before a preacher in a little Baptist Church and he pronounced us man and wife. We settled in a six room house, for which we paid ten dollars a month rent,

Thomas Dixon, Sr., and His Three Sons, Thomas, Frank, and Clarence, 1888

Thomas Dixon and His Wife Harriet, 1903

situated on Washington Street in Shelby, and I found a peace, poise, and harmony never known before—a peace destined to revolutionize life.[23]

Dr. Bussey was dismayed at the deed, not becoming reconciled to the couple until several years had passed.

Now at last Dixon felt that his life had meaning, that he had a sense of direction which would bring him every happiness. But as the months went by, he became more and more dissatisfied with the legal profession. He and Harriet talked many hours of his future law career, which no longer held much attraction for him. For weeks on end, he could not bear to enter his law office, and his clients, not finding him, frequently turned in other directions for help. Dixon's practice fell off alarmingly, and Frank, losing patience with his brother's indolence, upbraided him for letting a promising career come to nothing.

Dixon agonized over the problem as he sat alone or with Harriet. Was there something wrong with him or with the life around him? The question plagued him endlessly. His future appeared indefinite and his past successes now seemed tasteless. Harriet sensed the spiritual conflict disturbing her husband; she consoled him and urged him to follow whatever principle he felt was best for him. Dixon reviewed the whole course of his youth. He could not find meaning in a life that, in spite of its brilliance as student and legislator, seemed erratic and without purpose. In this frame of mind he visited Wilmington Beach, North Carolina, and climbed the high dunes overlooking the ocean.

As far away as my eye could reach, I saw huge white, thundering, foaming, mountains rolling in on the beach from out of the mists of eternity. I stood rooted in my tracks for more than an hour in breathless awe.

> For the first time in life I became conscious of the Spirit of God expressing omnipotence in nature—of the universal, infinite mind in action. It was sublime. With uncovered head I walked in the secret place of the Almighty. And I seemed to realize clearly that the marvelous power behind the glory of the sweep of the sun and tide was somehow the same force within me that drove the beat of my heart. I was one with it all.
>
> I descended from the sand dune a different man. A light was shining in my heart that would not go out. I breathed deeply and took a new hold on life. It had a new meaning.[24]

The faded memory of his experience as a child in New Prospect Church, his agnostic inclinations at Wake Forest, and the earnest prayers of his father now came back to him with clarity. Finally he told Harriet that a voice inside was calling him to a life better than he had known before. "You must hear that inner voice," Harriet answered. "Nothing else matters."[25] Dixon went immediately to his father and announced his decision. The elder Dixon replied happily, "It has come then, the call of God to a higher life! Of course, I knew it would. The Lord has promised that all my sons will preach the gospel of Jesus Christ."[26]

IV

Pulpit and Platform

The years of indecision and doubt now seemed behind. Dixon was ordained on October 6, 1886, in the old campus church at Wake Forest College, after a sermon preached by the father of Dr. William Royall, Dixon's former teacher. Four weeks later Dixon was called to a pastorate in Goldsboro, North Carolina. The fiery young preacher in turn pleased and antagonized his congregation. The church members had never before been confronted by a minister who preached a theology that was lulling to the senses one Sunday and devasting to them the next. With feelings of mixed awe and exasperation, the members saw that here was a man to be reckoned with. In the pulpit Dixon showed no compromise of principle, no fear of criticism; his boldness and forthright sincerity soon brought him more than local prominence. The weeks that followed were happy and exciting. Now he had the opportunity to tell the people all that was bubbling up from his mind and heart.

In November Dixon preached several sermons at a meeting of the Neuse-Atlantic Baptist Association held in Kinston, North Carolina, at which the ministers could keep a portion of their collections as "salary." On the third night of the convention week, Dixon preached to an unusually large congregation who had heard of his forceful personality. Though he impressed the listeners by his oratorical abilities, he evidently did not inspire their charitable inclinations, for the collection of the evening totaled only $6.64.[1] This small amount is interesting in view of the fact that only a few years later Dixon was to receive as much as a thousand dollars for a single lecture.

Dixon had served his Goldsboro pastorate scarcely six months when, on April 10, 1887, he was offered a charge at the Second Baptist Church in Raleigh. Since the church had been without a pastor for more than two months, the committee urged him to accept at once. The salary for the year was set at fourteen hundred dollars, an attractive figure to Dixon at the time. Added to the great increase in salary was the thought that he would be able to preach from a larger church in the capital of the state. His experiences in Raleigh as a legislator had left him with the desire to exert his influence as much as possible against the corruption that had driven him from politics. Later in the month he accepted the offer and began an energetic pastorate in his new home.

Dixon's reputation as an eloquent, persuasive young minister spread rapidly, even as far away as New England, and before the end of another six months the Dudley Street Church in Boston, Massachusetts, had made him a very flattering offer. The possibility of preaching in a great city fired Dixon's imagination, for he now saw as his goal the spreading of a message of hope to the great masses who swarmed the city streets. With impetuous enthusiasm he persuaded his wife Harriet, or "Pink" as he called her, to start packing for the trip. A son, Thomas Dixon III, had recently been born to them, and on the journey north they took along a Negro nurse. Upon arriving in Boston, they proceeded to a hotel in the middle of the city, where the manager informed them that the nurse could not remain with them in the hotel. Dixon answered heatedly that the nurse had stayed with the family wherever it had stopped in the past. The manager was firm, however, in his refusal. Dixon, invoking the spirit of the two great abolitionists from Massachusetts, departed in anger:

> In the name of William Lloyd Garrison and Wendell Phillips I gave him a piece of my mind.
>
> I shook the dust of the place from my feet and moved that night to a small hotel far out in Roxbury.[2]

Dixon's first Sunday with his new congregation was not an auspicious one. The feeling of self-confidence that had persuaded him to accept the new charge now suddenly left him:

> I shall never forget my first experience in a great city church. I was fresh from the far-off South, full of fire and zeal. I knew the church building had a capacity of 1,500 and that they had 1,600 members. My own little village church [at Shelby] barely held 400. I dreamed of a sea of eager living faces. I trusted to the inspiration of the hour to give me my best thought. The eventful morning in my life came. Shall I ever forget it? I sat shivering in the pulpit, the blood in my veins fairly frozen at the sight before me—a desert of empty benches with just 80 human beings scattered among them. I stumbled through the ser-

vice somehow. I tried to preach but I could not. The sight of that silent and solemn mausoleum . . . took all the soul out of me. I made the most stupid failure of my life. It makes me shiver to think of that December morning now.[3]

The inexperienced, twenty-three-year-old preacher had allowed his enthusiasm, it seemed, to place him in a situation that he was not certain he could cope with. The solemn, unsmiling faces in the new large church panicked him. The first several services were ordeals that he dreaded from one Sunday to the next. Feeling extremely self-conscious and adopting a defensive, serious attitude to hide his nervousness, he was greatly disconcerted during his sermon one morning by repeated interruptions from a crying baby in the rear of the church. At last, in exasperation, Dixon called out impatiently, "Will the mother of that baby kindly take the child out!"[4] Great was his mortification to see his wife Harriet arise and convey the squealing infant Tommie up the aisle and out the rear door of the church. As an ill-suppressed titter arose throughout the congregation, Dixon colored violently and then, suddenly swept by the humor of his awkward situation, broke into hearty laughter. The congregation joined him, and from that point on, Dixon once more was the enthusiastic young minister who was determined to carry his message to the people.

Dixon's congregation stimulated him to very careful preparation of his sermons, for among the members of his church were men of considerable intellectual curiosity. Through them Dixon became acquainted with the Boston bookstores, where he spent many hours browsing among the shelves and meeting new friends of similar interests. Among his closest friends at the time was Dr. Francis L.

Goss, a graduate of the Harvard Medical School, who attended at the birth of Dixon's daughter Louise. With Goss, Dixon spent many hours discussing the many religious, political, and scientific ideas of the day.

In the fall of 1887, not long after he had begun his pastorate at the Dudley Street Church, Dixon went to the Tremont Temple to attend a lecture entitled "The Southern Problem." The speaker, Justin D. Fulton, had recently returned from a six weeks' study of the Southern scene. He reported that the South was a hotbed of revolution and that the North must brace itself against the impending upheaval. Dixon was so much antagonized by the views expressed that he sprang to his feet in the middle of the lecture and denounced the speaker as a liar and a fool. After heated debate and after almost being arrested, Dixon was persuaded to resume his seat until the end of the program. He now decided that he must someday tell the world what he knew of the South at first hand. From that night forward he set himself to studying closely the history of the Civil War and Reconstruction. Greatly disturbed by the sectional feeling in various parts of the country, he thought that by presenting a full account of Reconstruction from the Southern viewpoint he might bring about a closer sympathy between people of Northern and Southern views. The best medium for presenting his views seemed to be a trilogy of novels modeled upon the work of the Polish writer, Henryk Sienkiewicz. Dixon greatly admired the works of this novelist, whose stories of oppression at the hands of conquerors suggested to Dixon a similarity between his native South and Poland. The Southerners, like the people of Poland, had suffered indignity and brutality from military occupational forces. In such novels as Sienkiewicz's *The Deluge, With Fire and Sword, Children of the Soil,* and *Knights of the Cross,* which cover the period of the Polish struggle with the Military Order of Teutonic Knights, Dixon saw that the woes of the Polish people were in many respects like those of the South during Reconstruction.

Through the spring of 1888 Dixon's prominence as a dynamic pulpit personality steadily grew. Members of his congregation jokingly remarked that if their young preacher's fire and zeal did not land him in jail, he was destined for great accomplishments. In May, much to his surprise, Dixon was invited to make the commencement address at Wake Forest College. Such an invitation was extremely flattering to a young man of twenty-four who only five years before had left his Baptist alma mater an agnostic! After working over his sources again and again, Dixon delivered a speech that left his audience enthusiastically applauding. The Reverend J. D. Hufham, a prominent member of the Board of Trustees at the college, praised the speaker highly and said that he supposed young Dixon would, in the near future, be nominated to receive the honorary degree of Doctor of Divinity. Dixon dismissed the possibility as being rather unlikely, but after pausing a moment, he suddenly said that he could nominate another person, a young man who, Dixon thought, was better qualified to receive an honorary degree. The several members of the Board who were present expressed interest in Dixon's words, and for the next hour or so Dixon elaborated glowingly upon the qualifications of his classmate at Johns Hopkins, Woodrow Wilson, as a young man of brilliant promise. Dixon outlined in detail the career of Wilson up to that time and concluded:

His study of our form of government will become a classic in the literature of Democracy. He has chosen the profession of teaching. He will make a great institution out of any college that calls him. He is the type of man we need as President of the United States, and on that platform I name him for the degree.[5]

As a result of the nomination, Wilson received the Doctor of Laws degree. This was the first honorary degree awarded the young scholar, and the occasion brought him wide publicity in the press. In later years Wilson would repay Dixon for his good turn in a way that could not have been foreseen at the Wake Forest commencement exercises.

Upon his return to Boston, Dixon learned that he was being considered for a charge at the Twenty-third Street Baptist Church in New York City. Upon receiving the official request to come to New York, Dixon pondered the matter for several weeks until, late in July, he offered his resignation to the Boston church, indicating that if his purpose had been to be a pastor of a family church, he would not have considered leaving. His aim now appeared to be, however, to work among the great unreached masses in Manhattan, and his acceptance of the New York charge would be a step in that direction.[6]

Dixon's ministry in Boston, although antagonizing some of the older members of the congregation, had been especially appealing to young men whose problems he understood and boldly discussed from the pulpit. The Board of Deacons, realizing that they were about to lose a vital force in their community, offered immediately to double his salary if he would remain, but Dixon would not be dissuaded.

Soon after accepting his new charge in August, 1889, Dixon was shocked by the abrupt change from the comparative serenity of his pastorate in Boston to the turmoil of

Manhattan, where the crowds seemed indifferent to appeal or reason, jostling one another blindly. It appeared that Dixon's voice would surely be drowned in the great waves of humanity that seemed to engulf him from every side. With a sickening realization of the apparent impossibility of being heard or heeded, he sank into a dejection as dark as the misgivings that had beset him about his career as a lawyer. In churches that were capable of holding hundreds of people, he was dispirited to see only a few persons in what appeared to be a kind of death house. Was he here to die spiritually like so many other ministers who had learned the coldness of the great city? New York seemed to him a huge spiritual gulf awaiting those persons who were foolish enough to hope that they could make the slightest ripple on its waters of indifference. Later, in a book concerning his New York ministry, Dixon indicated that the city seemed to be a fascinating, deadly lure for the unsuspecting preacher:

> New York is the biggest graveyard of Protestant preachers in America. Toward the dazzling light of its metropolitan life they eagerly flock from the smaller cities. Against its adamantine surface they dash their brains out like bewildered birds around a lighthouse.[7]

The unfavorable impression that Dixon received in his first months as a minister in New York never wholly left him thereafter, though he was to live there much of his later life. Always bold and explicit in his statements, he was prompted to say:

> New York is one of the most *godless* [cities], if not the most godless city in America. The growth of churches and the growth of population shows that the vitality of Protestantism has declined steadily during the last forty years.[8]

The indifference that seemed to confront Dixon on every side sometimes colored his evaluation of the many people about him, and in a burst of impatience he once wrote:

I have encountered nothing on this earth that compares to the average half-well-to-do New Yorker. He has little brains, no culture—not even the rudiments of common sense—but being a New Yorker, he assumes everything![9]

Greatly concerned about the apathy he encountered in his church and in those he visited, Dixon realized that he must throw off the oppressiveness of his situation or leave New York City entirely. It was true that the Twenty-third Street Church was much larger than any other charge he had held, but the hundreds of empty seats mocked him at every service. He worked upon his sermons with great care, repeating them over and over, sometimes to his patient, long-suffering wife, until he could say them without hesitation or repetition. Studying far into the night, he worked to give his congregations fresh, vital messages. Searching through literature in Greek, Latin, and French, he sought for allusion and exposition. As he later recalled, this period was a reminder of his days as a college student when he had struggled so hard to win the French Medal:

I studied and worked as never before. I prepared my addresses with infinite care. I put in them not only all the strength of scholarly thought that my mind could summon, I put into them my immortal soul. When I fumbled my way down from the platform on Sunday nights after two services, my eyes were dim and every nerve was quivering with exhaustion. I had given all that was in me.[10]

Such preaching got reactions. A. C. Wheeler, the senior dramatic critic of the city, heard of the powerful sermons being preached by the youthful minister and decided to see and hear Dixon in person. Much impressed by the forceful personality in the pulpit, he wrote a long article praising Dixon and giving him widespread publicity in the press. Soon the church at the corner of Twenty-third Street and Lexington Avenue became a center of intellectual ferment. "His handsome appearance, his deep, musical voice"[11] made Dixon's church one of the best attended in the city. By the spring of 1889, the church could hold little more than a fraction of the crowds that flocked to criticize or praise the brilliant speaker. The Young Men's Christian Association, which was located a block away and had a much larger auditorium, was rented for the Sunday services.

Noting that services in the city were attended mostly by women, Dixon dramatically appealed to men by boldly discussing local government, saloons, gambling, or whatever he felt would interest them:

> With the increase of my congregation I found myself in the leading role of a daily drama of tremendous excitement. All sorts and conditions of men thronged the services.[12]

Sunday after Sunday Dixon hammered away at the problems of alcohol, religious apathy, denominational narrowness, and politics. Frequently, when matters of church policy or belief arose within his congregation, he decried uniformity for its own sake, maintaining that any attempt to force conformity only destroyed the quality that the churches were seeking—a unity of ideals:

> Uniformity gained by force does not mean unity. The belief that it does is the one tragic superstition of our history. To preserve this "unity" of the Jewish religion the constituted authorities crucified Jesus Christ. Such is the record of the thumbscrew, the rack, the wheel, the torch. This spirit drenched England in blood, bathed the world in Huguenot tears, sent Alva into the

Netherlands to butcher 18,000 victims in six years, and in Protestant history burned Servetus in the Old World, the witches in New England, and imprisoned and whipped the Baptists in Virginia.[13]

Dixon condemned the lack of vitality in the modern practice of Christianity, stating that Christian practice had been weakened to such a great extent that it was hardly recognizable as the embodiment of those principles set forth in the New Testament. In spite of his own interest in Greek and Roman history and literature, he later recorded that the influences of the Greek and Roman cultures had contributed greatly toward weakening the purity of Christian ideals:

> Christianity is yet burdened with the legacy of pagan theology. The astrology of the Chaldeans is still a potent force in too many lives. The Greek and Roman Fates wove their accursed threads not only into the web of ancient life, but through literature, philosophy, and religion, those three old hags are still spinning, weaving, and cutting the tangled threads of human destiny.[14]

The rapidly developing mechanistic and pragmatic philosophy of the nineteenth century also often evoked Dixon's sermons. Deploring a lack of faith in everything that cannot be proved by modern scientific testimony, Dixon remarked, concerning the historians of the past and present:

> According to such a theory, Plutarch, Caesar, Tacitus, Xenophon, and Herodotus, are not credible witnesses, because forsooth they did not live in our day. According to such a theory, we would crucify Xenophon and crown Zola, the modern apostle of putrefaction; we would outlaw Plutarch, and canonize Ingersoll as a teacher of men![15]

Dixon's sermons soon held a tremendous attraction, even

for many persons not accustomed to attending church. His appeal, inspiring and forthright, had an almost hypnotic effect upon his listeners. Here was something new to people accustomed to hearing the average sermon. The impression that a reluctant newcomer to the services received upon his first visit is indicative of the compelling personality in the pulpit:

> In the view which I had of him he appeared to be six feet three in stature and almost weirdly gaunt. He did not stand erect in the parade sense, and his long limbs betokened an enormous sinewy power rather than grace or symmetry. His dark, spare, close-shaven face, his plentiful coal-black hair, carelessly pushed backward from his temples, his strong, almost cadaverous jaw, and his black, deep-set, and scintillant eyes made up a personality that arrested my interest at once. It was a type of man especially forged for hard, earnest, fearless work in some direction.
>
> He had not spoken five minutes before some instinct which I could not analyze told me that he had something to say to the world and meant to say it.[16]

Dixon spoke with an air of authority, yet tenderly, and in spite of his bold convictions, with an intonation that conveyed a sense of humility before vital truths. He developed his subject clearly, never resorting to involved abstractions but always using the precise phrasing necessary to lead his audience. Sometimes, when a particular illustration of his argument appealed strongly to him, his face would light up and his voice would rise resonantly; again, his manner would drop to the colloquial level. At no time, however, would he permit the dignity of his theme to be lowered or lost. Whatever the allusion or however tempting the illustration, he never let his enthusiasm lead him very far from his stated subject.

In Dixon's sermons there was no puling hesitancy or weak sentimentality. He made no attempt to modify Christianity to suit jaded senses or convenient rationalizations. There was a fascinating, powerful appeal about him that caused A. C. Wheeler to write that "the energizing young apostle marked the renaissance of new Christian endeavor and a new Christian socialism."[17]

The meteoric popularity of Dixon's sermons soon came to the attention of John D. Rockefeller, the multimillionaire, who was at that time a member of the fashionable Fifth Avenue Baptist Church. He attended one of Dixon's sermons and was impressed by the pulpit presence and forthrightness of the young minister. At the end of the service, he greeted Dixon and invited him and his family to dine at the Rockefeller home. After the meal, when the ladies had withdrawn to another room, Rockefeller probed Dixon with incisive questions concerning the young minister's ideals and plans for the future. Dixon enthusiastically expressed a long-cherished dream of someday building a great temple in the heart of Manhattan so that he might reach the thousands of people who thronged the New York streets. Dixon said that he wanted to teach "the presence of God in all life."[18] In order to proclaim this doctrine he said that he had dreamed of constructing a great building forty stories high, with classrooms, offices, and an auditorium that would seat three thousand people. Going straight to the point, the practical-minded oil magnate looked penetratingly at Dixon and asked:

"What will your building cost?"

"A million in cash. The lot [office rentals and investments] will carry the rest."

"Good. It's a great ideal. I'm with you heart and soul. I'll give you half a million. The others must do as much. When the subscriptions are in, let me know and I'll draw my check."[19]

In the next several weeks, Dixon and Rockefeller spent much time together. Young Dixon came to admire greatly the man who was one of the most controversial figures of the time. Rockefeller taught Dixon to ice skate on the private rink at his home on West Fifty-fourth Street, and amid laughter at the precarious positions assumed by Dixon's lanky frame and his ludicrous falls upon the ice, the men enthusiastically laid plans to build a structure and religious program that would draw the attention of the world.

Dixon thought that he could raise the other half of the cost in his own congregation, for many of the members had already heard Dixon discuss his plans of someday founding an interdenominational temple in downtown Manhattan—plans to which they had reacted favorably. Dixon was unprepared, however, for the fierce intradenominational struggle that his proposal stirred up. Other Baptist churches of the city became envious of the great sum of money Rockefeller had pledged.

In the weeks that followed, Dixon saw his dreams fading. His strongest opposition came from Calvary Church on West Fifty-seventh Street. The congregation there had erected a large church and maintained a membership of twenty-five hundred persons; it claimed to be the largest congregation in the entire Baptist church. A trustee of this congregation led the opposition against Dixon. In spite of the fact that he had the sympathy and encouragement of such outstanding men as Rockefeller and Charles Evans

Thomas Dixon, the Young Minister, Age 28

Dixon's Home on West Ninety-fourth Street,
New York, 1893

Hughes, Dixon at last realized that for the time being he would have to forsake his plans to build the temple.

Bitterly disappointed by his failure and quick to reveal his feelings, Dixon antagonized some members of his congregation, who in turn sought to weaken his efforts. He cared little for the formality of his position, and his actions were always prompted by a personal code of ethics that at times shocked the members of his church. His profession did not in the least restrict him from speaking upon any subject that he thought needed attention. To Dixon, no special privileges or restraints applied to the minister as differentiated from the layman, a principle he expressed both from the pulpit and on the printed page:

> The so-called "sacredness" of the office has never and never will oppress me. I am worth just as much as a minister as I am a man, and no more. . . . The letters R E V that men put before my name add nothing to its weight. They mean nothing; they are nothing.[20]

Occasionally Dixon's brother Clarence, who now held a pastorate in Brooklyn, assisted Dixon in the Sunday services. Their different interpretations of certain points of doctrine, however, sometimes caused friction between them. Clarence, more conservative than his younger brother, was at times alarmed by the daring and seemingly cavalier manner in which Dixon faced issues. Dixon in turn was dissatisfied with certain fundamentalistic aspects of Clarence's theology. Dixon's approach to existing evils was abrupt, militant, and uncompromising. He sometimes lost patience with Clarence's more pacifistic approach. Their differences reached a climax in late June, 1891, when Dixon publicly denounced several of Clarence's theological principles in a letter to the *New York Herald and Advertiser.* As soon as Dixon saw the letter in print, he felt ashamed of his hasty action and immediately wrote to Clarence, deploring the letter's lack of tact and consideration:

DEAR CLARENCE,

On reading over my note in the Herald and Advertiser, I was pained and shocked at the harshness and unbrotherlyness [*sic*] of its phraseology.

I do wish I had said it in a sweeter way. It sounds differently in cold type from what it did in my heart. I hope you will forget it.[21]

Dixon was not alone in regretting the letter. His brother Frank, now living in Oakland, California, saw the letter in the paper and wrote to Clarence on the sixteenth of July concerning Dixon's action:

I was deeply pained to read Tom's letter in the "Herald" respecting you. Oh I deplore it so deeply. Tom is too impulsive and inconsiderate. His heart is warm, though, and the promptings of it are toward goodness. His error is in theory. He thinks the scourge of John the Baptist more effectual than Christlike gentleness.

He is making of himself a prophet rather than a preacher of the Gospel. He believes too much in laying the axe to the throat of the trees. I thought his axe must have flown off the handle when it struck you.

Most likely I don't agree with your theology any more than Tom does, but dear me! I love you. If a man's theology doesn't give him a sweeter spirit than Tom's, it is mere rot. I'm sorry, sorry, sorry about this matter.[22]

Though the relations between the brothers were strained for a short time, Dixon's impulsive plea to be forgiven and Clarence's lasting affection for his younger brother soon smoothed the ruffled feelings. The divergence of their views, nevertheless, occasionally caused disagreements in the future.

However much Dixon and Clarence may have differed on certain points of theology, they were strongly unified in their view of the teachings of Colonel Robert G. Ingersoll. Ingersoll, an eloquent platform personality, drew large audiences wherever he appeared. Dixon had acquired an especial aversion to the facile, brilliant Ingersoll. He attacked his teachings on many occasions, sometimes quixotically, and placed himself in situations from which only an unflinching, unbending forthrightness could extricate him. Dixon even brought his attacks together in a volume entitled *Dixon on Ingersoll: Ten Discourses Delivered in Association Hall.*[23] The book systematically attempts to refute ten previous lectures by Ingersoll. The refutations reveal strong conservative, even reactionary, principles. Dixon's early home training accounts for many passages defending motherhood, the sanctity of the home, and man-made laws. Dixon and Ingersoll had frequently condemned each other in the columns of the newspapers,[24] and in the book Dixon expanded his newspaper attacks.

At the same time that Dixon was preparing his volume for the press, his brother Clarence was also engaged in a heated controversy with Ingersoll. Noticing that some of the younger members of his church were being influenced by the lectures of Ingersoll, Clarence gave a series of sermons on agnosticism, with "Ingersollism" the special target of his texts. Ingersoll, who had been educated for the legal profession in his native Illinois, had entered the political field but, after losing an election to the United States Senate, had turned to the lecture platform with tremendous success. As chairman of the Liberal League, Ingersoll had, in 1878, advanced a petition of seventy thousand signatures urging the repeal of the "Comstock Law," an enactment designed to curb such books, papers, pictures, and establishments as might be considered injurious to public morals. On February 8, 1892, Clarence received from Ingersoll the following communication:

MY DEAR SIR:

My attention was called for the first time, this morning, to a report that appeared in the Brooklyn Edition of the New York *World* on February 1st, 1892, of a lecture delivered by you on the 31st of January at the Hansen Place Baptist Church, and in the report the following is said to have been uttered by you: "A few years ago it was found that pictures and impure publications were passing through the mails. Anthony Comstock decided to stop it. On investigation, whom should he find representing the publishers of impure literature but Colonel Ingersoll—*paid to pollute the minds of the young of this generation*." I write for the purpose of giving you an opportunity to retract, whether by stating that you used no such language, or that the statements are absolutely untrue. If you do not make such retraction I shall commence an action against you for having uttered a malicious libel.[25]

Undaunted, Clarence refused to retract his statement and answered with two and a half columns in the *New York World*, giving documentary evidence that Ingersoll had represented the publishers in their efforts to influence Congress to repeal the Comstock Law.

Soon after, Ingersoll brought suit against Clarence for five thousand dollars, but Clarence continued his series of sermons on agnosticism while awaiting the trial. At last Ingersoll wrote through his attorney that he had indeed represented the publishers of "liberal" literature in their efforts to repeal the law because he feared that some of his own works might be excluded. His chief objection was to Clarence Dixon's statement that he had been *paid* for his services by these publishers. If the minister would retract that portion of the statement about paid services, Ingersoll would dismiss the suit. Clarence replied immediately, urging that the trial be held as originally scheduled and concluding that, for the sake of Ingersoll's reputation, it would be far better should it be shown that Ingersoll's services *had* been paid for rather than given free of charge, to Clarence a much worse act from an ethical standpoint.

At the trial, the judge held that it was not libelous to say that a lawyer had been paid for his services. The question before the court was, "Did Mr. Ingersoll represent the publishers of obscene literature in their efforts to have the Comstock Law repealed?"[26] It was found that Anthony Comstock had provided documentary evidence of the fact in one of his books, and Ingersoll, having already admitted this, asked his attorney to have the suit dropped immediately. After the trial, in the months that followed, both Clarence and Thomas Dixon continued to attack Ingersoll in the pulpit and in the newspapers.

The experience Dixon had gained in his Boston church and the challenging life he now led in New York gave him a sense of enthusiasm and determination which, coupled with his magnetic personality, brought him more and more prominence.

In addition to his preaching engagements, Dixon frequently lectured to large secular crowds throughout greater New York City. His reputation as a bold, fearless critic of the city government gave him enthusiastic supporters and dangerous enemies. Dixon's activities were now ceaseless, and he seemed to be a human dynamo that derived its energy from some hidden, ineluctable source. Sometimes going all night without sleep, he pursued his objectives with an obsessive dedication that, when he found himself trembling with fatigue and excitement, boded ill for his gaunt, nearly six-foot four-inch frame.

During his early residence in New York, Dixon changed homes frequently, always trying to find more healthful and comfortable quarters. He first moved to a small apartment far uptown, close to the elevated train, which was a constant reminder of his lack of privacy. The family then moved to larger quarters with six rooms, but, as Dixon said later, the iron grillwork around the back of the apartment gave them the feeling of being incarcerated. Desiring a place still closer to his work, Dixon tried a boarding house dominated by an old lady whose eye could freeze a child into immobility. While here, Dixon's little daughter Louise became gravely ill of pneumonia and was attended by two doctors and two trained nurses for six weeks.

Constantly beset by the noises and crowds of the city, Dixon dreamed of someday getting away to a setting removed from the smoke, sounds, and pressures of Manhattan. He thought that he had found such a place when a vacant lot at Bensonhurst, with a sixty-foot waterfront, was offered for sale. He immediately bought the lot and started building a house on it. Now at last his dream of a beautiful suburban home would come true. But the dream faded soon after the family had moved in. Dixon was kept busy in his hours at home clearing the waterfront of tin cans, driftwood, dead cats and dogs, and various other flotsam and jetsam that confronted the family each morning. After services on the first Sunday following the move into his new home, Dixon was caught up in an enormous crowd on the way to Coney Island by way of Bensonhurst and was unable to make his way to the trains. Struggling for more than two hours to buy a ticket and board one of the excursion cars, he finally gave up the venture and returned to Manhattan, where he remained until the next morning.

When winter arrived, the first snowstorm covered the trolley rails, broke down the telephone lines, and prevented Dixon from getting home for two days. After only a few months in his new home, he was ready to move almost anywhere. After advertising for four weeks, he found a buyer whom he termed a bigger fool than he was to want such a place.

Dixon now turned to a five-acre lot on Staten Island, with the house sitting on top of the highest hill. In spite of the magnificent view of Sandy Hook and the sea, the mosquitoes were so numerous and venomous that life was miserable for the Dixons. Little Jordan, their third child, suffered particularly. His legs would swell greatly each time the mosquitoes bit him. By the end of the summer he had fallen into a perilous malarial fever, and the family for a time despaired of his life. He finally recovered from the attack, but another serious illness, probably poliomyelitis, left him paralyzed in both legs.

To get away from the miasmal situation on Staten Island, Dixon turned once more to Manhattan and, in the autumn of 1893, settled on West Ninety-fourth Street, in the block that faces Central Park. The house, which Dixon called "a nineteen-foot slit in a block of scorched mud with a brownstone veneer in front,"[27] had narrow, dark halls and a paved "cat-yard" nineteen by twenty feet. His dream of a beautiful, comfortable home seemed impossible to attain.

The constant demands of his lectures and sermons, the anxiety over his family in their frequent moves from house to house, and a burning zeal for accomplishment finally undermined Dixon's health. The long-predicted breakdown, of which Dixon had encountered the premonitory urgings in recent months and against which his physician, Dr. John Woodham, had repeatedly warned him, came at long last. As Dixon later recalled, "I flopped in bed and the lights went out."[28] The weeks of December, 1893, were dark for Dixon and his family. Not yet thirty years of age and with great plans of future accomplishment simmering in his brain, he now found himself dangerously ill, with grave doubts as to his sanity and life. Light and noises were torturing to him, and the three children moved silently about the house in awe of the unbelievable power that could lay their father, always filled with such boundless energy, pale and silent upon the bed. Dr. Woodham urged Harriet to remove her husband to a restful location far away from the pressures of his New York activities.

As the weeks of the new year progressed, Dixon and his wife made plans to move to Cape Charles, Virginia, where a substantial home was found on Chesapeake Bay. Dixon's condition was now somewhat improved, and the thought of living by the sea, always fascinating to Dixon, caused him daily to regain strength. In the late winter of 1894, the move to Cape Charles was made, and almost immediately the signs of Dixon's recovery could be seen. The smell of grass and flowers, the exhilarating breath from the sea, the quiet woodland walks—all of these were a wonderful tonic for Dixon. Though he remained still a man of extremely angular frame, he daily gained strength and resolved to return wholeheartedly to his work. His congregation had been generous and sympathetic during his illness, and the lectures he had given had provided him with comfortable circumstances. From Monday through Thursday, Dixon worked on his sermons and lectures at Cape Charles. Early on Friday morning he caught the train for New York and remained at his downtown Manhattan quarters through the Sunday services. Although the weekly commuting journey from Virginia to New York was tiring, Dixon felt that he had found a permanent situation at last. Once more he entered upon his activities with vigor and perspective.

By the beginning of 1895, Dixon felt that he could no longer remain a pastor of a denominational church. The restrictions of the Baptists, he thought, hampered him in the expression of his ideals for a more universally appealing religion. Always expansive in his actions and aims, he thought his congregation was too cautious, too conservative; if he was to reach the masses, he must withdraw from the denomination and establish a new church founded on principles closer to his desires. The failure to build the great temple in downtown Manhattan had also added to Dixon's dissatisfaction with his pastorate. Toward the end of March, Dixon decided that he must definitely sever his connections with the Twenty-third Street church within a month. The whole aim of denominationalism now seemed to him at variance with all his concepts of religious freedom. On March 11, the *New York Times*, which now regularly reported the activities of the remarkable young minister, gave the following account of Dixon's resignation:

The Rev. Thomas Dixon, pastor of the Twenty-third Street Baptist Church, yesterday morning announced his determina-

> tion to sever his connection with the church, and to found a new one on a broad and popular platform. Instead of speaking on "Spectacle versus Sensation," in reply to exceptions of "An Old Fashioned Clergyman," as had been announced, Mr. Dixon read his resignation to the congregation . . . .[29]

After reading his resignation, Dixon added: "I wish to have a perfectly free pulpit, in which to preach to their last logical conclusion those things which have become to me of supreme importance."[30] Dixon said that he was most concerned for the great masses of people who did not attend the average church service. To attract and convert these people was his ambition. "I believe," he concluded, "it is more important to lift many men out of the ditch than to spend my time making a few men Baptists."[31]

The effect of Dixon's announcement to the packed church was electric. Murmurs of dissent at his views swept through the congregation. Though many members of the church had heard Dixon voice from the pulpit in a general way the advantages of a nondenominational church, they had accepted it as in keeping with his enthusiastic personality. Alfred D. Clinch, clerk of the Board of Trustees, was chagrined at Dixon's resignation and intimated that the action was an insult to the Baptist ministry. The following week was stormy with accusations and denials. Some persons charged that Dixon was forced to resign; others that he had an income of over twenty thousand dollars a year, that he was living off the "fat of the land," and that he wanted a still larger income than his present pastorate could supply. The following Sunday Dixon vehemently denied the accusation and, running his hands down his bony frame, said that it was quite evident that he was not living nearly so well as had been charged. Dixon contended that his sole desire in leaving the Baptist church was to reach a wider audience. He said that during the five years and nine months in which he had been pastor of the Twenty-third Street Baptist Church, the congregation had contributed more than eighty-one thousand dollars, a greater amount than had been given in the previous twenty years; his own income, however, had never exceeded nine thousand dollars a year and had been as low as one thousand. James A. Bennett, president of the Board of Trustees for the church, wrote a public letter clarifying the reasons for Dixon's resignation and relieving him of all charges. But Dixon left the Twenty-third Street Baptist Church amid strong criticism.

Planning to open a new "Church of the People" in April, Dixon publicly outlined the organization and aims of his new venture. Half the members of the Board of Deacons would be women, a decision that called forth the enduring gratitude of the female sex. In the new church Dixon planned to have three assistants, one of them a Universalist. The motto of the new church, "In essentials unity; in nonessentials, liberty; in all things charity," was widely advertised in the days that followed. On the first Sunday in April, 1895, after days of intense preparation, Dixon opened his new, nondenominational church in the Academy of Music, the largest building available, where eleven years before, on his first day in New York, the young college student had celebrated his twentieth birthday by hearing Adelina Patti sing. But even the immense auditorium of the Academy of Music could not hold the congregation. A large cordon of policemen was required to handle the hundreds of people seeking entrance to the building.

Since he boldly proclaimed his political views from the

pulpit, Dixon made firm friends of those who agreed with him and enemies of those who disagreed. He drew to his services the largest congregations in the country as he fearlessly discussed the men and issues of the day. Policemen were now frequently required to maintain order. On September 6, 1896, while Dixon was denouncing William Jennings Bryan as a Presidential candidate, many members of the congregation got up from their seats and left the service:

> It was when Mr. Dixon was denouncing the free coinage of silver as a "bunko-steering business" that the demonstration began. Several shouted, "You don't know what you are talking about!" One gray-haired man arose and exclaimed: "I won't stand this any longer," and rushed from the building. He was followed by fifty others, some applying unkind epithets to the preacher as they left. The exodus unnerved Mr. Dixon for the moment, but he was quickly reassured by the applause from those who endorsed his views.[32]

A short time later one of Dixon's services was again the scene of a near riot. On this occasion violence was averted by a special detail of determined policemen. There was a mixture of threats, shouts, hisses, and applause as the minister denounced the "Chicago Platform" of Bryan. Dixon, now accustomed to dealing with unruly audiences, paid little attention to his hecklers and continued the service while the disorder was going on.

As a result of his open condemnation of the Tammany machine and his opposition to the appointment of Joseph Koch as chairman of the Board of Excise, Dixon was arrested during the second week in September and released under a bond of twenty-five hundred dollars. Dixon claimed that Koch had been charged with two felonies, and a newspaper reporter found that the jury which had freed Koch had been packed by Tammany Hall. The Sunday following his release, Dixon again openly denounced Tammany Hall from the pulpit. The editor of the *New York Sun,* Charles A. Dana, attacked the minister vigorously. Dixon replied through a lawyer that should his name again be libeled in the newspaper, he would sue for half a million dollars. Significantly, Dixon's name did not further appear in a discreditable light, but for a time he felt that he was going to be "railroaded" to jail by the powerful forces in Tammany Hall. Only his unflinching boldness before the threats of his enemies at last convinced them that they were dealing with a fearless personality who might seriously embarrass them should they press further charges of libel.

A few days later Dixon went hunting on Staten Island and killed seventeen robins for a pie. Although he said that he was unaware of a city ordinance against shooting robins, he was arrested and fined twenty-five dollars. Immediately upon hearing of his arrest and fine, Dixon's enemies in Tammany Hall maneuvered through a legal technicality to have his case tried again. The result was that this time Dixon had to pay a fine of fifteen hundred and twenty-five dollars! The publicity that attended the event raised Dixon's lecture fee, five hundred dollars at the time, to one thousand dollars.

During the fall of 1896, Dixon had become vitally interested in the cause of Cuba's independence from Spain. He and Charles A. Dana, also a supporter of this cause, soon forgot their former enmity and became very close friends in the work. When Dixon spoke on the subject, he draped the stage with American and Cuban flags. The

Academy of Music became the national revolutionary headquarters for the Cuban cause, and Dixon was kept endlessly busy with meetings and lectures. His popularity as a speaker was now such that he was in constant demand for lecturing engagements, despite the one-thousand-dollar fee.

On September 20, while he was preaching on the Cuban cause, an amusing incident occurred to break the tension of the explosive sermon. In expectation of possible disorder during the service, policemen had stationed themselves at strategic points to prevent any interruptions from the audience. When a member of the congregation toward the rear quickly stood up, Dixon, thinking the man was going to criticize the sermon, called out sharply to the policemen to arrest the would-be heckler. The audience was thrown into an uproar when the man meekly but hurriedly intimated that he had gotten up just to go to the men's room.

Maintaining a strong interest in the issues of the day, Dixon continued to speak frequently on political subjects. A reading of his sermons reveals that they sometimes smacked more of the subjects heard at political rallies than of those usually heard at church services. Speaking frequently now at the Grand Opera House, Dixon drew crowds that halted traffic for blocks. The following titles, taken from a collection of his sermons, are indicative of the political nature of many of his messages: "The Anglo-Saxon Alliance," "Traitors at Washington," "Kitchener and Dewey," "A Letter from Santiago," "McKinley as War President," and "Roosevelt's Personality." Early in his New York ministry, Dixon had become acquainted with Theodore Roosevelt, and later when Roosevelt ran for governor, Dixon campaigned strongly for him, both in and out of the pulpit.

From the beginning of his residence at Cape Charles, Dixon's eye had been taken by a great mansion across the bay in Gloucester County. The area in which the house was set appealed to him particularly, for it was said to have been once owned by Powhatan, the famed Indian chieftain and father of the still more famed Pocahontas. The idea of owning "Elmington Manor," as the estate was called, was a dream that Dixon had hoped someday to see fulfilled, but when he had first moved to Cape Charles, his finances, though entirely adequate to provide comfortably for his family, had not been sufficient to enable him to own so pretentious a residence as Elmington Manor. Not long before the Spanish-American War, however, Dixon's income from his lectures had made him moderately wealthy. To the young man, born and raised in near poverty, the ownership of the great estate across the bay represented one of the ambitions of a lifetime. So, early in the fall of 1897, Dixon bought the new home and entered upon an extensive remodeling and decorating program. When Dixon acquired Elmington Manor, it was only a great square brick edifice finished with portland cement and painted brown. The house, built by Dr. John Prosser Tabb, the wealthiest man of the area, had been completed fifty-seven years before. The walls, three feet thick, were constructed of brick more than two hundred years old dating from colonial days. Built by hundreds of slaves, the house revealed a solid massiveness in every feature. The stairs and stair rails were constructed of polished mahogany, and the window and door sills were formed of fine Italian marble. The straight lines of the building permitted Dixon to turn the structure effectively into a modified form of a Greek revival house by adding façades and pillars on two sides. Upon completing the outside remodeling, Dixon commissioned Wanamaker's of Philadelphia to furnish and decorate the interior. The thirty-five-room,[33] three-and-a-half-story mansion was set amid five hundred acres of virgin timber. A great expanse of lawn, reaching to the edge of the bay, was bordered and dotted by over three hundred great shade trees, predominantly elm, from which the estate took its name. Here Dixon and his family began a period of gracious outdoor living which had a remarkable effect upon the general health and well-being of both children and parents.

Soon after moving to Cape Charles, Dixon had become very much interested in boats of both the sailing and the powered variety. As his enthusiasm progressed, he learned much about boat design and began to desire larger and more seaworthy craft. The first in a series of increasingly expensive boats that he owned was the "Chattahoochee," so named, Dixon said, in memory of the river on whose banks he had proposed to Harriet. After two seasons, Dixon had another, more powerful, craft built, modeled after one of the then-popular United States lifesaving boats. Though this craft was capable of going to sea, it lacked many of the conveniences and comforts for which Dixon was searching. Progressing through several more crafts and types of motive power, Dixon had built to his specifications the "Swannanoa," a naphtha-powered cruiser finished in mahogany, silk, and plush. She was a beautiful craft and handled magnificently, but Dixon soon learned that such spotless appointments were not appropriate for rough cruising while

Dixon's Home, Elmington Manor,
Gloucester County, Virginia

The "Dixie"

Interior View of Elmington Manor

hunting or fishing. After one season of operation, Dixon piloted her to New York, where he sold her before he had been at dock two hours.

Finally, early in 1897, Dixon planned a full-sized yacht capable of crossing the ocean, yet of a draught shallow enough to thread the inland waterways of Tidewater Virginia during the hunting season. After considerable searching among shipbuilders, Dixon found the man he was looking for in E. J. Tull of Pocomoke, Maryland, who built a hull about whose beautiful lines Dixon never tired of rhapsodizing. The fittings and appointments of the vessel, made in New York and New Jersey, when added to the hull, resulted in a craft of grace, durability, and comfort. Equipped with sails and a powerful naphtha engine, the "Dixie," as she was called, was launched in December, 1897. The name had been given in allusion to Dixon's name and to the fact that the craft sailed in Southern waters.

Dixon had had the "Dixie" in operation only one month when he and his family had an experience that they would remember all their lives. During the first week in February, 1898, Dixon planned a major sailing and hunting trip in search of wild fowl. For a week before the sailing date, Dixon and the crew were kept busy storing provisions and gear aboard the yacht, rigging the sails, and laying in spare equipment. As the craft at last pulled away from the dock and moved out into the channel toward Chesapeake Bay, dark clouds were sweeping across the face of the sun. Within a short time the bay was a mass of whitecaps. The great masts heeled over in the wind, and the shrouds popped like pistol shots. Somewhat perturbed by the ominous-looking clouds, Dixon asked the Captain,

George Isdell, if he thought it safe to continue; but Isdell reassured him by saying that the craft could take care of herself.

Within four hours the group had reached the spot where they expected to find wild geese. Anchoring the yacht not far from one of the numerous inlets along Chesapeake Bay, Dixon and his companions made their way in a fifteen-foot lifeboat to the famous Boss blind, built fifty years before by "Uncle" Nathan Cobb, the best-known fowl-hunter in the area at that time. Although the increasing velocity of the wind caused Dixon some alarm, he consoled himself by rationalizing that geese are best hunted in windy weather because they are then most attracted to the bobbing decoys.

The highest expectations of the hunters were realized in the several days that followed. Numerous fowl of various species were brought aboard the "Dixie" and hung to the great foreboom. The wind, after blowing fiercely and continuously for days, now stopped abruptly. But Dixon, his family, and the crew soon began to realize that the lull in the wind was the preface to a matter much more serious than the buffeting gusts that had caused the group concern after leaving the harbor. Already low, the temperature dropped steadily, hour by hour. When the mercury had reached nine degrees below zero, the group knew that they were being caught in one of the greatest freezes in three hundred years of Virginia history. The great bay, rarely frozen for more than a day or so in previous winters, became on February 13 a massive expanse of ice. The "Dixie," now anchored fifteen miles out in the bay, where it had been blown by the high winds, looked like a ship caught in a great polar ice pack.

Unprepared for an experience of this kind, the group

soon found their fuel resources giving out. Luckily, the abundant game aboard forestalled any fear of hunger; the main consideration now was fuel with which to cook the food and heat the cabins. As the days went by, with no softening of the ice pack, the crew searched the deck and hold for wood to replace the exhausted supplies of coal and oil. At first the wooden decoys, then the shelving from the forecastle, and finally the lifeboats were chopped into splinters for the greedy flames of the stoves. A week went by, and the winds, which had ceased before the freeze, now returned with double fury. Great flocks of wild fowl, bewildered and tossed about by the storm, could be seen hurling themselves against the lens of a lighthouse in the distance.

Another week passed, and the group now began to entertain serious doubts of their survival. Finally, on the fifteenth day, a steady, warm downpour, followed by brilliant sunshine, began to thaw the ice. The "Dixie" dropped "Sleep Easy," the front anchor chain, to cut the ice field, started the screws, and headed toward the dock at Dixondale. Happy indeed were the "sailors" as they heard the ice, broken by the great chain, sweeping by the cabins with a booming roar. Now that the danger was past, all aboard felt exultant. Young Thomas III and Jordan were especially proud at having experienced such a wonderful adventure.

During the spring and summer of 1898, numerous friends and relatives came to visit the Dixons, and the house rang with laughter, song, and conversation. Dixon was proud to see his sister Delia, whom he, along with Clarence, had helped through medical school and had seen complete her studies and enter upon a promising career. Delia's achievement was the culmination of a long period of overcoming obstacles to the pursuit of her chosen profession. During her early years, she had been a sprightly shadow of her brother Tom, who thought that his sister, in spite of the disadvantage in being "just a girl," could be tolerated because of her intrepidity and her intelligent interest in the important schemes of boyhood. When Delia had shown an inclination to study medicine, her father had expressed himself in unmistakable terms, saying that he did not care to have the family disgraced by a "female doctor." To the elder Dixon, unacquainted with such an anomaly and the product of an age that did not favor women in professional life, the ambition of his daughter seemed less than respectable for a young lady. In spite of the arguments by Delia, Frank, Clarence, and Thomas, the father remained firm in his opinion throughout Delia's training. Only after Delia had established herself as an outstanding physician did the old man relent, and from that period on, he delighted in praising the skill of his daughter and wanted to be attended by no other doctor.

After two years at Cornell University, where in her entrance examination she had made the highest average in New York State, Delia had furthered her training at the Woman's Medical College in New York City, where she earned her diploma in 1895. In an examination for an internship in Blockley (later Philadelphia General) Hospital, Delia ranked third in a group of six hundred aspirants otherwise all male. Denied the position because of the prejudice against women in the medical profession, Delia demanded a hearing and persuaded the examining board to recognize her abilities, regardless of sex. The senior medical officer of the great hospital was so impressed with the skill of the young woman that he appointed her his immediate assistant. Upon the strong recommendation of the hospital physicians, Delia, early in 1898, was engaged by Mrs. Vanderpool, a wealthy woman who desired the services of a personal physician during a fifteen-month journey around the world. Immediately upon her return in the summer of 1899, Delia was called to serve as professor of physiology and hygiene and physician in residence at Meredith College in Raleigh, North Carolina, where she established herself as one of the most outstanding women physicians in the country. The far-reaching influence of this feminine pioneer in the medical field is shown in the attention commanded by her funeral in 1934, at which the pallbearers included the governor of North Carolina, the ambassador to Mexico, a United States senator, and two justices of the Supreme Court. After her death, Dixon remarked: "Of all the work I've done in life, the part I played in shaping her career gives me most joy."[34]

By 1898 Dixon was so much in demand as a lecturer that he could afford to take only the more lucrative commitments. Frequently a speaking engagement would take him to the Midwestern part of the country, making it difficult for him to get back to New York in time for Sunday services at either the Academy of Music or the Grand Opera House. Though his services were always attended by capacity crowds, Dixon felt that somehow he was not reaching as many people as he desired. Through the fall of 1898, Dixon pondered the purposes and ultimate success of the People's Church, which he had established to supplant denominationalism. The goal of a united brotherhood of all denominations had not been forthcoming. Then, too, the maintenance of a church in one location hampered greatly Dixon's desire to reach thousands of people over wide geographical areas. In spite of the great crowds who came to hear him preach, his permanent congregation numbered no more than six hundred members, and he had had to turn elsewhere for the bulk of his income. As the year drew to a close, Dixon determined to sever his connection with the People's Church and to resume his ministry in the Baptist church. On January 14, 1899, he informed his congregation of his intentions:

> While our church is now in as good condition as at any time in its history, I can see no sure future for it along the lines on which it was projected. Four years ago, desiring to continue my work among the down-town masses of New York, I resigned my pastorate of the Twenty-third Street Baptist Church. I organized the People's Church on the principle of Christian union, personal faith in Christ being the sole basis of its active membership.
>
> . . . .
>
> I have been disillusioned as to the idea of organic Christian union. There is no real call for such a thing. What we gained in breadth we have lost in vital force. Denominationalism is merely the personal equation in religious life. Its destruction would not be a gain but a distinct loss to Christianity. I have determined, therefore, to resume my position in the regular Baptist ministry.[35]

Despite his resolution to return to the Baptist church, Dixon never accepted another charge, though he was referred to as "Reverend" for many years. Declaring that he must bring his "message" to as many people as possible, he entered upon a strenuous lecturing program during the next four years. His success as a platform speaker eclipsed even his career in the pulpit. So thoroughly did he enjoy lecturing that he said he never considered public speaking a job, but merely a pastime. Never referring to notes in his speeches, he nevertheless spent long hours in preparation, laboring with great care to achieve just the right intonation and emphasis for the desired effect. Once he had perfected his platform technique, he spoke with such ease that frequently he thought of matters far removed from the announced subject, while at the same time noting and responding to the laughter or applause of his audience.

The great Chautauqua program, first formed in 1874, had by the turn of the century reached its most popular development. Hundreds of agencies throughout the country maintained, during the summer season, lecture programs which were attended by millions of people. As one of the most striking personalities ever to grace the lecture circuits, Dixon was always assured of overflow audiences wherever he appeared. Persons who heard Dixon lecture were enthusiastic about his ability as an orator, in a day when people placed more importance upon oratory than they now do. He was repeatedly referred to as "the best" lecturer in the country. During a four-year period, Dixon was heard by more than five million people, an unusually large number when it is recalled that his lecturing career occurred before the day of radio and television. For a program of two hundred lectures a year, Dixon's audiences averaged more than six thousand listeners on each occasion. His favorite lectures were "Backbone," "The New Woman," "Municipal Corruption," and "Fools," the last of which he delivered more than five hundred times. Though many persons disagreed with Dixon's approach to a given subject, the eloquence and magnetism of his speeches was such that his program was usually sold to capacity long before the season began. Such a statement as "We have been listening for nigh on to twenty years to speakers . . . and Thomas Dixon leads them all"[36] was typical of the effect that Dixon's lectures had upon his listeners.

Constantly meeting new ideas and seeing new places was tremendously exciting to Dixon. The great sweep of the Western plains, the throbbing life of the great cities, the towering peaks of the Rockies—all of these, which he saw in his lecture tours, fired his imagination and inspired him to heights of eloquence as he attempted to analyze the greatness, the diversity, the complexity that is America. Every day offered challenging experiences. In spite of the constant problem of catching trains, living in hotels, and seeing his family irregularly, Dixon thought that this was the life for which he was destined.

On one occasion, while en route to fill an engagement in the Midwest, Dixon and his fellow train passengers had a close call with possible disaster. The train, expected to stop at a small village, roared by the station. Then, picking up speed rapidly, the train lurched forward, careening around curves and throwing the passengers from their seats. Realizing that something was seriously amiss, the conductor made his way forward amid the shouts and screams of the passengers. Crawling with great care over the now dangerously rocking coal tender, the conductor was confronted by a startling picture. The engineer, holding the throttle wide open, was leaning out of the window, his hair streaming from his head, while from his lips poured the unintelligible screams of a mind gone mad. Upon reaching the engineer, the conductor crashed a heavy stick over his head, and as the pathetic figure slumped to the floor of the cab, the conductor closed the throttle and applied the air brakes. The incident was later used effectively in Dixon's lectures to illustrate the principle that man's life is like a runaway locomotive unless his mind, refreshed by repose and new ideas, is constantly alert at the throttle of reason.

Ever since the evening, years before, at the Tremont Temple in Boston, when Dixon had heard Fulton's lecture on "The Southern Problem" and had leaped to his feet denouncing the speech as false and biased, he had determined that someday he would write the true account of the South's agonies and survival during the Reconstruction era. Much of his study in the years following had been given to the history of the Civil War and Reconstruction. Early in 1901, Dixon attended a dramatization of *Uncle Tom's Cabin,* which had become very popular on the stage. Angered by what seemed to be a great injustice in the play's attitude toward the South, he could hardly keep from jumping to his feet and denouncing the drama as false. Finally, when the performance was over, he arose, vowing that he would tell the "true story" of the South if it was the last act of his life.

To give up the profession of lecturing and write a trilogy of novels treating the Reconstruction period now became a passion with Dixon. Despite the pressure of a strenuous speaking tour through the summer of 1901, he started to work. For the remainder of the year, while still lecturing, he brought together and studied the materials he had accumulated during fourteen years, gleaning more than a thousand pages of notes dealing with Reconstruction history. Up to this time, according to Dixon, the "Southern viewpoint" had not been adequately treated in fiction, and he was determined to set the record straight. He felt that the South's actions during Reconstruction had been maligned and misunderstood. Since Harriet Beecher Stowe's *Uncle Tom's Cabin* was the most famous indictment of the

South in fiction, Dixon maintained that the best answer to her charges would be a sequel, pointed to reveal her errors about the South. Not interested in his book as literature, Dixon said that he wanted merely "to make a merciless record of the facts."[37] The first title he considered for his book was "The Rise of Simon Legree," suggested by W. D. Howells' popular novel, *The Rise of Silas Lapham.* Since Simon Legree was an important character in *Uncle Tom's Cabin,* Dixon thought it would be fitting to make Legree a central figure in his "sequel."

Through all manner of distraction, Dixon pushed ahead, planning the novel. In trains, hotels, and waiting rooms, he consulted his notes and worked out the plot. So great was his zeal that after a train on which he was traveling in the Midwest had been wrecked, he continued his writing while the railroad crews worked frantically trying to clear the tracks. Once when staying at the Hotel Metropole in Saint Joseph, Missouri, he became so absorbed in his work that he absent-mindedly appeared at a formal dinner without necktie or collar!

In spite of the long period of fourteen years that had gone into the accumulation of background material for the novel, Dixon completed the actual writing in a remarkably short period. Within sixty days after beginning the first chapter, he had the manuscript ready to submit to a publisher. He had finally settled upon the title *The Leopard's Spots,* derived from the Biblical question (Jeremiah 13:23) "Can the Ethiopian change his skin, or the leopard his spots?" Since the novel was to involve the Negro problem in the South during the Reconstruction period, Dixon thought this title more pointed and appropriate than the original one he had chosen.

In considering a possible publisher for his first effort in fiction, Dixon immediately thought of his old friend, Walter Hines Page, who was now a member of Doubleday, Page and Company. Then it occurred to Dixon that it might be embarrassing for Page to have a friend submit for consideration a novel that might not be acceptable. After all, Dixon reasoned, Page was in the publishing business to make a living, not to do favors for would-be authors. Dixon had had no experience as a novelist; he had no way of knowing how the book might be received or whether it was even publishable. Then, too, his wife Harriet was somewhat alarmed by his idea of setting out, unproved, upon a new career at thirty-eight years of age. But Harriet Dixon had learned long since that once her husband had accepted the challenge of a new endeavor, it was impossible to divert his determination to give it every ounce of his being. Finally, after spending several days worrying over the matter, Dixon impulsively wrapped the completed manuscript, tied it with heavy cord, and addressed it to Page. Good or bad, acceptable or not, the book was finished. The sooner he got it out of the house, the sooner he would know its fate. With some misgivings as to the wisdom of his newly-chosen "career," Dixon mailed the heavy package and returned to Elmington Manor, reconciled to whatever might come from his efforts.

V

"*His Luxuriant Imagination*"

The press of morning traffic was already heavy when Walter Hines Page left his quarters at the Everett House and headed toward a restaurant near his publishing firm at the corner of Union Square and Sixteenth Street in New York City. Late the afternoon before, he had received a bulky package in the mail and, upon opening it, had found a manuscript written by his old friend from the days when Page had been editor of the Raleigh *State Chronicle*. Ordinarily, he would have laid the manuscript on his desk to be read later during routine business hours, but the memory of the dynamic young Tom Dixon in the legislative halls of the capitol at Raleigh excited his imagination as he wondered what sort of novel his friend might have written. Then, too, Page had followed the meteoric career of the young preacher and lecturer with great interest in the several years past. Though their paths had crossed only infrequently since Dixon had left Raleigh, they had renewed their relationship warmly each time they saw each other. Therefore, instead of leaving the manuscript, Page thrust it under his arm to take it home with him.

After a late dinner and a social engagement, Page sat down with the manuscript and began to read, hoping to cover two or three chapters before he had to retire. So absorbed in the novel did he become, however, that he continued to read in spite of the lateness of the hour. Before he realized it, the sunlight of a new day was pouring through the blinds. Groggy from lack of sleep but now much excited about the manuscript in his hands, he hurriedly shaved and left his quarters in search of breakfast. Stepping aside abruptly from time to time to avoid other pedestrians, he continued reading as he walked along. Unaware that he had reached a busy thoroughfare, he stepped out into the flow of traffic at Fourth Avenue. Suddenly there was a loud cry, a scream, and before he knew what was happening, Page found himself knocked flat by a streetcar. Still clutching the manuscript, he arose shakily to his feet, alarmed by the blood on his hands and face and the pain in his arm.

As a crowd of onlookers gathered, a doctor was summoned to determine the extent of Page's injury. After a brief examination, the physician found Page to be shaken considerably and a bit dazed but fortunately not injured beyond a few cuts and bruises. The manuscript, however, which Page had in some way held during all the excitement, was covered with blood. After regaining his equilibrium and dusting off his clothing, Page insisted no harm was done and proceeded on his way.

On the afternoon of the day of Page's accident, Dixon was busy gathering oysters from the mile-long beds on his estate at Elmington Manor. Hearing an excited voice call from the porch, he looked up and saw his son Thomas III running toward him, waving a telegram in his hand. Only a glance at the first line was needed to tell Dixon that Page had accepted the book. Though Dixon had expected no reply at all in less than at least three weeks, here was the answer within forty-eight hours of mailing the manuscript. The telegram, the longest ever received at Dixondale, Virginia, was bursting with enthusiasm and congratulations. Saying that he believed Dixon to have written a good "seller," Page urged him to come to New York on the next train to discuss a publication contract.

When Dixon arrived the next day at the publishing firm, he was cordially received by Page, Frank Doubleday, Henry W. Lanier, and Sam Everett, the active agents of the company. Here also he met the brilliant young Frank Norris, whose promise as one of the great novelists of his era was cut short by his death later in the year.

The acceptance of the novel had raised Dixon's enthusiasm tremendously, and he exclaimed that he hoped the novel would sell a hundred thousand copies, a figure that brought a burst of laughter from Page:

> "Forget such nonsense! Books don't sell by the hundred thousands. Press agents talk about such sales, but as a rule they are not made. A sale of twenty-five thousand copies of a novel is a big success. Thomas Nelson Page has taken the wind out of your *sails*—if I may make a pun. You're about fifteen years late for a sensation on this subject."[1]

Since Page had little hope of the novel's selling more than twenty-five thousand copies, a number that would be highly satisfactory to his company, he laughingly told Dixon to write his own scale of royalties after twenty-five thousand copies, the royalty up to this number being 10 per cent of sales. Dixon thereupon replied that he would like to have 12.5 per cent for the next twenty-five thousand, 15 per cent for the third twenty-five thousand, and 20 per cent for all sales over seventy-five thousand copies. Page, amused at Dixon's imaginative flights of fancy, readily assented to the proposal.

Upon his return to Elmington Manor, Dixon was greeted enthusiastically by his family, everyone demanding to know the details of his trip to the publishers. Harriet no longer had misgivings about his ability to make a career as a novelist; indeed, there now seemed to her nothing that her husband could not do if he set his energies to the task.

Through the month of February, 1902, Dixon, now between lecture tours, eagerly awaited the appearance of his first novel. True, he had already published three books on religion during his ministry, but they had not enjoyed any great circulation. Then, too, this was his first attempt at fiction, and he was greatly interested to see if he could be successful in a new profession. Always searching for newer and richer experiences, he now found the goal of novelist infinitely appealing.

For the design of the cover of *The Leopard's Spots,* Dixon chose a tobacco plant, the symbol of his home country in North Carolina, placed against a deep red background. When the finished book arrived during the second week in March, Dixon feverishly tore off the wrapper, eager to see how well his design had been carried out. To his extreme disgust and disappointment, he saw that his suggestion had not been followed at all. Instead of the cover he had chosen, the book was bound in dull red and the symbol was a hangman's noose encircling a burglar's mask; through the whole was thrust a dagger. "I dropped the thing on the floor as if it had been a rattlesnake and drew away from it with a sense of nausea."[2] Harriet quietly picked up the book and handed it back to him. As he thumbed through its pages, it seemed to him to be "the deadest, flattest, stupidest rubbish" that he had ever read. "The words had no meaning. The pages said nothing. I stared at it until my eyes grew dim and tears blurred the words."[3]

Greatly vexed with the publishers for having released the book with such an offensive design, Dixon sat down and immediately wrote Page to burn the entire first edition of fifteen thousand copies and to send him the bill for them. By return mail Page answered in a tactfully worded reply that the first edition had been sold in advance and that the cover had not hurt the sales; he would, however, be glad to change the design in any further editions.

The public response to *The Leopard's Spots* was immediate. Rarely has a first novel been so highly praised or so violently condemned. The sales passed one hundred thousand copies within a few months, and when Dixon received the first semiannual report with a royalty check of only thirty thousand dollars, he gleefully reminded Page of the ascending scale in the contract to which Page had so readily agreed. So popular did the book become in the first year that numerous foreign translations appeared, and Dixon's fame became international. The sales, which eventually passed the million mark, helped to establish Doubleday, Page as a major publisher and made Dixon several hundred thousand dollars in royalties.

THOMAS DIXON AT WORK IN HIS CABIN
AT ELMINGTON MANOR

Dixon with Brothers and Sisters, 1902

Thomas, A. C., and Frank

Addie (Mrs. Ernest Thacker) and Delia (Dr. Delia Dixon Carroll)

The reviews of the novel rarely took a moderate view—it was either all good or all bad. One critic boldly proclaimed:

> *The Leopard's Spots* is a masterpiece by a master hand. No other book on the subject has ever approached it in power or fearlessness of expression.[4]

Lilian Bell, reviewing the book in the *Saturday Evening Post,* also praised it highly and urged her readers to learn that aspect of American history which was treated in the novel:

> I shall be speaking only the truth if I say that to read the book, nay, to learn certain portions of it by heart, would be a liberal education, for most of the stern facts marshaled by the author are quite unknown to even the so-called enlightened people. . . .
>
> . . . .
>
> . . . whether you believe it all, accept it all, or like it all, have the justice to read it. . . . Now for the first time there speaks through the medium of the novel the history of thirty-five awful, never-to-be-forgotten years.[5]

Extravagant praise came from many quarters. Frank L. Stanton, the popular Southern poet, said: "It is genius. It speaks out in meeting."[6] Dr. Max Nordau, the famous German physician and author, was so impressed that he communicated his sentiments to Dixon immediately after reading the book:

> "The Leopard's Spots" is the most powerful novel I have read for years. Powerful by its plot, more so by the greatness of the issues treated, most so by the nobleness and lofty force of its good characters. The incidents are stirring, the emotional parts rend the heart, the arguing passages reveal the scholar and the

thinker. But precisely by reason of the first-rate qualities of this masterwork, I put it down with a quivering heart. Man! are you conscious of your immense responsibility? You have deliberately undone the work of Harriet Beecher Stowe![7]

Other critics were quick to note the relationship of *The Leopard's Spots* and *Uncle Tom's Cabin.* In nearly every situation where the similarity between the novels was noticed, *The Leopard's Spots* was judged the more effective and superior work. The words of one critic among those writing on the subject are typical:

> It is the most thrilling book that has been written since the war [War Between the States]. It is an epoch-making book, and a worthy successor to "Uncle Tom's Cabin." It is superior in power of thought and graphic description. Unlike most other novels, it is packed with truth stranger than fiction.
>
> He has certainly studied the great masters of fiction and given us a book that is likely to produce an impression on the world second to no book issued in modern times.[8]

The reviews, however, were by no means all favorable. Some critics regarded the work as radical, prejudiced, and highly colored. Kelly Miller, somewhat later, in condemning *The Leopard's Spots* for its treatment of the Negro, addressed an open letter to Dixon, in which he wrote in part:

> Voltaire tells us it is more difficult and more meritorious to wean men of their prejudices than it is to civilize the barbarian. Race hatred is the most malignant poison that can afflict the mind. It freezes up the fount of inspiration and chills the higher faculties of the soul. You are a greater enemy to your own race than you are to mine.[9]

He then went on to castigate the author more severely: "Your teachings subvert the foundations of law and established order. You are the high priest of lawlessness, the prophet of anarchy."[10] Another writer called the work "perhaps the most bigoted of American novels."[11]

In *The Hindered Hand,* the most elaborate attack upon Dixon in American fiction, Sutton E. Griggs wrote in 1905 that "in the long line of men of letters of the Anglo-Saxon race we find no counterpart to Mr. Dixon." Griggs concluded with an epitaph for the white author:

> The misguided soul ignored all of the good in the aspiring Negro; made every vicious off-shoot that he pictured typical of the entire race; presented all mistakes independent of their environments and provocations; ignored or minimized all the evil in the more vicious elements of whites; said and did all things which he deemed necessary to leave behind him the greatest heritage of hate the world has ever known. Humanity claims him not as one of her children.[12]

The literary style of *The Leopard's Spots* was both praised and condemned. One reviewer stated:

> His luxuriant imagination and sympathetic nature have given him a natural power of creating, with a few swift touches, human characters that live and love and suffer before your eyes.[13]

Another critic's view shows how widely opinions differed on the literary quality of the work:

> . . . the love, passion and pathos sections, introduced to buoy up the book as a whole, are done imperfectly if not extraordinarily badly, and may be very shortly dismissed.[14]

One review, signed "Now-and-Then," called the novel "good in purpose and bad in workmanship" and attacked the occasional shaky grammar of the book by quoting humorous pronominal references in a passage from the story:

> Tom was entering the gate of his modest home in as fine style

as possible, seated on a stack of bones that had once been a horse, an old piece of wool on his head that had once been a hat, and a wooden peg fitted into a stump where once was a leg.[15]

Quick to defend his work, Dixon was most affected by the criticism that came from a totally unexpected quarter. His brother Clarence reproved Dixon strongly for the inflammatory nature of the book and questioned the motive he had had in writing it. Answering from Hartford, Connecticut, where he was filling a lecture engagement, Dixon wrote in part:

I assure you I cherish no hard feelings toward you—I've quite made up my mind always to love you as my "big brother" in spite of your hideous theology. I'm sure you can't help it now, and you're getting too old to ever learn any better.

What did hurt me just a little bit was a remark you made about my book in discussing the *purpose* of the study—You said what my bitterest critics who wrote with Prussic Acid never thought of—that my *purpose* was to make money. This is of course true, just as your purpose is to make money preaching—and I confess the fact, but I thought it rather brutal for you to *say* so. After all it's the truth that hurts.[16]

Clarence had also expressed concern over Dixon's apparent neglect of religious observances, and now in answer Dixon added:

Much you said to Pink [Harriet] is true. It was simply foolish for *you* to say it. I do say nasty words in a close place at sea sometimes, I don't have family prayers, & I manage to make Pink or Junior say grace most of the time—for I confess that as I grow older, those things bore me more and more—*all formalism* does.[17]

Dixon concluded the letter by reassuring his "big brother" of his lasting love and esteem, but the essentially different views of the men, aggravated at a crucial period by Clarence's criticism of a sensitive facet of Dixon's nature, served to erect a wall of coolness between them for a time. The differences between the brothers were further accentuated at this time by Clarence's probable misunderstanding of Dixon's efforts to persuade their younger brother Frank, now also a minister, to leave the pulpit and go on the lecture platform. In answer to Clarence's criticism that Dixon was exerting a bad influence upon Frank, Dixon explained:

> I've done my best to get him a church for 5 years & his name has been presented to over 50 churches in that time & the moment they discern his lameness, it kills him. Broughton told me he had the same experience with his [Frank's] name in the South. Last year Frank was bordering on a complete nervous collapse when he thought his trustees here [Hartford, Connecticut] were going to pitch him out. I offered him a temporary position with me at Elmington to have the children for a year till he could get on his feet if the worst came to worst. You are vastly mistaken if you feel I am playing *Mephisto* to Frank's *Faust*. He certainly cherishes no such illusions. All I want is that he get a field fit for his talent & where he can support his wife and babies—and I have laid aside my literary work & given all my spare time since last January, forcing him on my bureaux to give him a start lecturing that he might not feel so pitiably helpless & at the mercy of the brutes who sometimes masquerade as officers of the church of Christ. I've gotten out of the Chautauquas South and West & worked him in my place this summer.[18]

The effort to help Frank get started as a Chautauqua lecturer came at a propitious moment. Frank, already possessing considerable talent as a public speaker, entered the lecturing field during a period when the public was very much interested in his brother Thomas. During the next few years Frank Dixon became one of the most effective lecturers in the country. Ultimately becoming president of the American Chautauqua Association, he brought to his profession a charm and appeal that gave him wide recognition during his twenty-three years as a platform speaker.

Throughout the spring and summer of 1902, Dixon was prompted time and again to respond to the welter of mixed criticism that surged about his ears concerning his book. The "truth" of the story probably aroused more controversy than any other single feature of the work. Some critics maintained that the novel was filled with falsehoods about the South, and they criticized it as "quasi-historical" and highly partisan in its treatment. Others answered that the story was merely dramatized fact.

Writing from Elmington Manor in July, Dixon made an impassioned defense of the authenticity of the novel. He denied any effort to arouse race hatred or prejudices and maintained that he had "the friendliest feelings and the profoundest pity"[19] for the Negro. In summarizing his defense, he wrote: "I claim the book is an authentic human document, and I know it is the most important moral deed of my life. There is not a bitter or malignant sentence in it."[20] Despite his avowals, however, *The Leopard's Spots* continued to be highly controversial and in some quarters was considered an evil literary force.

The manifest purpose of *The Leopard's Spots* was to trace the racial problem in the South generally and to reveal the history of the problem in North Carolina from 1885 to 1900 as typical.

Dixon had often said that he despised the degradation of slavery. In his ministry he frequently voiced his opinion about the evil of subjecting one person to the will of another, and in a speech in 1889 before the New England Paint and Oil Club, after saying that the Negro and white populations of the South must be segregated, he added:

> All this I say with the kindliest and tenderest feelings for the Negro race. Yes, I say it by the memories of the dear old nurse in whose arms the weary head of my childhood so often found rest, at whose feet I sat and heard the sad story of the life of a slave until I learned to hate slavery as much as I hate hell.[21]

Dixon maintained early in his ministry that the South lifted the Negro from the "bondage of savagery into the light and strength of Christian civilization," and he held that the ending of slavery was one of the greatest advances of mankind:

> I thank God that there is not today the clang of a single slave chain on this continent. Slavery may have had its beneficent aspects, but democracy is the destiny of the race, because all men are bound together in the bonds of fraternal equality with one common father above.[22]

The last clause in this quotation of Dixon's words as a minister is at variance with his attitude as set forth in his novel. As vehemently as he denounced slavery, he maintained that there is a fundamental difference between the Negroes and the whites that would make equality impossible. The primary assumption of *The Leopard's Spots* is that the "Anglo-Saxon race" is superior to the Negro race. Dixon contends, through the chief characters in the novel, that the Negro has certain inherent qualities that make him incapable of high culture. He quotes Lincoln in reinforcing his argument that the physical difference between the races will "forever forbid them living together on terms of social and political equality."[23]

Negro political activity, Dixon maintains, does not operate by itself; it derives its significance from the deeper meanings of society. Since the foundation of society rests within the family, equality of suffrage connotes social equality; social equality implies amalgamation of the races. The last implication, Dixon writes, is repugnant to the white man; only bloodshed will result from attempts to place the two peoples on the same social level. If these races must not amalgamate, they must exist separately. The words of the Reverend John Durham, one of the characters of the novel, present the great problem facing America: "*In a democracy you cannot build a nation inside a nation of two antagonistic races; and therefore the future American must be either an Anglo-Saxon or a Mulatto.*" The minister's words, always italicized, occur several times in the course of the novel; they serve as the refrain for Dixon's view that the race problem can be resolved in only one of two ways: the Negro must submit to the superiority of the white population, or he must be entirely removed from contact with whites.

In an article that Dixon wrote for the *Saturday Evening Post* in 1905, he suggested that the race problem could be solved by colonizing the American Negro in Liberia. He stated that the American government had spent about eight hundred million dollars on Negro education since the Civil War; one-half of that sum, he held, would have been sufficient to make Liberia a powerful Negro state. "Liberia is capable of supporting every Negro in America. Why not face this question squarely?"[24]

In urging this solution of the problem, Dixon concluded:

> I have for the Negro race only pity and sympathy, though every large convention of Negroes since the appearance of my first historical novel on the race problem has gone out of its way to denounce me and declare my books caricatures and libels on

their people. Their mistake is a natural one. My books are hard reading for a Negro, and yet the Negroes, in denouncing them, are unwittingly denouncing one of their best friends.

. . . .

As a friend of the Negro race I claim that he should have the opportunity for the highest, noblest and freest development of his full, rounded manhood. He has never had this opportunity in America, either North or South, and he never can have it. The forces against him are overwhelming.[25]

Interwoven with the history of the racial problem as revealed in *The Leopard's Spots* is a love story in which the hero, Charles Gaston, romantically courts Sallie Worth. Gaston, a young man whose childhood has been saddened by the dark hours of the Reconstruction period, was modeled upon Charles B. Aycock, the governor of North Carolina at the time the novel was published.

Simon Legree, the brutal slaveholder in Mrs. Stowe's *Uncle Tom's Cabin,* appears again in *The Leopard's Spots,* but this time as a "champion" of the freed slaves. After inciting the Negroes to violence in their demand for full citizenship, Legree takes his choice of the spoils. The only educated Negro in the story is George Harris, the son of Eliza Harris, who in *Uncle Tom's Cabin* had escaped from slavery with her child and fled across the ice-packed Ohio. George Harris is revealed in Dixon's novel as a graduate of Harvard, a poet, and a scholar. His intimate white friend, the Honorable Everett Lowell, is an enthusiastic defender of the Negro cause until Harris asks the hand of Lowell's daughter.

The Ku Klux Klan, under the leadership of Major Stuart Dameron, is glorified by Dixon for its work in bringing order out of the turmoil that followed the war. Major

Dameron realizes, however, that the Klan has served its purpose once its mission has been accomplished, and he orders that the Klan be disbanded forever so that irresponsible persons may not abuse its tremendous power. Such abuse as Major Dameron feared is represented by a lynching under the leadership of Allan McLeod, a scalawag. Charles Gaston makes a valiant effort to prevent the violence, but he is knocked down by the lynchers.

The success of *The Leopard's Spots* and the continuing demand for Dixon as a lecturer kept him traveling to every part of the country. While on a speaking tour of the Southwest, Dixon received a telegram that his mother Amanda was dying. Though she had not approved of some of her son's views or actions during his active career as a minister and lecturer, she and her son had achieved an unusually close relationship of spirit during the year preceding her death. Unable to reach North Carolina in time, Dixon was represented at the funeral by his wife.

Hardly had *The Leopard's Spots* appeared before the public when Dixon began research for the second novel of his trilogy on the Reconstruction era and its aftermath. At the same time that he was studying materials for this new work, he was also writing a novel that was destined to have a wide reception as the first of a trilogy on socialism. Dixon had little patience with a social order based upon collective or governmental control of property and distribution of goods. His philosophy on the subject had already been forcefully shown in his individualism as a lawyer and minister and in his famous lectures, "Backbone" and "The Fool." Very adept at making socialistic theory appear in a ridiculous or contemptible light, Dixon shows his skill nowhere better than in *The One Woman,* published in 1903. In this novel Dixon attempts to show that socialism undermines the roots of society. In the space of two pages, he quotes radical doctrines from Fourier, William Morris, Robert Owen, Grant Allen, and Karl Pearson. Dixon's theories on socialism are revealed as he selects from the writers passages that the reader is to understand are most objectionable to the author. A quotation from Fourier is a case in point:

> Monogamy and private property are the main characteristics of Civilization. They are the breastworks behind which the army of the rich crouch and from which they sally to rob the poor.[26]

A further quotation from Robert Owen reveals Dixon's main objections to socialism:

> In the new Moral World the irrational names of husband, wife, parent and child will be heard no more. Children will undoubtedly be the property of the whole community.[27]

Dixon maintains that socialism weakens the foundations of the family. Without the family as the social unit, chaos will ultimately result. In pressing home his argument, Dixon has one character say to another:

> Observe in all these long-haired philosophers how closely the idea of private property is linked with the family. That is why the moment you attack private property in your pulpit your wife instinctively knows that you are attacking the basis of her life and home. Private property had its origin in the family. The family is the source of all monopolistic instincts, and your reign of moonshine brotherhood can never be brought to pass until you destroy monogamic marriage.[28]

Here in *The One Woman* is the story of the Reverend Frank Gordon, a dynamic minister of socialistic leanings who plans to establish a great independent church to which all interested persons will be welcomed. An enthusiastic, wealthy, and beautiful woman remains after one of Gordon's inspiringly idealistic sermons and confesses that she loves him. It is interesting to note that just such a confession had been made to Dixon after one of his sermons early in his New York ministry. He had extricated himself from the delicate situation with as much grace as he could muster, but the matter did not end there. The young woman was a writer, and she made the situation the basis for a story in a popular magazine. Dixon's wife Harriet read the story, and, though she never mentioned the matter to him, he knew that she had recognized her husband in the fictional account when he saw her toss the magazine into the trash as soon as she had completed the tale.[29] There are other strong autobiographical hints in the novel, for Frank Gordon's personality closely resembles that of the author, and Gordon's idealistic establishment of a new independent church is similar to Dixon's own experience as a minister.

Frank Gordon's absorption in his work and his growing interest in the wealthy young woman, Kate Ransom, gradually widen the gulf between himself and his family. At last he divorces his wife Ruth and marries the charming Kate, who has previously given a million dollars toward the establishment of his new church.

Dixon demonstrates the evils of "shared wealth" as Gordon's best friend, Mark Overman, falls in love with Gordon's wife Kate and wins her. Gordon kills Overman and is twice sentenced to death. Only at the last minute is his life spared by Morris King, governor of New York and an old sweetheart of Gordon's first wife, Ruth.

Frank Gordon epitomizes the naive, inspired dreamer

who sees society as a group of clear-eyed children who will instinctively turn to goodness if it but be shown to them. He is the champion of the masses, the opponent of the capitalistic monopolies that perpetuate the deplorable working conditions of the weak. As Dixon characterizes him, Gordon unfortunately lacks the practical insight of his cynical friend, Mark Overman, who foresees the inevitable end of unrestrained emotions.

When Dixon submitted the manuscript of *The One Woman* to Doubleday, Page and Company, he was told to name his own royalties. The shock of such a communication was probably one that most authors only dream about.

The One Woman aroused much controversy as a novel of "doubtful propriety." It had been for sale only a short time when it was noted that "no book published in recent times has received such a torrent of savage abuse from unknown critics, and such enthusiastic praise from the leaders of thought."[30] As one critic thought of the matter: "Socialism, with Mr. Dixon, means sexual license and the disruption of the family."[31] On the other hand, this novel of "doubtful propriety" was highly recommended by outstanding clergymen, who considered it a strong plea for the sanctity of the home. A verbal battle ensued in the press concerning the quality of the work. The following review indicates the attention given to the book:

It is doubtful if any book of the year has excited quite the amount of controversy that has been accorded "The One Woman." It murders Socialism with the same animalism with which the hero kills his friend. It paints in colors that are not to be mistaken the consequences of the too common social evil. The action is terrifically and breathlessly rapid. You will read it over and over in whole or piecemeal. You will be enraptured and angered. You will think about it and dream about it. You will praise it and condemn it, admire and despise it. And after all you will decide that it is a great book.[32]

The popularity of *The One Woman* was enormous, almost as great as that of *The Leopard's Spots.*

For his second novel on the Reconstruction period, Dixon sifted more than five thousand pamphlets and books for source material during a year of obsessive, unrelenting labor. The historical novelist, Dixon believed, should spend a long period of study in order to understand thoroughly the significance of the period of history he is treating; yet once he has reached the stage where he thinks that he is ready to begin writing, he should not hinder the train of his thought by constant interruptions. He should write in the heat of the moment; corroboration of details can be taken care of after the work is completed. In this way, the novelist can more effectively dramatize his story.

Dixon wrote with a large, heavy pencil and wrote rapidly. In the heat of creative effort, he drove himself unmercifully. Sometimes he wrote for seventeen hours at a time, finally falling to sleep from exhaustion. When he had completed the draft in pencil, he gave the manuscript to his wife Harriet for typing. After the typed manuscript was completed, he went over it again carefully before submitting it to a publisher. Thirty days after Dixon had begun writing it, the manuscript was ready. Now there was no question about where Dixon would market his third novel, for the firm of Doubleday, Page and Company had assured him that it was eager to have anything he wrote.

The storm that broke over the appearance of *The Clansman* was even greater than that which had resulted from the publication of *The Leopard's Spots.* Again the historical record was questioned. Dixon had written the first full-length fictional account of Thaddeus Stevens. E. L. Shuman, the dean of literary critics in the West, had praised the first novel highly in the *Chicago Record-Herald.* Now he severely criticized Dixon for what seemed to be an unwarranted and unjust attack on Stevens through his fictional counterpart, Austin Stoneman, one of the leading characters in the novel. In a carefully documented letter, Dixon answered Shuman's charges, citing the sources for his delineation of Stevens' character. The reply that Dixon received was unexpected. Shuman apologized in a long newspaper article and acknowledged his lack of information on the subject. But some other critics did not swerve in their denunciation of Dixon's portrayal of Stevens. Years after the appearance of the novel, people were still discussing the historical accuracy of the work.

Dixon quickly met each challenge of his critics. In answer to an anonymous article in the *Charlotte* (N.C.) *Daily Observer* as to the accuracy of the novel, Dixon replied heatedly:

> My critic uses the history of North Carolina with which to contradict "The Clansman," when he knows, if he has read the book, that the scene is laid in South Carolina.
>
> . . . .
>
> I drew of old Thaddeus Stevens the first full length portrait of history. I showed him to be, what he was, the greatest and the vilest man who ever trod the halls of the American Congress. I dare my critic to come out from under his cover and put his finger on a single word, line, sentence, paragraph, page, or chapter in "The Clansman" in which I have done Thad Stevens an injustice.[33]

As historical background for *The Clansman,* Dixon had made use of many experiences of his boyhood and of stories that had been related to him. That he could not have had any intimate first-hand knowledge of the events related in Book I of *The Clansman* is evident when it is remembered that he was less than a year and a half old at the time of the events related. The extent to which he borrowed from the writings of Walt Whitman[34] may be seen in parallel accounts by the two authors. The enthusiasm of the Union soldiers at the outbreak of the war is told by Dixon in the opening paragraphs of *The Clansman*:

The Thirteenth Brooklyn marched gayly Southward on a thirty days' jaunt, with pieces of rope conspicuously tied to their muskets with which to bring back each man a Southern prisoner to be led in a noose through the streets on their early triumphant return![35]

Whitman's eyewitness account of the same event appears in *Specimen Days* as follows:

I remember, too, that a couple of companies of the Thirteenth Brooklyn, who rendezvou'd at the city armory, and started thence as thirty days' men, were all provided with pieces of rope, conspicuously tied to their musket-barrels, with which to bring back each man a prisoner from the audacious South, to be led in a noose, on our men's early and triumphant return![36]

A few pages later, under the entry "Death of a Wisconsin Officer," we find these words by Whitman, who served as a hospital attendant during the Civil War:

The poor young man is struggling painfully for breath, his great dark eyes with a glaze already upon them, and the choking faint but audible in his throat. An attendant sits by him, and will not leave him till the last; yet little or nothing can be done. He will die here in an hour or two, without the presence of kith or kin. Meanwhile the ordinary chat and business of the ward a little way off goes on indifferently. Some of the inmates are laughing and joking, others are playing checkers or cards, others are reading, &c.[37]

The hospital scene in *The Clansman* in which Ben Cameron lies wounded is derived directly from *Specimen Days*, as the following lines reveal:

A little farther along the same row a soldier was dying, a faint choking just audible in his throat. An attendant sat beside him and would not leave till the last. The ordinary chat and hum of the ward went on indifferent to peace, victory, life, or death. Before the finality of the hospital all other events of earth fade. Some were playing cards or checkers, some laughing and joking, and others reading.[38]

In other particulars Dixon reveals his dependence upon Whitman, especially in relating Lincoln's assassination. That Dixon followed Whitman so closely is surprising, especially in view of the popularity of Whitman's work. A critic, in summarizing Dixon's dependence upon the poet, concluded as follows:

So indirectly, directly, in general, in particular, Dixon the Champion of the unreconstructed Southerner, borrowed from Walt Whitman, the staunch Unionist. Surely there is irony here, but, if the borrowing got out of hand, there is assurance too that Whitman, far from being perturbed, would not have minded in the least.[39]

The Clansman considers the terrible days of Reconstruction between the years 1865 and 1870. The novel is divided into four sections, each section emphasizing a locale and time after the Civil War. The scene of Book I is Washington, D.C., immediately after the end of the war, where thousands of soldiers lie sick and wounded in the makeshift hospitals of the city. The principal characters of the novel are introduced to the reader as they struggle with the grave problems presented by the chaotic conditions after the war. President Lincoln is treated with great sympathy, and the men who oppose his policies are pictured as men of bitter and malevolent antagonisms. Thaddeus Stevens, thinly disguised as the Honorable Austin Stoneman, is a brilliant but diabolical man contriving for full control of the government.

Book II relates the events that followed the assassination of Lincoln and Andrew Johnson's succession to the Presidency. Johnson is shown as a weak, misguided man at the mercy of malign creatures who are determined to bring about his downfall.

In Book III the scene shifts to South Carolina at the home of the Camerons. Austin Stoneman, now in very bad health, is urged by his doctor to move to the South. He settles with his son and daughter in the little town of Piedmont, South Carolina, the home of the Camerons. A romance between Phil Stoneman and Margaret Cameron develops, while at the same time Elsie Stoneman and Ben Cameron become sweethearts. The book also treats at length the poverty, shame, and degradation suffered by the Southerners at the hands of the Negroes and unscrupulous Northerners. A young girl, Marian Lenoir, is attacked by Negroes; because of her shame, she and her mother commit suicide by leaping from a cliff.

In Book IV Dixon relates in some detail the organization of the "Invisible Empire." Martial law is declared, and several thousand United States troops are sent to put down the insurrection brought about by the Ku Klux

Klan. Phil Stoneman kills a Negro who acts in a familiar manner toward Margaret Cameron. Phil's father thinks that the murder was committed by Ben Cameron, and he gleefully urges that Ben be executed. At the last moment Ben and Phil exchange places in the death cell, and old Stoneman is almost mad with grief and fury when he learns that his own son is to be killed. The Ku Klux Klan saves Phil, however, and that night the victory of the South is complete as the Klan defeats the Federal troops throughout the state.

The novel is told at a breath-taking pace. Events occur so rapidly that the reader has hardly collected his thoughts before he is swept along into another adventure. The attacker of Marian Lenoir is identified within a few moments by Dr. Cameron's use of a microscope with which he sees the image of the Negro attacker imprinted upon the retina of the dead girl's eye!

The sales of *The Clansman* surpassed even the spectacular successes of *The Leopard's Spots* and *The One Woman*. Bookstores could not keep up with the demands of readers throughout the country. Before many months had passed, Dixon saw the sale go far beyond a million copies. If his family had held doubts of his ability to succeed as a novelist, they were now fully reassured. Indeed, Thomas Dixon seemed to them "destined" as a writer.

From this time on, the announcement that a new book by Thomas Dixon had just been released was sufficient to engender an excited interest in the reading public. Yet, even before *The Clansman* had reached the bookstalls, Dixon was becoming restless and uncertain of his future. The knowledge that he had spoken to millions of people through the printed page was indeed a great satisfaction. Nevertheless, there was a lurking uneasiness that would not be ignored. The first flush of accomplishment had now worn off. Life was once more a rather routine, humdrum affair. Cruising the waters of Chesapeake Bay in the "Dixie" had lost its former zestfulness; the quiet, shaded walks now seemed boring; and, sitting in the cabin that he had built as a study on the lawn of Elmington Manor, Dixon ruminated at length about the future and the past. He recalled with growing dissatisfaction his failure as a young actor. Added to this failure of two decades past was a more recent failure at Elmington Manor. Deciding to become a gentleman farmer on a large scale, Dixon had, in the preceding two years, placed several hundred acres of land under cultivation as a great experiment in vegetable farming. He had dreamed of shipping tons of vegetables monthly to outlets in New York City. But as the months progressed in his experiment, problems seemed to multiply overnight. He was constantly having to recruit laborers in order to maintain the enormous project; heavy rains, freezes, and plant diseases made severe inroads upon the crops; and worst of all, the vegetables, once harvested, could not be delivered to the New York markets before spoiling. On one occasion, Dixon was confronted with the problem of having to dispose of thousands of heads of cabbage that had rotted before reaching their destination. It was not that Dixon was concerned about the great sums of money he had poured into the project, for he felt confident that, at any time he wanted to do so, he could earn enough to multiply his wealth. What was most galling was the realization that in this particular endeavor he had not been successful. To a man who could not recognize failure, the farming project was one of the most trying episodes of his life.

As he thought of his failure as a master farmer, the other failure of his short stage career returned relentlessly, again and again. Standing at the window of his home one winter morning in 1905, Dixon meditated for a long while, looking out over the white expanse of snow which had come, as if by magic, the night before. From another part of the house came the soft strains of a piano melody. Harriet's music had always been a source of great pleasure to him, but now the notes seemed tinged with sadness. The Old Dominion steamer, sweeping around the bend of the river not far from Elmington Manor, blew its deep bass note three times through the chilly atmosphere, sounding for all the world like some lost monster wandering the wasteland, sick and desolate. With an effort Dixon roused himself. What could be the matter? Perhaps he was not well. But no, his face was bronzed by the wind and his body seemed to be stronger than ever. Perhaps he was a bit tired from his hunting trip. The quail he had shot yesterday had fluttered pathetically in his hand before it died and had left a little fleck of blood on his finger. This morning his quail on toast did not appeal to him as usual. The flames in the great open fireplace somehow did not seem to take the chill out of the room. As he stood gazing into the flickering fire, his mind wandered into a dreamy contemplation of the exciting years in New York. The lure of the great city came mysteriously, overwhelmingly, as he later recorded:

> The old fever is in my blood. I have not lived it down. Why should I strangle the impulse, if God put it within. After all, it is His breath. This longing for fellowship, this consciousness of

kinship with the herd is in me and my heart is beating to its wild music. I lift my head and sniff from afar the dust of their hoofbeat and my soul answers with a cry.[40]

That night Dixon started preparing to move back to New York, eager to enter the great rush of humanity once more.

VI

"*The Greatest Play of the South*"

Once Dixon had decided to move back to New York, Elmington Manor no longer held the charm of previous years. The many qualities of privacy and spaciousness that had drawn him so strongly to the estate now appeared dull and uninteresting. The long months spent there as a novelist seemed to drag on interminably. As he later recalled, the fascination that lured him back to the city would not be denied:

> On the horizon of the night I see the city's lambent flame, the light that never grows dim, the life that never sleeps.
>
> Again I plunge into its human tides and feel the enfolding contagion of their animal and spiritual magnetism. Again I bathe in my favourite pool—the whirlpool at Madison Square—the vortex into which swift human rivers pour their waters. At this spot, he who has ears can always hear the roar of Niagara more thrilling than the music of the leap of rivers from granite cliffs.

I see the miles of electric lights flash brighter than the stars, and the glow and splendour and mystery of it all stirs my soul.

Warm hands clasp mine, and the faces of friends smile their greetings.

I hear the music of the orchestra, the tumult and the shouts of Broadway on gala nights of grand opera, the voices of my favourites singing as never before—and I am glad.

I slip into my study hard by the Square—I confess I have always kept it there—and turn up the lights with a sneaking joy at my inconsistency. I hate consistent people, anyhow.[1]

The great success of *The Clansman* as a novel prompted Dixon to think of its possibilities as a drama. His determination to try once again to succeed in the theater had become increasingly strong during his last months at Elmington Manor. He was still searching about for a suitable story for the stage when *The Clansman* appeared, and its immediate and tremendous popularity gave him the answer. He would rewrite the novel as a play. After working on the project for several weeks, Dixon, early in the spring of 1905, adopted a plan. Enrolling in a course in dramatic technique under William Thompson Price, who had a reputation as an excellent teacher, he applied his energies to studying the principles of the theater. After several weeks of intensive study, he came away from his training greatly inspired and thinking that Price was "the ablest critic of the theatre since Aristotle."[2]

Crosby Gaige, lately come from Cornell University, was, at the time of Dixon's training under Price, on the staff of Alice Kauser, one of the foremost dramatists' agents in the country. When Gaige read the manuscript of the play,[3] he enthusiastically predicted a great success for it. George Brennan, a young newspaperman, had recently established a production office on Broadway, and when

Gaige submitted the play to him, Brennan immediately sent for the author. Dixon, interested in more than future royalties, offered to buy a half interest in the play, much to the surprise of the producer. A contract was drawn up in which Dixon received half the stock of the Southern Amusement Company, the name of the corporation that would produce the play. Dixon's friends were startled that he should invest such a large sum of money in this new venture, and his household "thought a guardian should be appointed without delay."[4]

The weeks of selecting the cast and working out the details of producing the play were among the most exciting in Dixon's life. He never considered his long hours with the production as anything more than recreation.

Before presenting the play to the public, Dixon submitted a copy of the script to John Hay, Secretary of State, who strongly endorsed the document for its historical accuracy and asked that he might keep the copy that Dixon had sent him. Albert Bigelow Paine, the editor who was to become the biographer and literary executor of Mark Twain, read the draft of the play and expressed his admiration for it.

A brief glance at the plot of the play will reveal its closeness to both *The Clansman* and *The Leopard's Spots*. The setting is Piedmont, South Carolina. The time covers six months in 1867–68. The main characters include the elder Cameron, his son Ben, and a thirteen-year-old daughter, Flora. Austin Stoneman, a Northerner, has moved to Piedmont after the war and has become the commander of the Black League. With him is his daughter, Elsie, who becomes romantically linked with Ben Cameron. Silas Lynch, a Negro protégé of Stoneman's, is soon to be elected lieutenant governor of the state. In the play Lynch is a symbol of the tragedy that, Dixon believed, occurs when "do-gooders" strive to elevate the Negro. Stoneman constantly encourages Lynch: "Come, lift up your head! Have I showed you the pathway to the stars for nothing? Stand erect in the presence of every white man! God Almighty can do nothing for a coward!"[5] Stoneman reverses his philosophy abruptly, however, when Lynch informs him that he is in love with Elsie, Stoneman's daughter. As Stoneman listens incredulously, Lynch presses his point with a passionate justification of his stand:

> What have you done for me? Trained my eyes to see, ears to hear, heart to feel, that you might deny every cry of my body and soul. . . . You've stripped the rags of slavery from a black skin, but what are you going to do with the man? This man with a heart that can ache and break, oh! if I could take the stain from this skin, the kink from this hair, I'd bathe in hell fire!

As Stoneman replies, "Surely, Lynch, you have gone mad!" Ben Cameron and members of the Ku Klux Klan rush in to rescue Elsie, who is held by one of Lynch's henchmen. After his capture, Lynch is kicked down the steps of the capitol by Ben, who takes Elsie as his bride.

Along with the main story is a subplot in which Negro Gus, a former field hand, accidentally kills Flora Cameron. The Klan lynches Gus, drags his body through the streets, and leaves it at the doorway of the lieutenant governor. A tableau of the Klan members at the foot of the fiery cross is the climactic point of the play.

When "The Clansman" began to tour, the advertisements frequently read as follows: "The Greatest Play of the South. . . . A Daring, Thrilling Romance of the Ku

Klux Klan. . . . A Specially Selected Metropolitan Cast—50 People. . . . A Splendid Scenic Production—Two Carloads of Scenery. . . . A Small Army of Supernumeraries, Horses, etc."

A certain success for the play was expected, but the opening night in Norfolk, Virginia, on September 22, 1905, was one of the tensest experiences in Dixon's career. The reception of the play might be greatly affected by certain problems of production that had not been successfully solved by the opening date. For example, one of the actors seemed to become more confused in his lines the more he spoke them. Finally, his lines were cut to two words; still he could not say them with feeling. Several horses were to gallop across the stage bearing members of the Ku Klux Klan. The constant fear of the cast was that, at any moment, the nervous animals might leap over the footlights into the laps of the audience. At rehearsals, one of the horses had frequently stamped on the stage with one of its front hooves in a manner that boded ill.

The first act concluded without mishap, however, and as the curtain went down, the audience was completely captivated—laughing, cheering, shouting its approval. Brennan, the associate producer, grasped Dixon's hand and exclaimed excitedly: "Congratulations. We've got 'em. It's tremendous. I never felt anything like it in my life. Our fortune's made."[6]

Realizing that the play would be attacked on many sides because of its theme, Dixon had previously planned to give a short speech between acts, while the play was on tour, justifying his treatment of the racial problem. On the opening night, therefore, he said in part at the end of the third act:

> My object is to teach the north, the young north, what it has never known—the awful suffering of the white man during the dreadful reconstruction period. I believe that Almighty God anointed the white men of the south by their suffering during that time immediately after the Civil War to demonstrate to the world that the white man must and shall be supreme. To every man of color here to-night I want to say that not for one moment would I do him an injury. . . . I have nothing but the best feeling for the Negro.[7]

Dixon's speech was greeted with great enthusiasm. An account in the Norfolk *Virginian-Pilot* the next morning recorded that at Dixon's appearance on the stage, "pandemonium broke loose."[8] The same paper reported the success of the play with a seven-column heading across the top of the page: "THE CLANSMAN A TREMENDOUS SENSATION." The reviewer predicted that the force of the play was so great that it would be "like a runaway car loaded with dynamite."[9]

Three days later the play was presented in Richmond; again its success was phenomenal. Although crowds flocked to the drama, most of the newspaper reviews were unfavorable. A writer for the Richmond *Times-Dispatch* asserted: "Uncontrolled desires, primal passions, race hatred and race supremacy are the warp of the Clansman."[10] An old man who had been a member of the original Klan deplored the play and was quoted as remarking: "It would be . . . better if the play were strangled in its infancy."[11] Another Richmond paper, the *News Leader*, reported that the play was hardly more elevating than a lynching. In conclusion it stated that Dixon had committed "a distinct evil"[12] in writing the play. A third Richmond paper, the *Evening Journal*, provided a favorable review, however, and said in part that "we have little patience with the squeamish timidity that would shrink from seeing portrayed on the stage conditions that our fathers were men enough to grapple with in their stern reality and to conquer."[13] The producers of the play had no fear for the financial success of "The Clansman," for the receipts of the first weeks in the South paid the entire cost of the production.

When the presentation came to Dixon's native state of North Carolina during the first week in October, it was enthusiastically and boisterously attended wherever it appeared. In Winston-Salem, according to a newspaper report, "men fought madly for choice seats,"[14] and a special police force armed with fire hoses stood ready to rout the crowd should the situation get out of hand. When the play was performed in Raleigh, the audience was "wildly enthusiastic."[15] A reviewer for the Raleigh *News and Observer* stated that the play was "above the necessity for good acting. . . . Through it all runs the lure of sex, the appeal to the pride of race, the grip of the blood-call that is like a strangle hold."[16] A favorable note was sounded when Robert B. Glenn, governor of the state, publicly endorsed the play for its "great historical truth" and for its effort "to correct the foul misrepresentations done this beloved section."[17]

By mid-October, the troupe had proceeded into South Carolina. The effect of the play upon the audience at Columbia was volcanic. Some of the crowd showed their enthusiastic approval by clapping, shouting, and stamping upon the floor. Others registered their distaste by booing and hissing throughout the drama. When Dixon appeared on the stage, the diverse factions in the audience kept up a battle of "boos" and "bravos" for a full two minutes.

Later that night, many prominent young men who had objected strongly to the play gathered at Dixon's hotel and taunted him to come down from his room. The next morning the editor of the Columbia *State* vigorously attacked the drama as dangerously inflammatory and "full of inconsistency and historical inaccuracies."[18] Dixon, who prided himself on having done much research to substantiate the historical elements of the play, immediately wrote to the editor:

> I will refer the issue of historical accuracy between us to a jury of 12 to be appointed by the American Historical Society. If they decide that you are right, I will not only agree to pay $1,000 for the errors established, but I will . . . withdraw the play from the boards—on the condition that if . . . the verdict goes against you, you forfeit $1,000 and resign as editor of the "State." I repeat the motif of my play: "A Lighthouse of Historic Truth Built on the Sands of Reconstruction."[19]

Whether the editor was convinced of Dixon's sincerity or whether he did not care to respond to what he may have thought a "grandstand play" is not known. In any event, the editor did not accept the challenge, although he did direct the following remarks to the departing troupe: "We shall be agreeably surprised if innocent blood is not upon the head of the Reverend Thomas Dixon Junior, before he reaches New Orleans."[20]

From Columbia, Dixon and his group moved on to Charleston, where "The Clansman" was performed twice at the Academy of Music. As usual, crowds were turned away at both performances. The publicity that now preceded the play made it a sellout wherever it appeared. The editor of the Charleston *News and Courier* remarked that the presentation he attended was "one of the most remarkable exhibitions of hysterics to which we have been treated in many long days."[21]

When the play opened a three-day stand in Atlanta, the first-night audience, which included Governor Terrell, applauded the play loudly, and when Dixon appeared on the stage, the crowd cheered him "for several minutes."[22] Though the audience heartily approved of the play, some of the Atlanta clergy spoke against it. The Reverend Doctor L. G. Broughton, pastor of the Baptist Tabernacle, referred to the drama as "a disgrace," and spoke thus of Dixon:

> To claim that it is necessary . . . for him to go girating about over the south, stirring up such passions of hell, to keep the races apart and thus prevent, what he imagines, an impending amalgamation of the whites and blacks into one race of mixed bloods, is a slander of the white people of the south . . . so vile . . . that I cannot find words sufficiently strong to denounce it. . . . For God's sake, the negro's sake, and our sake, give the negro a rest from abuse and incendiarism![23]

After the play was shown in Montgomery, Alabama, on November 3, Governor Jelks of that state denounced it bitterly. Although admitting that the drama "was well sustained and even thrilling throughout," Jelks nevertheless said it was "a nightmare."[24] "Undertaking to teach Southern white people something of the horrors of social equality," he added, "is absolutely useless. They are already taught. The situations and suggestions are disgusting and beyond expression. It is bad, top, bottom and sides, and it hurts."[25] Another critic, writing in the *Montgomery Advertiser*, remarked with asperity: "It is mere folly for Tom Dixon to pretend that he is performing a public service in producing such a play. He is after dollars and he will get them. What a pity there is no way to suppress 'The Clansman.' "[26]

Wherever the play appeared, the story was much the same. The editor of the *Chattanooga* (Tennessee) *Daily Times* called the play "a riot breeder . . . designed to excite rage and race hatred."[27] Before the drama was presented in Knoxville, on Saturday, November 11, the editor of the *Journal and Tribune* had attacked it from what he had heard of its theme. He referred to Dixon as "a servant of the devil," and added: "How the mind of a man who preaches love, and peace, and extols the principles embodied in the Golden Rule, could conceive of such a thing as 'The Clansman' seems to be, is beyond ordinary comprehension."[28] He later stated that "the only charitable conclusion" that could be reached concerning Dixon, who, he said, "never was well balanced," was that Dixon had "gone crazy."[29]

On November 17 and 18 "The Clansman" was presented at the Vendome Theatre in Nashville, where the *Banner* reported that the audience was stirred "to the very depths of their souls."[30] The reviewer went on to say that the lesson of the play was that social equality between the races could "only end in crime, bloodshed and death." The North, more than the South, he explained, needed this lesson. He said that the only thing served by showing the play in the South was "to stir to boiling point the already hot blood of a Southerner."

"The Clansman" was now being billed as "the greatest theatrical triumph in the history of the South."[31] A news report that preceded the play in New Orleans asserted: "Such a phenomenal success has never before been seen in the theatrical world. The simple truth is that in no city or town has it been possible to find theatres large enough to accommodate crowds that have thronged to see this play."[32]

From New Orleans "The Clansman" moved into the Middle West, where it played to overflowing crowds in such cities as Columbus, Ohio; Indianapolis, Indiana; and Topeka, Kansas. While the troupe was continuing through the West, Dixon returned to New York to help rehearse another cast for the metropolitan opening scheduled for January, 1906. In a speech on December 21, 1905, to the King's Crown Association at Columbia University, Dixon refused to "tone down" certain features of the play that had proved offensive to some viewers, stating that should he do so he would be compromising his determination to tell the whole truth of Reconstruction. A reporter, who reviewed the speech for the *New York Evening Journal*, described Dixon's physical appearance at this time:

> He is a tall spare man. He is past his forties [Dixon was actually not quite forty-two]. His hair is iron gray. His heavy eyebrows are still black. He has small, shining, black eyes. He has a long, narrow face with a straight and delicate nose and a firm, thin-lipped mouth. The man will have till long past middle age the energy of youth.[33]

As a result of the unprecedented success of "The Clansman" throughout the South and the West, the publicity preceding the New York opening was enormous. The newspapers of the city were filled with protests, pictures, and advertisements relating to the coming presentation. Despite the many objections offered by individual persons and organizations, the play opened on schedule on January 8 to the largest crowd ever to attend a performance at the Liberty Theatre. Unexpectedly, the New York theatergoers responded enthusiastically, filling the seats at every performance, night after night. The reviews ranged from "commonplace"[34] and "boisterous but harmless"[35] to "obnoxious" and "abominable."[36] So great did the demand become, as a result of the New York showing, that two additional companies were formed to fill the bookings for the play outside the city.

On January 22, 1906, there occurred in New York an event that, because of its nature and juxtaposition in time and place to "The Clansman," provided a rare bonanza for the Manhattan newspapers. Booker T. Washington, the noted Negro educator and president of Tuskegee Institute in Alabama, was in the city for the purpose of raising one million, eight hundred thousand dollars in celebration of the silver anniversary of the Negro school. As an impetus to the drive, a great mass meeting was scheduled for January 22 at Carnegie Hall. More than two thousand people were turned away from the meeting, at which such prominent persons as Washington, Joseph H. Choate, former ambassador to Great Britain, and Mark Twain were listed as principal speakers. The boxes were occupied by such well-known personages as George Foster Peabody, Nicholas Murray Butler, Mrs. John D. Rockefeller, Mrs. Cleveland Dodge, and Mrs. Richard Watson Gilder. The fact that "The Clansman" was at the same time drawing great crowds and much comment caused the city to look with great interest on Washington's meeting. Just before Washington was to appear on the stage, he was handed a note from Dixon stating that Dixon would donate ten thousand dollars to Tuskegee Institute if Washington would declare at the meeting that he did not want social equality and that his school was opposed to racial amalgamation. To this challenge Washington made no answer, and Dixon, determined to press the point, gave an address the following week at the Baptist Church of the Epiphany, where he attacked Washington's cause bitterly, saying in part:

> And this thing, half devil and half child, is supposed to be your equal and actually claims that equality. He does not get it now, but fifty years from now 60,000,000 negroes will claim those equal rights and will take them if they are refused.
>
> . . . .
>
> We must remove the negro or we will have to fight him. He will not continue to submit to the injustice with which we treat him in the North and South. The negro makes a magnificent fighting animal. . . . When the negro smashes into your drawing room . . . his flat nostrils dilated, his yellow eyes and teeth gleaming, you will make good on your protestations of absolute equality or he will know the reason why.[37]

The controversy progressed heatedly in the newspapers in the following weeks, and adherents of both views had their say in articles, interviews, and letters.

By spring, the attention of the country was diverted to Tuskegee, Alabama, where the twenty-fifth anniversary of Tuskegee Institute was being celebrated and where such prominent speakers were on hand as Andrew Carnegie, President Charles W. Eliot of Harvard, Lyman Abbott, and Secretary of War William Howard Taft, whose speech was enthusiastically reported as being of presidential presage, a prophecy that was fulfilled two years later. Many newspapers covered the event, and the reports, on the whole favorable, may be summarized in the following excerpt:

> The splendid success of Tuskegee Institute . . . is the best

answer that could possibly be made to the libelous play of "The Clansman" in which the author, Ex-Rev. Thomas Dixon, insidiously seeks to promote the idea that to educate the Negro is to increase his powers for mischief. . . . The cruel slanders of "The Clansman" are abundantly refuted in the magnificent achievements of Tuskegee which is the conception of a Negro and has been under Negro management for a quarter of a century.[38]

The controversy between Dixon and Washington had excited much interest in the months past. Now headline attention across the nation was given to Andrew Carnegie's nomination of Booker T. Washington as one of the five greatest living men in the world. A critic, in reviewing Carnegie's statement, concluded: "Who the other four were I have no idea. But I do not think the list included the name of the Reverend Thomas Dixon, Jr., author of 'The Clansman.' "[39]

Before "The Clansman" was to open at the Wheiting Opera House in Syracuse, New York, Dixon had been warned by a friend that the company ran the risk of mob violence from people of the city. Before the Civil War, the Wheiting Opera House had been a famous station for the Underground Railroad, by which Negro slaves who had escaped their masters were led into Canada. Opening night was a tense occasion for the cast as they saw every seat of the theater being filled. Mob action, in which someone might be injured or killed, would not be good publicity for the drama. The racial theme might at any moment provoke old enmities into angry violence. But the performance closed without incident, the viewers were enthusiastic, and the entire first-floor audience shook hands with Dixon when he appeared on stage at the end of the play.

The drama did not fare so well in Philadelphia. After playing for four weeks at the Walnut Street Theatre, the play was stopped when a riot occurred during the performance. Elsewhere, "The Clansman" was presented to capacity audiences—breaking all records for theater attendance in Brooklyn, playing one week in Washington, D.C., two weeks in Pittsburgh, and all summer in Chicago. In the border states and in the Northwest it established new records wherever it appeared. When "The Clansman" was presented in Baltimore, the Baltimore *Sun* highly approved of it and referred to the unfavorable criticism of the Washington and New York critics as the "sheerest prejudice."[40]

Although the crowds that flocked to see "The Clansman" abated somewhat after its feverish first year of showings, the drama continued to tour the country for five years, with two companies operating simultaneously, setting a record for touring productions.

When a second group to tour the South came to Shelby, North Carolina, Dixon's boyhood home town, in 1906, the crowd filled the yard of the new school building, where the play was to be presented, an hour before the doors were opened. The response to the play was exuberant. After the curtain had fallen on the last act, only one person offered any adverse criticism—Dixon's father, now an old man. Gravely he spoke to his son: "My only criticism is, Son, I felt once or twice you bore down a little too hard on the Negro. He wasn't to blame for the Reconstruction. Low vicious white men corrupted and misled him."[41] When Dixon replied that he had tried to make that fact plain, his father answered: "I wish you had made it a little plainer. You couldn't make it too strong."[42]

The elder Dixon was to live only three more years. In his eighty-seventh year, not long before he died, he went to live with his daughter Delia, who was practicing medicine in Raleigh. On May 1, 1909, the elder Dixon arose, dressed himself, and then lay down upon his couch. When a servant came in, he found the old minister's eyes fixed in death. Two days later, the Reverend A. C. Irvin, who had officiated at the burial of Amanda seven years before, preached the elder Dixon's funeral to more than seven thousand persons who crowded the churchyard. In looking back over the long career of the man, the Reverend Mr. Irvin reminded his listeners that this devout preacher had established twenty churches, had been the leading force in building as many church houses, and had baptized more than six thousand converts.

Sometime prior to the death of his father, Dixon, from his first three novels and the dramatization of *The Clansman,* had made a fortune which permitted him to indulge himself in many luxuries. Owning a fashionable residence at 867 Riverside Drive, New York City, Dixon and his family lived an exciting life, enjoying the excursions, concerts, and plays that their wealth made possible.

Dixon's association with several New York brokers prompted him to attempt his luck in the exchanges of Wall Street. Becoming fascinated by the rise and fall of the stock market, he spent long hours in the brokers' offices, laughing, trembling, perspiring as the quotations spelled loss or gain. After a few weeks of intense study of the market, Dixon felt that he knew just where to place his investments for the greatest profits. Buying good stocks, mainly United States Steel, on margin, Dixon in a short time invested three hundred and fifty thousand dollars, intending to hold for the big rise certain to come. In the meantime, recalling his father's dependence upon cotton for a livelihood, he sentimentally invested in that commodity a few thousand dollars, which was multiplied to forty thousand in three weeks. Now convinced, as he said later, that he was a "commercial genius," Dixon immediately reinvested the forty thousand, hoping to multiply his winnings once more.

Then something went wrong. The cotton market took a downward plunge, and he lost twenty thousand dollars in three days. Within two more weeks he had lost the remainder and had to draw five thousand dollars from his broker in order to settle his account. The visions of financial wizardry were becoming distorted and dim, but Dixon was reassured by his many holdings in stocks. Soon his setback would be but a memory, and he would, he felt, have his money back several times over. Then came the panic of 1907. Suddenly, the very foundations of the stock market crumbled. The interest on Dixon's indebtedness was pushed to 127 per cent, and within a few days Dixon stood in the exchange, shaking with apprehension and the realization that he had lost every dollar. Later he commented: " . . . that night my hair turned gray."[43]

Of all the ventures of his life, Dixon recalled his fiasco in Wall Street as "the most stupid and futile."[44] From this experience he came away with a distaste for the stock market that remained with him for the rest of his life. The long days he had spent at the exchanges were recalled with disgust:

> It was not only a waste of time, it did something to me that poisoned the sources of life. Gambling is gambling whether at the race track, a card table, or a lottery drawing. It is the at-

tempt to get something for nothing, to take another man's money without a valuable consideration. It is a violation of the fundamental law of sane life: "Thou shalt eat bread in the sweat of thy brow."[45]

From the pinnacle of wealth, Dixon now found that he had fallen into serious financial trouble. In spite of royalties coming in occasionally from his literary efforts, he found that it would be difficult to maintain the standard of living to which he was now accustomed. But bemoaning his plight would not help him to overcome it. Already his teeming brain was hard at work on a plan to recoup his fortunes. The manuscript of the last novel of his trilogy on Reconstruction, though laid aside for a time while he was an habitué of the brokerage offices, he now brought out again and worked upon feverishly.

In July, 1907, Doubleday, Page and Company published *The Traitor: A Story of the Fall of the Invisible Empire.* This last novel of the trilogy is more subdued in tone than are *The Leopard's Spots* and *The Clansman.* The story opens with General Nathan Bedford Forrest's order for the dissolution of the Klan, and the scene is set in the atmosphere of the fierce neighborhood feuds that marked the Klan's downfall in the Piedmont region of the South. John Graham, the hero of *The Traitor* and leader of the Klan, disbands the Klan when he realizes that it will soon get out of hand, and he says he will fight "to the death" any man who attempts to reorganize it.

Like the other two novels in the trilogy, *The Traitor* had an enormous popularity, selling nearly a million copies. The three novels constituted the first trilogy of historical romances to achieve wide recognition in America, and two legislative bills were enacted as a direct result of them.

The royalties from *The Traitor* were helping Dixon to establish himself once more. Though he had by no means regained his former fortune, he no longer feared that he would lose his home on Riverside Drive. The novel was hardly out before he was making plans to dramatize *The One Woman.* The finished play, though criticized in some quarters as a work of doubtful propriety, was nevertheless highly praised by several clergymen.

In the last few weeks of 1907, Dixon and Channing Pollock collaborated in writing a stage version of *The Traitor.* Dixon was to receive 45 per cent of the royalties; Pollock, 45 per cent; and Alice Kauser, the agent, 10 per cent. When the play was produced early in the spring of 1908, it had a considerable success, probably due in part to the popularity of the novel, which had appeared the summer before. Though "The Traitor" appeared on the drama circuits for several seasons, it did not achieve the immediate popularity of "The Clansman."

Dixon, engrossed in his work with the theater, thought that he had at last found his medium. With the drama, he believed that he was capable of reaching more people and speaking to them more effectively than he could with the novel. As he toured the country with his productions, he came more and more to appreciate the problems and challenges of the actor, who, under every kind of adversity of body and spirit, must dedicate himself to the principle that the show must go on.

In 1909 Dixon completed a drama that he had long contemplated. To him, one of the greatest dangers in the close association of Negroes and whites was the possibility of miscegenation. The subject, taboo in many quarters of the South, was an especially delicate one to be treated in a drama during the first decade of the twentieth century. But, as he had done with other explosive subjects, Dixon boldly set about to bring his thesis to the stage. Several weeks of intensive writing resulted in "Sins of the Father," a title traced through Shakespeare's "The Merchant of Venice" (Act III, Scene 5) to the fragmentary "Phrixus" of Euripides ("The gods visit the sins of the fathers upon the children") or to the Book of Exodus.

In "Sins of the Father," Major Norton, the principal character, has a daughter by Cleo, a mulatto. Years later, when Norton's son Tom by his white wife has grown up, Cleo contrives to have her daughter Helen come from the private school she is attending and meet young Tom. A love affair ensues, and they marry secretly. When Major Norton learns of the marriage, he tells Tom of his past relationship with Cleo. Tom, believing that he has married his half-sister, urges that he and his father commit suicide. The elder Norton dies in the suicide attempt, but Tom lives to find out that his wife is not his sister after all. Cleo's child had died in infancy, and Cleo had adopted another secretly, later pretending that it was her own. During all the years that Helen and Tom were growing up, Cleo had been the house servant of Major Norton, for his wife, an invalid, had died. Norton had treated Cleo with utter contempt during these years and had not allowed her to stay in his presence. He considered her as one of the devil's clan because her charms had called forth his baser instincts in the past.

Because of its thesis, the drama aroused considerable

comment. Some critics condemned Dixon for the theme, but others praised him for his forthrightness. The play was later developed into a full-length novel. Dixon's treatment of the problem of miscegenation provoked two direct retorts in Negro fiction. In 1915 Thomas H. B. Walker attempted to counteract the work of Dixon by glorifying the Negro. The heroine of Walker's novel, *J. Johnson; or, "The Unknown Man,"*[46] maintained that the Negro has a fierce race pride that makes amalgamation unthinkable. Herman Dreer, in *The Immediate Jewel of His Soul,*[47] told in 1919 of the opposition that confronted William Smith, a leading exponent of the "new Negro." Dreer's work is interesting in its literary treatment of the militant Negro program for equal rights after World War I. It is also a direct attack on *The Clansman.*

When "Sins of the Father" was first presented in 1910 at Wilmington, North Carolina, Dixon and the cast decided to remain a day or so enjoying the surf at Wrightsville Beach. In the midst of their fun in the waves, someone shouted that sharks were near. Before the bathers could leave the water, the leading man in the play was killed. Dixon was the only member of the cast who knew the dead man's lines. With misgivings that he would ruin the performance, he took the leading part the next night at Fayetteville, North Carolina.

The reviewers were so enthusiastic about his portrayal of the leading character that Dixon decided to give his whole time to acting. Brennan started putting his name in two-foot electric lights as preliminary billing for the famous actor-manager-author. For nearly a year Dixon toured with the company, increasing his respect for the actor, with his often lonely, monotonous life. At the end of forty weeks, the company had cleared twenty-five thousand dollars, and Dixon had acquired in many cities a popularity as an actor almost equal to that which he enjoyed as a novelist and playwright. He had learned every facet of the play and could fill any part at will. By the time the troupe reached Chicago, Dixon, tired from the strenuous one-night stands, had decided to end his acting affiliation with the company and returned to New York to widen his dramatic horizons. For the next two years he served by turns as playwright, director, producer, occasional leading actor, and novelist.

In the midst of his activities with the stage, Dixon was pushing ahead tirelessly to complete his trilogy of novels on socialism, begun in 1903 with *The One Woman.* In 1909, he published *Comrades,* the story of a utopian colony whose leaders attempt to establish a socialistic state on an island off the California coast. The difficulties they encounter in the effort to force an unregenerate humanity into following impossible ideals emphasize in sharp satirical lines Dixon's social creeds. He shows little patience with the various "isms" that beset society, considering the ideologies outside the established order as "wild" or "half-baked."

In *Comrades* Dixon attempts to show that it is impossible for people of all classes and degrees of attainment to be completely leveled as a social group. In the colony of a few hundred persons, there are scores of would-be "preachers," "actresses," and "writers." There is no one left to do the domestic work. A new aristocracy arises among the scrubwomen, whose services are so dear that they become the highest-paid workers of the colony. The working day is eventually reduced to two hours in an effort to satisfy the demands of the workers. The society, as Dixon pictures it, is doomed to fall.

Two years later, in 1911, Dixon completed *The Root of Evil,* the last of his trilogy on socialism. The novel departs considerably from the theme of the first two books, and only indirectly is it a novel on socialism. It is more a refutation of extreme capitalistic principles than it is a sermon against socialistic ideologies. Here Dixon's argument is that the salvation of society lies in the "golden mean" between the extremes of "capitalistic greed" and "socialistic idealism."

Through each of the novels in the trilogy on socialism, Dixon wove an intense love story. In this way he managed to insure a wide popularity for all three books and to arouse interest in his theories among readers who might know little about the socialistic philosophies he thought were undermining the foundations of American society.

The strenuous demands of writing and his enthusiasm for the stage finally began to tell upon Dixon's health. He was urged to go abroad and forget the details of his work. His brother Clarence was now pastor of the Spurgeon Tabernacle in London, a charge to which he had been called the previous year. Clarence's sermons in London and in Scotland had engendered a remarkable response, and Dixon looked forward to visiting his brother in his new home. On May 2, 1912, he and his wife Harriet embarked from New York for England. Their first day in London was not a propitious one, for at the St. Regis Hotel, Dixon, who was dressed rather casually, was firmly informed that he would not be permitted to register because he was not wearing correct attire. The unpleasant occasion was soon forgotten, however, in Dixon's enjoyment of the sights of London. He felt a great affinity for the metropolis and its people and later recalled his first day in the great city:

> I was overwhelmed with the impression that I had arrived at home. I loved her old streets. I loved her historic buildings. I loved her countryside. I knew that I had grown out of it. My soul answered with a cry of joyous kinship.[48]

After a visit with Clarence, Dixon and his wife left London and proceeded to the continent for a holiday of several weeks. As they journeyed from country to country, Dixon found that no other part of Europe impressed him quite so much as Italy. Fond of seeing the relationships between European culture and that of his native state, he never tired of describing the Italian scene as viewed through the eyes of a North Carolinian. He enthusiastically recorded his impressions, writing of the great similarity between the Italian Alps and the "Land of the Sky" around Asheville. To be in Italy was like a return to childhood, for he remarked: "I waked every morning with the dim, sweet consciousness that I was a boy at home again in the foothills of my native State—even the fleas in Italy seemed to bite exactly as they used to at home."[49]

On his return trip to the United States, Dixon, now refreshed by his holiday, spent long hours in his deck chair thinking of the career still ahead of him. Should he continue as an actor and playwright? If the success of the past several years was any indication of his future in the drama, he had bright days ahead. Dixon had, as an actor, already added considerably to the stature of his career. Some reviewers were convinced that, should he return to full-time acting, he would achieve even greater fame than he had enjoyed as a novelist. Of a passionate, compelling, and dramatic nature, he dominated any scene in which he appeared. A critic, referring to Dixon's ability as an actor, spoke for thousands of persons who had seen him perform:

> Mr. Dixon had histrionic ability which indicated that his sphere in life was on the stage. His admirers believed he would have made a great actor. Eloquent in his presentation of any subject, with a commanding presence and power to move audiences, his friends were doubtless right in thinking his throne was the stage.[50]

But new horizons were constantly beckoning to this man of remarkable versatility. Disappointed in his youthful attempt to become an actor, he had become determined through the years to drive himself to eventual success. *Failure* was a word Dixon could not endure, and he would go to any lengths to avoid it. When he found that he had at last reached the goal he had so long sought, he began to lose interest. The life of an actor was exciting, but it had its deadening, prosaic side as well. A play, over a period of time, might reach a wide audience, but the endless repetitions of plot and scene before relatively few people at a time made Dixon impatient of the drama as a medium for the dissemination of ideas. Books, too, were limited in their appeal. A new medium, called "motion pictures," just becoming known in the first decade of the twentieth century, lured Dixon like the words of a vaguely-heard song. Though the acting profession in general held an outspoken contempt for this new toy, Dixon's interest was not diminished. What if this novelty, so lately sprung up in America, could be dignified by a serious, historically vital story—would it not be the potential means of reaching and influencing millions of people? The question came to him repeatedly as he neared New York and in the weeks that followed. His efforts to discover the answer finally led him through several years of discouragement that would have defeated a man with less determination than Thomas Dixon.

Thomas Dixon, the Actor

VII

"Writing History With Lightning"

The morning of February 20, 1915, was bitterly cold in New York City, and as Theodore Mitchell left his Bandbox Theatre and started walking through a cutting wind toward a huge, barnlike structure at Broadway and Fifty-third Street, his temper became progressively more ruffled. Mitchell at the time was one of the most highly successful publicity men in the American theater. Earlier, he had devoted much time to promoting the career of Miss Lillian Russell and had profited greatly by her popularity. He had since, however, become very much interested in presenting drama as a serious artistic genre. He headed an acting group known as the Washington Square Players, later called the Theater Guild, which was to wield great influence in the development of the twentieth-century American stage. The weather, plus Mitchell's interest in drama as high art, made him disgruntled that, of all things, he had promised to watch a private showing of a "movie." Motion pictures were thought of by mature persons as hardly a degree above peep shows, and Mitchell was not happy about this appointment. As he pushed unsteadily closer to his destination through a near blizzard, Mitchell was far from realizing that he was about to view something that would revolutionize the stage and much of American culture.

In the months following his return from Europe in 1912, Dixon had worked earnestly to persuade a producer in the infant motion picture industry to accept his scenario of *The Clansman*. Again and again he had been rejected by every established agency. His persistence had evoked only laughter or polite refusals from the successful companies. The taste of the public at the time was for low comedies, light farce, and short action sequences with little plot. The motion picture companies, intent upon providing what their patrons demanded, wanted nothing of Dixon's "historical beeswax." No producer cared to risk bankruptcy in accepting serious stories such as Dixon's.[1]

Dixon knew early in his efforts that a difficult task awaited him. Even back in September, 1911, he had tried to form a corporation for producing a film version of *The Clansman*. The organization was to have been known as the Kinemacolor-Clansman Corporation. The capital stock had been set at ten thousand dollars to be divided equally among the stockholders. But the venture had failed because of disagreement and lack of interest. Dixon, seeing that he would not succeed in the venture, had put the idea aside for the time being.

As the months wore on, it had become increasingly apparent to Dixon that he would never be able to market his scenario among the well-known companies. Reluctantly he had turned to the little, unstable agencies that were leading a precarious existence on the fringes of the industry. But even these little companies were afraid to risk producing his work.

Finally, late in 1913, when he had about accepted the idea that such a manuscript as his had no future in the film industry, Dixon had met Harry E. Aitken, who had formed a small company which, in spite of fitful efforts, had not made a motion picture. Frank Woods was in charge of scenarios, and the director for the company was a young man who had come to his newly found profession after a varied background of jobs such as newspaper reporting, part-time acting, and day laboring. Just prior to his association with Aitken, this young man, David Wark Griffith, had been doing scenarios for one-reel motion pictures at five to fifteen dollars each. He had several years before been hired and then rejected as an actor in "The One Woman." A Southerner from Kentucky, he had been an interested reader of *The Clansman* as a novel. Now he urged Aitken to see what could be done with Dixon's scenario. Whereas Griffith had heretofore taken his work casually, even half-apologetically, referring to each new production as "grinding out another sausage,"[2] his attitude toward this new venture was entirely different.

For the rights to his scenario Dixon asked ten thousand dollars. He would have asked a higher price but for the lesson he had learned in frequent rebuffs from other agencies. This price, therefore, was a compromise between what he wanted and what he thought he could get. But the little company could not give him an amount even half that figure. After much discussion as to the merits of the scenario and after almost giving up the idea of letting Aitken use the manuscript, Dixon at last reluctantly agreed to accept a 25 per cent interest in the picture.

In the weeks that followed, Dixon worked closely with Griffith in a dirty loft in Union Square which housed the meager facilities of The Epoch Producing Corporation, the name of the newly formed company. At last, when the scenario was ready for production, Dixon filled Griffith's trunk with books and papers to be used in getting up background material for the historical features of the story and, wishing the little group success in their undertaking, saw them off on their journey to Hollywood, where the picture was to be filmed.

Establishing headquarters in a studio on Sunset Boulevard, Griffith set about energetically recruiting actors, stagehands, and properties with which to produce the film. The actors and actresses whom he hired were, for the most part, newcomers to the motion picture world, for Griffith could not afford to pay very much. The main characters from *The Clansman* were acted by the following persons: Lillian Gish (Elsie Stoneman), Henry B. Walthall (Ben Cameron, the "little Colonel"), Mae Marsh (Flora Cameron, the "little sister"), Ralph Lewis (Austin Stoneman), Elmer Clifton (Phil Stoneman), Wallace Reed (Jeff the Blacksmith), Howard Gaye (General Lee), Raoul Walsh (John Wilkes Booth), Joseph Henabery (Abraham Lincoln), and Donald Crisp (General Grant). In addition to the main actors, hundreds of extras were hired to participate in the war scenes and in the forays of the Ku Klux Klan.

Griffith planned to push the project forward as rapidly as possible so that the picture might be finished within a few months. But unexpected difficulties caused him to fall constantly behind schedule. Horses to be used in the Ku Klux Klan scenes were difficult to obtain because of the urgent need for them in the European war. Thousands of yards of cotton sheeting were needed for the actors; the pressure of war made this item scarce also. The greatest burden of all was the relentless struggle for money with which to pay the actors and production men. All Griffith had was poured into this undertaking. He staked everything on the success of his production. Borrowing on all hands, begging aid from every source he could, Griffith pushed on, day after day, as the list of his creditors grew longer and the number of his supporters grew smaller.

Three times Griffith had to suspend production because of lack of funds, and each time the members of the production, including actors, barbers, stagehands, and chambermaids, donated their salaries and savings so that the work could be resumed. The Gish sisters, Lillian and Dorothy, offered Griffith their total savings of three hundred dollars. Their mother made many of the costumes, and Lillian brought parcels and bags to work each day to help in making the scenery and other properties. At no time did any actor make more than seventy-five dollars a week.

Finally, after more than a year from the time that Dixon and Griffith had sat down together over the scenario, Griffith thought that the production was ready for shooting. Needing a large tract of land on which to film the battle scenes, Griffith rented an area about thirty minutes out of Los Angeles. The owners tried to sell the land to the company for five thousand dollars, but Griffith informed them that he could not buy it under any circumstances, having barely enough funds to finish the shooting alone. That same section of land, which Griffith was unable to purchase for his company, was later to be covered with oil wells valued at more than twenty-five million dollars.

The actual filming occupied nine weeks between July and October, 1914. Griffith's bold and inspired directing revolutionized a medium that had previously been somewhat static. Constantly trying new procedures, frequently against the advice of more experienced directors, Griffith achieved startling results. Where the motion picture prior to this time had been composed of a series of stilted poses taken at random distances and tagged together with little continuity, Griffith introduced principles of shooting that were to make the motion picture a new art form. His camera became a living, human eye, peering into the faces of grief and joy, ranging over great vistas of time and space, and resolving the whole into a meaningful flux, which created a sense of dramatic unity and rhythm to the story. Such technological devices as montage, the close-up, the fade-out, the cutback, the iris dissolve, the soft-focus close-up, and the climactic action sequence are now accepted so readily that it is hard to imagine a period in motion picture history when they did not exist; all of these procedures Griffith either introduced or brought to a level of high excellence in his picture. Often on the set by three in the morning in order to utilize every moment of daylight, Griffith would shout directions through a megaphone from a high platform, run perspiring from one part of the set to another, adjust a piece of scenery here, reorganize a sequence there, and study intently the progress of an action being filmed by his talented cameraman, G. W. (Billy) Bitzer.

The finished film, after many sections had been discarded, was still twelve reels long, an unheard-of length for that time. The rumors that had spread concerning the expense of producing the film prompted critics to say that it was a foolish and audacious waste. In a letter supposedly written by William DeMille to Samuel Goldwyn, two young producers at the time, there is evidence that men in the motion picture industry did not expect the film even to pay for itself:

I also heard rumors that the film cost nearly a hundred thousand dollars! This means, of course, that even though it is a hit, which it probably will be, it cannot possibly make any money. It would have to gross over a quarter of a million for Griffith to get his cost back and, as you know, that just isn't being done.[3]

A musical score for the film was composed by Joseph Carl Breil, who made adaptations from Negro folk songs and from passages in "Rienzi," "Die Walküre," and "Norma." In February, 1915, Griffith decided that the picture was at last completed. It was given a preliminary private showing at Clune's Auditorium in Los Angeles on February 8, under the title "The Clansman." After making a few minor adjustments in the film, Griffith hurried with it to New York in order to show it to the censors and the group who were to promote the picture.

The building that had been chosen for the showing was a large structure at the corner of Broadway and Fifty-third Street. As the appointed time drew near, the seventy-five people scattered among the seats kept looking back impatiently toward the projectionist to see when he would start the film. The damp, cold, and cheerless semidarkness of the large auditorium did not contribute to the enthusiasm of the group. Among the guests were Aitken, the producer; Theodore Mitchell, the possible publicity agent; and

Thomas Dixon. At one end of the large room, Breil, the composer of the musical score, was visibly irritated as he rehearsed with the orchestra.

Finally it was time to start. Dixon, not having seen any of the film and expecting the worst, crept upstairs to watch the picture away from the eyes of the other viewers. If the presentation proved to be a failure, Dixon did not want to be seen when it was over. After settling into a seat in the balcony, Dixon reacted to the preview showing in a way he had never expected:

> The last light dimmed, a weird cry came from the abyss below—the first note of the orchestra, a low cry of the anguished South being put to torture. It set my nerves tingling with its call. And then a faint bugle note of the Southern bivouac of the dead. In it no startling challenge to action. No trumpet signal to conflict. It came from the shrouded figures of the great shadow world.
>
> And then I saw my story enacted before my eyes in scenes of beauty and reality. And always the throb through the darkness of that orchestra raising the emotional power to undreamed heights.
>
> It was uncanny. When the last scene had faded, I wondered vaguely if the emotions that had strangled me were purely personal. I hesitated to go down to the little group in the lobby and hear their comments. I descended slowly, cautiously, only to be greeted by the loudest uproar I had ever heard from seventy-five people.[4]

Dixon immediately caught the infectious enthusiasm of the group; he shouted to Griffith across the auditorium that "The Clansman" was too tame a title for such a powerful story; it should be called "The Birth of a Nation."

Hardly had the private showing of the film ended when news of the event somehow found its way into the press. Opposition came from several unexpected quarters. The most powerful forces against showing "The Birth of a Nation" were headed by Oswald Garrison Villard, editor of the New York *Evening Post,* and Moorfield Storey, president of the American Bar Association, who were apprehensive of the racial theme of the picture. The Epoch Producing Corporation, which had brought out the film as an independent agent, had no recourse to the powerful support of the large film companies. Within a few days after its preview showing, the picture seemed doomed. Opposing factions threatened to suppress it completely.

Then Dixon, determined to carry his story to the nation, made a move remarkable even for a man of his energetic personality—a move that, for its outright boldness and originality, has scarcely been paralleled in the history of motion pictures or of American letters. If the President of the United States should give his approval to "The Birth of a Nation," would not the opposition be silenced? The members of the company had little hope of success in the matter, but they agreed that Dixon might at least try to persuade the President to see the film. Dixon thought that should he be able to reach the President before the politicians heard of his move, he might be able to persuade Wilson to help him. He wrote to Wilson requesting a thirty-minute interview; the President replied immediately and arranged a time. After Dixon had been received at President Wilson's desk in the White House, the two men reminisced a few moments about their college days at Johns Hopkins University. Dixon then broached the subject of the film for the first time. In relating the event, Dixon recalled:

I had a favor to ask of him, not as the Chief Magistrate of the Republic but as a former scholar and student of history and

> sociology. From the movement of his expressive eyebrows I saw that any anxiety that I might be an office seeker had been dissipated.
>
> As rapidly as possible I told him that I had a great motion picture which he should see, not because it was the greatest ever produced or because his classmate had written the story . . . but because this picture made clear for the first time that a new universal language had been invented. That in fact it was a new process of reasoning by which the will could be overwhelmed with conviction.[5]

Wilson immediately showed interest in the film, but he said that he could not go to the theater at that time. The recent death of Mrs. Wilson held the White House in mourning. After a moment of thought, he added that if the projection equipment could be brought to the East Room of the White House, he and his Cabinet could view the film there.

In closing the interview, President Wilson recalled the day that Dixon had successfully nominated him for an honorary degree at Wake Forest College:

> I want you to know, Tom, that I am pleased to be able to do this little thing for you, because a long time ago you took a day out of your busy life to do something for me. It came at a crisis in my career, and greatly helped me. I've always cherished the memory of it.[6]

On February 18, 1915, the motion picture was shown in the White House to Wilson, his daughter Margaret, and the members of the President's Cabinet and their families. When the two and a half hours of the story had ended, President Wilson gave to the film one of its highest tributes: "It is like writing history with lightning. And my only regret is that it is all so terribly true."[7]

If the film could be shown to the President of the United

States and his Cabinet, could it not also be shown to the Chief Justice of the Supreme Court? Nothing now seemed impossible to Dixon. As his enthusiasm mounted, he could visualize the film's being presented before the Supreme Court, and then later perhaps before both houses of Congress. He eagerly broached his thoughts to Griffith, who endorsed them heartily.

Early the next morning, on February 19, Dixon hurried to the office of a friend of early North Carolina days, Josephus Daniels, now Secretary of the Navy. Since he did not know Edward Douglass White personally and had heard of the difficulty of obtaining a conference with the Chief Justice, Dixon thought Daniels might be persuaded to arrange an introduction. When Dixon had stated the reason for his visit, Daniels urged him to drop the matter immediately, for he thought White would never consent to see him. When Dixon further persisted and asked about the personality of the man he wanted to see, Daniels replied:

> Well, he's a wonderful old fellow, but he's a bear. He never goes out of his library. He may see you a moment if I ask him, but if you don't get out pretty quick, he [will] push you out and slam the door. Do you want to risk it?[8]

Dixon answered that he did, and soon Daniels had arranged the appointment by telephone. Within a few minutes Dixon was at Chief Justice White's door. Mrs. White met him and directed him to the library. When he entered, he saw a grizzled head buried among papers. For some time White did not look up. Finally, when he did so, he flashed a half-angry look at Dixon: "Well, well, Sir," he growled, "what can I do for you? Mr. Daniels telephoned me that you were coming over."[9] Dixon realized that he must state his business at once, so he said that he wanted the Supreme

Court to view a picture. At this point White interrupted him:

> Picture! The Supreme Court of the United States see a picture! Of all the suggestions I have ever heard in my life that is the limit! What sort of picture?[10]

When Dixon answered that it was a motion picture, White said with a tone of finality:

> Moving Picture! It's absurd, Sir. I never saw one in my life and I haven't the slightest curiosity to see one. I'm very busy. I'll have to ask you to excuse me.[11]

Realizing that the interview was ending unsuccessfully, Dixon, in turning to leave, said in a Parthian shot that the motion picture told the true story of Reconstruction and the redemption of the South by the Ku Klux Klan. At these words, Chief Justice White made an unexpected move. He slowly took off his glasses, pushed his work aside, leaned forward in his chair, and said, "I was a member of the Klan, Sir."[12] After a few more words, he agreed to see the motion picture immediately.

Griffith, showing complete trust in Dixon's persuasive abilities, had followed Dixon's suggestion and engaged the ballroom of the Raleigh Hotel, even while Dixon was still at White's home. Griffith further had had programs printed, merely leaving a blank in which to insert the name of Chief Justice White, as guest of honor presiding over the occasion, as soon as Dixon should return with White's consent.

That evening, the members of the Supreme Court of the United States, with the Senate and the House of Representatives as their guests, witnessed a showing of "The Birth of a Nation." While the film was being shown, Dixon envisioned the incalculable influence, for good or for evil, of the motion picture of the future:

I watched the effects of the picture on the crowd of cultured spectators and realized for the first time the important fact that we had not only discovered a new universal language of man, but that an appeal to the human will through this tongue would be equally resistless to an audience of chauffeurs or a gathering of a thousand college professors.[13]

Dixon had promised President Wilson and Chief Justice White that he would not give the showings any publicity; nevertheless, his plan to have them view "The Birth of a Nation" in a private showing was a brilliant move. When the film was scheduled to make its first public appearance in New York, Dixon learned that his "sectional enemies," as he referred to them, were planning to close the theater on opening night. At a preliminary court session less than forty-eight hours before the film was to be shown, the opposition objected so strenuously that the sheriff received a warrant to close the theater; at this point a defense attorney mentioned that the film had recently been shown at the White House. The opposition was incredulous, and a long distance call was placed to the White House. President Wilson's daughter Margaret answered the phone and affirmed that "The Birth of a Nation" had indeed been shown there a short time before. She added that the film had been seen the following night by the Supreme Court and Congress. The chief magistrate of the city of New York therefore immediately withdrew the warrant for the suppression of the film.

"The Birth of a Nation" opened at the Liberty Theatre in New York, March 3, 1915, nine years after the play "The

Clansman" had been presented on the same stage. The public response was overwhelming. During the intermission, Dixon made a brief speech in which he told the audience that the performance they were seeing would revolutionize the history of the theater and that the "Wizard of Light" would be remembered as its prophet; whereupon he called D. W. Griffith from the wings and introduced him to the audience. Dixon was later to recall:

> My prediction has been fulfilled. A few years have passed and today the press of New York devotes as much space to motion pictures as to the spoken drama and employs as many and as able critics to review the productions.[14]

"The Birth of a Nation" became the sensation of the hour. Along with unstinted praise for the power of the story and the superb artistry of the photographic effects, came condemnation, from some quarters, of the prejudicial treatment of the Negro. In objecting to the racial theme, one critic heaped abuse upon Dixon:

> He is yellow because he recklessly distorts negro crimes, gives them a disproportionate place in life, and colors them dishonestly to inflame the ignorant and the credulous. And he is especially yellow, and quite disgustingly and contemptibly yellow, because his perversions are cunningly calculated to flatter the white man and provoke hatred and contempt for the negro.
> . . . It ["The Birth of a Nation"] degrades the censors that passed it and the white race that endures it.[15]

During the last week in March, the city was at fever pitch over the film. The New York Board of Censors, after much dissension and after hearing the city administration say that it had no authority to close the box office, finally voted to permit the continued showing of the picture. Rabbi Stephen Wise, a member of the censorship board, voiced a bitter denunciation of the production, saying in part:

> If it be true that the Mayor has no power to stop this indescribably foul and loathsome libel on a race of human beings, then it is true that Government has broken down. The Board of Censors which allowed this exhibition to go on is stupid or worse. I regret I am a member.[16]

On the second night following Wise's statement in the press, the Liberty Theatre was the scene of a near riot. At a particularly exciting part of the story, when young Flora Cameron was leaping over a cliff to escape Gus, the Negro servant, a group of persons in the front rows began throwing eggs at the screen. When policemen rushed in to quell the fighting that the disturbance had caused, one of the more vocal demonstrators was heard shouting, "Rotten, rotten"[17] as he was being rushed up the aisle. Whether the vociferous dissenter was referring to "The Birth of a Nation" or to the eggs is not recorded, but the reporter, who found himself in the midst of pandemonium, had other matters of interest for his newspaper. As egg yolks oozed down the face of the screen and spectators took short cuts over the backs of seats, it became apparent that the sacred injunction of the theater that "the show must go on" would be violated on that night.

Hard upon the release of the picture came determined opposition from several quarters. Moorfield Storey led a vigorous fight to suppress the picture in Massachusetts. The mayor of Boston was appealed to, but he ruled that he knew of no legal grounds upon which the picture could be suppressed. Consequently, he ordered the Boston police force to give protection adequate for the crowds. A rally of several thousand persons was called to protest the showing of the film, but it opened on schedule to a great crowd that jammed the seats and lobby of the Tremont Theatre. As in New York, the picture was an immediate sensation, many patrons coming again and again to see it. In the meantime, tension ran high. A crowd of twenty-five thousand persons demonstrated on the grounds of the Massachusetts state capitol, demanding that Governor David Walsh take steps to ban the picture. Impressed by the seriousness of the situation, the Governor hurriedly laid the matter before the legislature, pressing for a special act to suppress the film. A bill was submitted and rushed through the house, only to be found unconstitutional by the judiciary committee of the senate. As a result, it appeared for a time that the film would have no further opposition. But the calm was short-lived. After a few nights, a crowd of ten thousand people gathered on Boston Common opposite the theater, and as feelings mounted higher, a pitched battle with the police broke out which lasted twenty-four hours.

The publicity arising from the Boston incident boosted the notoriety of the film enormously. The subject of the rioting was soon on the lips of the whole nation, and everyone wanted to see the motion picture that was causing so much commotion. Controversy raged wherever the film appeared, and cries of bigotry and intolerance followed Dixon and Griffith everywhere. Charles W. Eliot, president of Harvard University, accused the film of perverting white ideals. Jane Addams, philanthropist and founder of Hull House, was greatly disturbed about the picture and wrote vigorously against it. Booker T. Washington denounced the film in the newspapers. To charges that he had falsified history, Dixon offered a reward of one thousand dollars to anyone who could prove one historical inaccuracy in the story.

Throughout the West the picture met opposition, but in

Thomas Dixon, Age 72

the weeks that followed the New York and Boston showings, no theater was closed to it. At first refused in Chicago by the board of censorship on May 1, 1915, it was soon accepted under a permanent injunction that restrained police interference provided children under eighteen years of age were not admitted. In nearly every large city in the North and West, the film had difficulties passing the boards of censorship but was ultimately passed by all. An official of the city of St. Louis said that it required the combined actions of the recreation division, the police department, and the prosecuting attorney's office to prevent the showing of the film. Even this opposition was finally prevailed over. Between February and June the producers of "The Birth of a Nation" spent more than a hundred thousand dollars in legal fees to meet the opposition of the critics in Los Angeles, New York, Boston, and Chicago alone. Still the film prospered greatly, bringing in thousands of dollars each day.

The tremendous interest created by "The Birth of a Nation" was typically expressed by Ward Greene, a feature writer for the *Atlanta Journal,* while the film was appearing at the Atlanta Theater in early December, 1915:

> The Birth of a Nation hit Atlanta like a tidal wave. The story of the Creation was told in eight words, but should the pen of another Moses be raised today he would need 10 times that number of pages to do credit to The Birth of a Nation. There has been nothing to equal it—nothing. . . .
>
> If you haven't seen it, spend the money, borrow it, beg it, get it any old way. But see The Birth of a Nation.[18]

The plot of "The Birth of a Nation" follows *The Clansman* in spirit if not in substance. After a short introductory sequence showing slaves being brought to America and an account of the abolitionist activity before the Civil War, the film shows Phil and Tod Stoneman of Pennsylvania at the home of their school friends, the Cameron brothers, in Piedmont, South Carolina. Phil Stoneman soon falls in love with Margaret Cameron; Ben Cameron at the same time dreams of the face of Phil's sister, Elsie, which he had seen in a daguerreotype. Into the midst of this idyl the Civil War suddenly erupts, and the Stoneman brothers return to Pennsylvania to join the Union forces. As the war progresses, the two younger Cameron brothers and Tod Stoneman are killed. Ben Cameron is wounded and is nursed by Elsie Stoneman as he lies a prisoner of Phil Stoneman. Elsie Stoneman's father, whom Dixon had portrayed in *The Clansman* as the counterpart of Thaddeus Stevens, is still presented as a diabolical figure who tricks the Negro, Silas Lynch, into leading his people in an advance against the Southern white population.

The story of the Reconstruction is told in vivid scenes of looting and lawlessness. Ben Cameron becomes the leader of the Ku Klux Klan as he is fired to revenge the wrongs he has seen perpetrated on his people. Gus, a Negro servant, makes advances to Ben's younger sister Flora; in her terror to escape him, she jumps from a cliff at the foot of which Ben discovers her dying.

When Elsie Stoneman comes to Silas Lynch to beg that he save her brother Phil from the Negro militia who have him besieged in a log cabin, Silas demands that Elsie marry him. The situation is resolved when the clansmen, with Ben as their leader, put the militia to flight, free Elsie from Lynch, and kill Gus. A double wedding takes place between the Stoneman and Cameron families, symbolic of the unification of the North and South. The people of the South now turn from the dark period of terror and desolation to a hopeful view of the future as the nation arises from the ashes of war.

That "The Birth of a Nation" took a biased view of the Negro there can be little doubt. The actions of the emancipated Negro were overdrawn to make him appear as obnoxious as possible. The idea that the Negro and the white man must remain distinctly segregated in all areas of society was passionately maintained in the picture. It is clear that the tremendous social significance of "The Birth of a Nation" cannot easily be dismissed. The white persons who held a natural prejudice against the Negro saw in the powerfully executed film a confirmation of their feelings. In stirring up enmity between the races, the film aroused the violent objections of Negroes especially. Many Negro groups which had been somewhat acquiescent in their programs for social and political equality now became militantly aggressive in denouncing the white man's treatment of them.

Curiously enough, some of the enmity aroused by "The Birth of a Nation" was offset by the positive effects for good that the film produced. Dixon had said that he wanted to give a faithful history of the suffering endured by the South during Reconstruction; in so doing, he believed that the world would be more prone to understand and sympathize with the South's attitude toward the Negro. Having lived through the terrors of Reconstruction, he considered himself a spokesman for the people who had shared his experience.

In general, the public who attended the film reacted favorably. In spite of the explosive theme, the artistry of the film captivated audiences everywhere. In Los Angeles, a ballot was distributed to patrons to get their reaction to the picture. At one showing, more than twenty-five hundred favorable comments were returned, as contrasted with only twenty-three objections. As to the technical and artistic achievements of the film, critics were of one accord. Vachel Lindsay, the poet, praised some of the scenes in enthusiastic terms, describing them as "tossing wildly and rhythmically like the sea."[19] From all sides the picture was acclaimed as the genesis of a new art form, more pervasive and powerful in its influence than anyone had ever dreamed a medium of communication could be. Though much has been learned about motion picture artistry since "The Birth of a Nation," the harshness of the lighting and the great skill of Griffith gave an authenticity to the film that can scarcely be equaled by the most modern techniques.

The force and superb artistry of "The Birth of a Nation" in relating the effects of the Civil War awakened the world to the social import of the motion picture medium. Perhaps masses of humanity, hitherto unreached by the written word, could now be profoundly moved by this new method of communication. Here was a powerful agency controlled by comparatively few men. These men could change the whole course of national culture by flashing pictures on a screen. Whether society admitted it or not, as Dixon said after World War I, the true capital of the world was not in the buildings of the League of Nations at Geneva, but in Hollywood, California, whose pervasive and incalculable power reached people everywhere. The realization caused Dixon later to write:

There has been nothing like this before in human history. The men who write and produce the pictures which these millions of boys and girls, men and women, see each week are making our life. The importance of this fact cannot be overestimated. There is a force in daily motion that may change the development of the race.[20]

In the motion picture, man had at last a truly universal language. In instituting this great educational program, no ponderous legislative action would be needed, no expenditure of great sums of money for the erection of buildings for the new "University of Man." The buildings were already in existence: "The classrooms, with row on row of seats in our Theatres, are already heated and lighted and provided with ushers."[21]

Dixon thought that, used properly in the best interests of humanity, the motion picture could be the answer to the wars that beset mankind:

> The whole problem of swift universal education of public opinion is thus solved by this invention. Civilization will be saved if we can stir and teach the slumbering millions behind the politician. By this device we can reach them. We can make them see things happen before their eyes until they cry in anguish. We can teach them the true living history of the race. Its scenes will be vivid realities, not cold works on printed pages, but scenes wet with tears and winged with hope.[22]

Dixon concluded that the motion picture could at last teach "the Fatherhood of God and the Brotherhood of Man, the horror of war, a new and nobler patriotism, and the true basis of human progress."

When the producers of "The Birth of a Nation" finally had time to collect their thoughts in the welter of controversy and acclaim that surged about them, they realized that they owned the most valuable piece of dramatic property in the history of mankind. Dixon had suggested that J. J. McCarthy, later vice-president of Fox Films, assume the responsibilities of promoting the film. McCarthy, who had been the agent for Dixon's play "The Clansman," urged Theodore Mitchell to take care of the publicity. Mitchell, who had gone so reluctantly to the first showing in New York, became a dynamo of energy and enthusiasm in his work as he showed the film to millions of Americans as well as to royalty and commoner in Europe. Under McCarthy's able management, twelve companies were kept employed full time to fill the bookings. These companies did not include other agencies that were organized to show the film in the New England states, sixteen Western states, and Canada.

Around "The Birth of a Nation" several legends arose, some of them without basis in fact. Many people thought that the film was the first to be "road-shown," but two Italian productions, "Cabiria" and an early "Quo Vadis," had previously toured the United States.[23] Some persons thought the film had the first especially adapted musical accompaniment, but in 1908 Saint-Saëns had composed a score for the French picture "*L'Assassinat du duc de Guise.*"[24] That the picture cost more than five hundred thousand dollars to produce and had a cast of eighteen thousand actors was believed by many people; actually the producers never had more than six hundred on the payroll, and the cost of production was between eighty-five and ninety thousand dollars.[25] But "The Birth of a Nation" was the first film to charge a two-dollar admission fee (at a time when the usual cost of admission was about fifteen cents), and the picture may have earned the highest profits for a single film in motion picture history.[26] After an official gross income of eighteen million dollars, the film was distributed among many small companies and was shown throughout Europe, Australia, South Africa, and South America, where millions of additional viewers saw it.

Throughout its history, the picture was to be a subject of controversy. It was suppressed in Paris because it was feared the film would insult the Negro citizens of the French Republic. In later years, when an attempt was made to revive the film in Chicago, Harold Ickes, later Secretary of the Interior, was attorney for the city in trying to prevent the showing of the picture. After excoriating the film all day at the hearing in the inimitable Ickes manner, he is said to have remarked behind his hand to Harry Aitken, the producer, "Best picture I ever saw in my life."[27]

VIII

"I Had a Message"

Convinced that "The Birth of a Nation" had created something new in the world, that "the producers of motion pictures are wielding a greater power than any monarch who rules the world, or ever ruled it," that "they can shape the destiny of humanity,"[1] Dixon in the summer of 1915 moved to California and built "The Dixon Studios, Laboratory, and Press," located at Sunset Boulevard and Western Avenue, Los Angeles. Here, in the midst of a large orange grove, he established an impressive array of buildings in which to house studios, darkrooms, machine shops, and living quarters for a number of workers. Here he planned to produce a motion picture greater than "The Birth of a Nation."

His conviction that the United States would be drawn into World War I caused him, in 1916, to publish *The Fall of a Nation.* While the novel was being prepared in book form, he had been producing and directing a film version in which he attempted to warn America that her false sense of security and her misdirected pacifism could again divide the nation and lead to its downfall.

Before producing the film, Dixon had written to President Wilson, telling of his plans to awaken the nation to the necessity of preparing for a war in which, he maintained, America was certain to become involved. Wilson answered in unequivocal terms, trying to dissuade Dixon from his plans:

> I must frankly say to you that I am sorry after reading the synopsis of your new enterprise, because I think the thing a great mistake. There is no need to stir the nation up in favor of national defense. It is already soberly and earnestly aware of its possible perils and of its duty, and I should deeply regret seeing any sort of excitement stirred in so grave a matter.[2]

Dixon was not to be deterred from his course, however, and he went ahead with his plans. In addition to hiring a large cast, he engaged Victor Herbert, the famous composer, to write an original orchestral score for the film. From September, 1915, through the spring of 1916, Herbert was busily engaged in the composition. Both Dixon and Herbert considered the musical score to be a major factor in the future success of the film industry. In an interview for the *New York Times,* Herbert was enthusiastic about his work, saying in part:

> For the first time in the history of American pictorial drama, a complete accompanying score will be played that has never been heard anywhere else. . . . In brief, the musical programme will not be a mosaic or patchwork of bits of Wagner, Grieg, Verdi, Bizet, and others, but will be strictly new, as individually written to each particular scene.[3]

After much advance publicity, "The Fall of a Nation" had its première at the Liberty Theatre in New York City on June 6, 1916. Present at the occasion, in addition to many celebrities from the film world, were both Dixon and Victor Herbert. The public, still agog over "The Birth of a Nation," was eager to see the sequel from Dixon's pen. Though the première performance was viewed with great interest, there was not evident the frenzy of acclaim and denunciation that had accompanied the first showing of "The Birth of a Nation." A critic, after viewing the première performance, expressed some doubt as to the success of the picture. After describing the film as "graphic," "exciting," "absurd," and "undeniably entertaining," he concluded: "And, like all big spectacular pictures, it must face the eternal question, 'Is it as good as "The Birth of a Nation"?' It has not yet been possible to answer this in the affirmative."[4]

While the film was being presented in the theaters, the story was enjoying a wide sale in bookstores. In spite of the popularity of the book, critics in general looked with disfavor upon it. One criticism is indicative of the consensus of the reviewers:

> It would be difficult to discover anything more futile and foolish than "The Fall of a Nation," even in the midst of an epoch that produces many futile and foolish books. . . . But it need hoodwink none of us into believing it to be a propagandist tract against pacifism. It is nothing but a story, and a very poor story at that. It is exactly the sort of story to be expected of the author of "The Clansman."[5]

The purpose of *The Fall of a Nation,* in both the novel and film versions, is to point up the danger of following misguided idealists, especially should these idealists be women who are motivated by pacifistic instincts. The Honorable Plato Barker, a pacifist in the film, seems to be a thinly disguised caricature of William Jennings Bryan.

In the story, Virginia Holland, a brilliant and beautiful young feminist, mirthfully derides the efforts of John Vassar, a congressman from New York, to introduce a bill in Congress for a considerable expenditure of funds for national defense. Since Miss Holland is secretary of the "National Campaign Committee," a country-wide organization for the emancipation of women, she wields great influence in her cause. Her compelling personality and power of public speech draw many people to her side as she campaigns against Vassar's plans for compulsory military training.

In his argument, Dixon postulates a boundless gulf between the democratic and the monarchic state. He tells of the bitterness that the crowned heads of Europe feel against America, the democratic thorn that pierces their sides and threatens to destroy their right to rule. This bitterness finally reaches a climax as the monarchs concentrate their might and swoop down upon the unsuspecting American people. Within a week the country is at the mercy of the "Imperial Confederation." Every business is at a standstill. The feminine idealists who have brought about America's downfall are vindicated, however, as secret word is passed over the country that on the anniversary of the *coup d'état* of the Imperial Federation, each young American woman is to stab her unsuspecting foreign escort at the stroke of midnight.

The popularity of both the film and the novel served to crystallize the attitudes of many persons toward America's part in the war raging in Europe. Although Dixon, who sometimes equated popularity with influence, was not altogether satisfied by the relative success of the film, he yet had a word to say for the picture as an effective medium of communication: "It reached more than thirty million people and was, therefore, thirty times more effective than any book I might have written."[6] But the picture must be counted a failure by Dixon's original standards, for it showed a great falling off from the stirring and brilliant artistry of "The Birth of a Nation." Dixon's aim to surpass his first great success had fallen short of its mark.

Somewhat taken aback by the fact that he had not produced the greatest of motion pictures, Dixon stopped to collect his thoughts and decide upon his next move. The royalties from "The Birth of a Nation" and his novels had made him a millionaire. He had, therefore, no financial problem. He could, if he chose, be assured of wealth and fame should he retire at this point. But inactivity was alien to the nature of Thomas Dixon. His brain, sensitive to every social force of the day and constantly searching for ways of expressing his newest ideas, was never idle. Even while he was trying unremittingly to find a motion picture producer for *The Clansman,* Dixon had been constantly writing.

In 1913, as a result of his great respect for Abraham Lincoln, he had published a fictional biography of the Civil War President, under the title *The Southerner.* The author here shows for his hero an admiration usually reserved for Southern leaders. He makes much of the fact that Lincoln was born in the South, and he considers the cast of Lincoln's thought and character peculiarly "Southern." Lincoln is shown as a man of infinite patience, gradually sinking under a burden of criticism, opposition, and sadness.

To balance his treatment of Civil War leaders, Dixon, the following year, had written *The Victim,* a study of Jefferson Davis, President of the Confederacy. The novel traces the whole span of Davis' life, beginning with his boyhood in Mississippi, proceeding through the war, and ending with his death. The book reveals considerable historical research by Dixon, especially into matters relating to Davis and the generals of the Confederacy. The gradual physical decline of Davis and his final flight from Richmond into Georgia are told. Under every sort of injury and insult, Davis is pictured as a man of indomitable courage and whole-hearted devotion to his cause.

In addition to his attention to socialism, Civil War history, and motion pictures during this period, Dixon had also been very much interested in the current matter of woman suffrage, with all the evils that, he thought, would accompany the "emancipation" of womanhood. Though he has no trilogy on the "new woman," he treats her in several of his works, one of which is *The Foolish Virgin,* published in 1915, not long after the first showings of "The Birth of a Nation." A young girl, innocent of the ways of life, will not listen to the advice of her more sophisticated friend. Her romantic, preconceived ideas about love and marriage lead her into an elopement with a charming criminal whose true nature she learns soon after they are married. In the novel, Dixon portrays woman as a creature of finer clay than man and "superior" to the baser instincts of the male. Any attempt on a woman's part to enter a man's world only degrades her and makes her a slave to ambition. Dixon emphasizes very strongly the danger of an inexperienced woman's acting through uncontrolled impulses. Ready belief in the words of strangers is especially to be guarded against.

The preceding several years had indeed been busy ones for Dixon. In addition to his novels, much incidental writing, and lecturing, he had written several plays.[7] Now the disappointment over the fact that "The Fall of a Nation" had not proved to be more successful than "The Birth of a Nation" gave him reason to pause. Although "The Fall of a Nation" was perhaps not what he had hoped for, was it not, after all, his first attempt? So he reasoned, as he prepared to move forward in his new career. Experimenting in new techniques of lighting, camera effects, and plot sequences, he hoped to bring freshness and originality to an industry now teeming with competitors.

The results of some of Dixon's experimentation came in 1918 in a motion picture version of his novel *The One Woman,* which had aroused so much controversy when it was first published in 1903. But now, fifteen years later, the "propriety" of the theme was not so questionable as it had been when the novel first appeared. Though "The One Woman" had no signal success beyond the average film of the time, it was interesting as an effort to employ new techniques in portraying on the screen the theme of this widely read and much-discussed novel.

Still undaunted by his failure to "conquer" Hollywood and determined to inform the public of a growing post-war Bolshevistic influence, Dixon in 1919 helped to produce "Bolshevism on Trial," based on *Comrades,* the second of his novels on socialism. Although the film was a fairly effective propaganda piece, its woodenness and weakness in casting earned for it only a moderate success.

Dixon had for years become increasingly concerned with the forces that had brought about the Russian Revolution of 1917. Though "Bolshevism on Trial" could not be counted a success, he hoped to accomplish his end by another production dealing with the menaces of communism. The result was a drama, "The Red Dawn," which he planned to adapt to the screen. The play, first presented at the Thirty-ninth Street Theater, New York City, on August 9, 1919, aroused a great deal of comment. Much attention was given to it in the press, and several critics characterized Dixon as a "prophet of doom," who was overstressing the dangers of Soviet-inspired world revolution. Having some similarities to *Comrades,* "The Red Dawn" likewise sets the scene on an island off the coast of California. John Duncan has founded a colony there to prove to the world that an ideal socialistic state can prosper. The drama opens quietly enough, with little to distinguish the settlement from many idealized socialistic colonies. Only when a Mr. Stanton, a communistic delegate from the "Central Soviet of Northern Europe," arrives does trouble start. He precipitates an upheaval that threatens to destroy the colony. A quarrel arises among the leaders concerning the right of each of four dancing girls to choose her own costume. Duncan disapproves of the dance and the costumes, but Stanton, an avid leftist, says that the first law of socialism is that no people must be placed under an authority not of their own choosing. The dance brings on a crisis, and Duncan's attempt to stop the dance is overruled. Stanton takes command of the colony, and when one of the dancing girls complains that Cargin, a lieutenant, has been executed without a trial, Stanton sends her to the stockade. Stanton now boldly asserts that the socialists (communists) are going to overthrow the government of the United States. Soviet troops are to march into Texas from Mexico. When Stanton's wife tries to dissuade him from his purpose, he has her imprisoned.

A group of counterrevolutionaries overpower Stanton, and Simpson, a man who had joined the colony as an ex-convict, proves himself instead to be a United States secret agent, who brings charges against Stanton. As the play ends, Simpson removes from his coat lapel the red bud of revolution and puts in its place the badge of a United States government official.

"The Red Dawn" is interesting as an example of Dixon's concept of Soviet political philosophy before the end of the second decade of the twentieth century. As in the novel *Comrades,* Dixon depicts socialistic principles in such a light that they will appear ridiculous or contemptible. Although he does not clearly distinguish between socialism and communism in the play—perhaps because the direction the new Soviet regime would take was not yet clearly revealed to the world—his writings and public utterances in later years contain the term "communism" with far greater frequency than they do any references to "socialism," the ideology he attacked in his works before 1920. In spite of his desire to use the play for the screen, its too-close similarity to "Bolshevism on Trial" finally persuaded him that it would not prove to be a financial success.

At the same time that "Bolshevism on Trial" and "The Red Dawn" were being written, Dixon was using his seemingly limitless energies in another area. In 1919 D. Appleton and Company published *The Way of a Man,* Dixon's most ambitious treatment of the "new woman." This novel created a sensation at the time for its bold treatment of "free love" and "emancipated sex." Ellen West, the heroine, is an unconventional young person who believes that certain principles of conduct are to be followed according to one's personal system of ethics rather than according to an established moral code. She believes in the complete emancipation of woman and in full equality with man in every phase of business and social life. Contending that the woman who is in earnest, the woman who is determined to gain the full rights of her sex, must demand freedom and independence in sexual matters, she boldly proclaims the theory of free love. When Ralph Manning asks her to marry him, she refuses on the ground that marriage is a degrading relationship of slavery on the one hand and authority on the other. She would readily accept, however, a situation that has no ties or responsibilities attached. Manning will not agree to such a relationship at first, but finally she persuades him to see the matter her way, and they are "married" in a remote mountain retreat with the murmur of the brook beneath their cabin as their "wedding march" and the mist of the waterfall as Ellen's "bridal veil."

The relationship continues several years, but the constant secrecy that must attend it causes the lovers to quarrel more and more. Finally, when a young niece comes to stay with Ellen, Manning is attracted by the ingenuous, though conventional, attitude of the girl. Not until Ellen loses Manning does she realize how empty her ideals have been. Dixon treats the heroine sympathetically, and in so doing, he is better able to show the disillusionment that finally comes to her as she sees the error of rebelling against the mores of society.

Dixon attacks socialism in *The Way of a Man* as the undermining enemy of the monogamous marriage. He contends that having the wife as the center of the home and the husband as its head is the most stable basis for an orderly society. Any departures from this arrangement can only bring a complete breakdown of moral and social values. The natural place for woman is in the home of a monogamic marriage, and those women who seek complete emancipation by following socialistic theory are "the sexless, the defectives and the oversexed, who can always be depended on to make the herd a lively place for its fighting male members."[8]

The great popularity of *The Way of a Man* through the summer of 1919, plus Dixon's reputation as the author of "The Birth of a Nation," enabled Dixon to sell the motion picture rights to Joseph M. Schenck on September 12, 1919, for a large sum.

Although Dixon's motion picture venture had thus far not achieved the success that he had at first been sure would be his, he was still a very wealthy man. For all his talent in making money, however, he was not a man interested in retaining what he had made. Generous and casual with respect to wealth, he had sometimes found himself in need of money; yet whenever his funds became depleted, he could call upon his creative brain for a new money-making endeavor. He gave large sums to charitable and civic organizations, invested heavily in numerous enterprises, and provided generously for his family. Jordan, Dixon's younger son, had been crippled by poliomyelitis since early childhood. Dixon sought every means to cure Jordan; he spent thousands of dollars for doctors and treatments in his efforts to bring comfort to his son, but his expenditures were useless. Jordan, a handsome, appealing young man, became progressively weaker through 1918, and at last died on March 18, 1919.

The depressing effect that Jordan's death had upon Dixon, coupled with his disappointment over his efforts at film-making, caused Dixon to consider moving back to New

York. Having maintained his Manhattan home at 867 Riverside Drive while he was working in Hollywood, Dixon decided early in 1920 to direct all further motion picture work from his New York headquarters.

No sooner was he back in New York than he returned to the subject of Abraham Lincoln in a drama entitled *A Man of the People,* published in book form. Although effectively recreating the atmosphere of pressure and confusion that surrounded Lincoln during his campaign for re-election, the drama offers little new interpretation of Lincoln's character beyond *The Southerner,* Dixon's fictional biography of him as Civil War President.

In the fall of 1922, while visiting friends in Shelby, North Carolina, Dixon became interested in erecting an equestrian statue of his uncle, Colonel Lee Roy McAfee, dressed in the robes of the Ku Klux Klan. His plans touched off a controversy which raged in newspaper editorials over the country in the weeks that followed. The aftermath of World War I had created its share of racial organizations, and the new Ku Klux Klan, as an organization that solved its problems by force and violence, was especially appealing to certain mentalities. The early twenties saw Klans burgeon into organizations with hundreds of thousands of members. Among the newspapers discussing Dixon's proposal, the *Charlotte Observer* declared that "it would be hard to conceive of a statue more grotesquely created."[9] The *Montgomery Advertiser,* on the other hand, called the *Observer*'s editorial "ridiculous" and further stated: "Kukluxism is an interesting phase of Southern civilization, an institution that rose up to do a definite thing, and disappeared when its purposes had been accomplished. It will always live in the lore of the people."[10] The *New York*

Times strongly agreed with the view of the *Advertiser*. If the controversy stirred up by his announcement deterred Dixon from his undertaking, the fact was not made public. In any event, the statue was never erected.

Some of Dixon's critics have said that his novels and "The Birth of a Nation" had a powerful influence on the revival of the Klan of the nineteen-twenties. Walter White, depicting the causes of the 1906 race riots in Atlanta, claimed that

> Fuel was added to the fire by a dramatization of Thomas Dixon's novel *The Clansman* in Atlanta. (This was later made by David Wark Griffith into *The Birth of a Nation*, and did more than anything else to make successful the revival of the Ku Klux Klan.) The late Ray Stannard Baker, telling the story of the Atlanta riot in *Along the Color Line*, characterized Dixon's fiction and its effect on Atlanta and the South as "incendiary and cruel." No more apt or accurate description could have been chosen.[11]

Since the first showing of "The Birth of a Nation," Dixon had been repeatedly approached for support of the new Klan, and after his announcement about the statue, Klan leaders tried to associate his name and influence with their cause. The leaders of the new Klan soon learned, however, that they had misinterpreted the actions of the man who had praised the historical Klan of Reconstruction days. On January 20, 1923, only a month after the newspaper controversy, Dixon vigorously attacked the new Klan in a speech before the American Unity League in New York City. With outspoken contempt, he excoriated the "Renegade Klan," as he called it, for its lawless acts. He stated that ignorance of the original purpose of the Klan had caused the modern, self-appointed "judges" of society to try to place themselves under a banner that would never have accepted them as suitable members. In conclusion, Dixon summarized his attitude toward the new Klan:

> Its proscription of the negro race under the conditions of modern life is utterly uncalled for, stupid and inhuman. . . . The Klan assault upon the foreigner is the acme of stupidity and inhumanity. We are all foreigners except the few Indians we haven't killed.[12]

Determined to make one more effort to capture the attention of the nation through motion pictures, Dixon worked unceasingly on his next film. On June 1, 1923, he addressed the Authors' League of America at Town Hall in New York City. In his speech he declared that motion picture stories were ten years behind the technological developments of the industry. Dixon added that in his new film, scheduled for release later that month, motion picture art would be brought up to date by putting the technological advances to their best use. In addition to using the latest techniques, Dixon said that he had tried to achieve a high degree of unity of action, based on the classical concept of the drama, by having a minimum number of actors. The film, in part based upon Dixon's novel *The Foolish Virgin*, was to be released under the title "The Mark of the Beast."

The thesis that man's nature is dualistic, one element good, the other bad, is set forth in the story. The young doctor in the tale believes that "while man sleeps the beast awakes." This "beast" in man affects the lives of the characters in New York City and the Catskill Mountains.

"The Mark of the Beast" was especially interesting in that Dixon here made a "psychological" study of his characters, a method of approach that has become common among motion picture producers in recent years. Attempting to achieve his effects by utilizing the changes in lighting techniques recently made available to the industry, he optimistically tried to bring the motion picture "up to date," but he overestimated the ability of his audience to understand his methods. At the film's première in late June, 1923, the young woman who played the heroine of the story and who years later was to become Dixon's second wife, accurately predicted the film's reception by saying that it was far too advanced psychologically for its time and would fail at the box office.[13]

With the failure of "The Mark of the Beast" to revolutionize the film industry, Dixon concluded that his career as a motion picture producer was at an end. His desire to surpass "The Birth of a Nation" had not been fulfilled. Nor was D. W. Griffith ever again to reach the success that had been his when he collaborated with the author of *The Clansman.* The peculiar talents of each man had been transmuted through their collaboration into an artistic performance of genius that neither of them afterward achieved in separate attempts.

As his novels appeared during this period, Dixon was frequently constrained to defend them against the charges that they lacked organic structure and an awareness of established literary principles. He insisted that his critics simply did not understand what he was trying to do. The works of some writers might be considered apart from their lives; their philosophies of life and their principles of literary art might have sharp lines of demarcation separating them. But such a demarcation could not be drawn in Dixon's works. In his literary career as a whole, there was evident from the beginning a fusion of his social philosophy and his literary principles. After his first novel, *The Leopard's Spots,* Dixon had written:

> I have made no effort to write literature. I had no ambition to shine as a literary gymnast. It has always seemed to me a waste of time to do such work. Every generation writes its own literature. My sole purpose in writing was to reach and influence with my argument the mind of millions. I had a message and I wrote it as vividly and simple as I know how.[14]

In the words "I had a message" Dixon summarized the motive behind his entire writing career. His constant aim was to reach a wider and wider audience with the message about which he was currently concerned. Those literary devices were used which, he believed, could best reach and move the greatest number of people. "A novel," he wrote late in life, "is the most vivid and accurate form in which history can be written."[15] He felt that by using historical facts as a basis for his thesis, the novelist can dramatically heighten the glory and significance of the past; he can make the reader more conscious and appreciative of his heritage. Dixon believed that the rich history of the American past had barely been touched by the novelist, and here was a vein of ore that could be mined for a long time.

In the dissemination of his "message" Dixon strongly disapproved of any form of censorship. Even while still a minister in New York, he had expressed his support for free speech and a free press in forthright terms:

> I believe in a free press and a free platform. I have no fear for the widest publicity given the utterance of any infidel. If any infidel can overturn my faith it is a weak thing.[16]

When Slattery, an ex-priest, was villifying the church to which he had once belonged, Dixon had denounced him vigorously from the pulpit for his action, but he had said that it was even worse when the mayor of Savannah, Georgia, refused to permit the ex-priest to lecture publicly.

Dixon maintained that men should be permitted to speak, whatever their views might be.

Dixon was conscious of the great dangers that attend censorship, and he made determined efforts to keep the press free. In a famous and electrifying speech to the American Booksellers Association in New York, he emphasized that censorship will lead to political graft and dictatorship:

> The itch for censorship is a contagious mental disease. Once it starts it goes on. It spreads from one nosey mind to another. . . .
>
> . . . A censorship would be that of a group of peanut politicians. It would not be an intellectual or moral censorship. It would be political. If there was a Democratic Administration we would have a Democratic board of censors and if there was a Republican Administration we would have a Republican board of censors.
>
> . . . .
>
> God Almighty never made a man or a woman good enough, broad enough, wise enough to hold the autocratic power to place hands on the throat of an author and say, "You shall think only as I think and write only what I say shall be written."[17]

While in Hollywood as a motion picture producer, Dixon joined forces with Jesse Lasky for a fight against censorship. For eighteen years he denounced censorship whenever he had an opportunity, appearing before the legislative bodies of the country in an effort to stem the encroaching powers of the censor. He held that a democratic form of government can never endure the destruction of a book, for in so doing, the destroying agency goes counter to the democratic principles of free speech and a free press.

In fighting against the power of the censor, Dixon did not imply that all material was suitable for mental consumption. The moral standards of society must be maintained at a high level, but censorship is not the medium through which these standards may be upheld. Rather, society must be guided by education; those writers responsible for tearing down moral values can then be scorned or ignored by persons who have acquired discrimination in their reading.

Dixon contended that true beauty cannot exist without morality, that "morality and beauty are in their essence, identical."[18] The writer or the artist must undertake his work with a deep sense of responsibility for the influence that his work may have. The "esthete" who considers himself not governed by the laws of morality, who attempts to achieve for art "freedom from the restraint of all moral laws as its noble privilege is certainly baser than the lowest scavenger."[19]

The writers who claimed membership in the realistic-naturalistic school drew Dixon's severest censure. This school, he said, informed the world that the day of romanticism had passed, that "Shakespeare and Scott and Thackeray and Dickens, and all those misguided, misled people who supposed they had power to understand the secrets of the human soul had made a mistake."[20] Dixon placed much of the blame at the door of Émile Zola, whom he called "the modern apostle of putrefaction."[21] When asked in an interview what he thought of the writings of the modern realists, Dixon answered: "I think that a lot of it is unspeakably filthy. I cannot understand how the publishers print it, and I don't understand why people buy it."[22]

According to Dixon, the writer who maintains that he must make use of everything that confronts him for the sake of making his work a true representation of life has no justification for his claim. Some of the realities of life, acceptable in their proper context, may be entirely inappropriate in a book, on the screen, or in a play:

> The plea of realism in this case is sheer bunk. There are many realities of life that are not fit for dramatic exhibition. Manure is a reality. It is a good thing in the right place, which is under the soil in contact with the roots of plants and flowers. Because manure is a reality is no reason why an author or producer should be allowed to cart a load of it into the theatre, dump it on the stage, put shovels in the hands of skilled actors and have them throw it into the faces of a decent audience.[23]

Dixon was greatly concerned about the moral quality of the modern stage. In his eyes the drama had sunk to a level that would make the stage of the seventeenth century seem tame by comparison. The desire to imitate the theater of Paris had caused the American stage to sink to the level of animalism:

> In our stupid way we have gone far beyond anything ever attempted on the legitimate stage of France. I do not speak of the vicious resorts, peep-shows and can-cans concocted for American eyes. We are producing in first class theatres in New York, and inviting our boys and girls to see plays that would not be tolerated a moment by the authorities of Paris, Rome, Berlin, Moscow or London. We have sunk to lower depths than any nation of the ancient or modern world. And there are those who call this "Progress." It is. Progress down grade to the Hell in which leper trash is consumed.[24]

When he turned to view the progress of motion pictures, Dixon was equally concerned. His words, written before the time of television, have a striking modernity about them, for they seem to apply to television as well:

> Our responsibilities are enormous and we have not been living up to them. We still allow sex obsession to hold the centre

of the screen. We still overwork morbid themes—gruesome, cruel, appalling. We still exploit murder as an integral part of our daily life. Thoughts are things. They make and unmake character. It is small wonder that we have the highest murder rate of any nation of modern times. We are still glorifying the gangster and applauding his crimes. We are still presenting on the screen a world that is false—a world that is not true to life or any cross section of it—but immeasurably worse.[25]

To all the questions about how to improve the moral quality of the novel, the motion picture, and the drama, Dixon had no ready answer. He saw increasingly the need for effectively curbing the pernicious influence of some literary works. But censorship was not the answer. Only by becoming aware of our great moral responsibilities to society can we effect any permanent change for good in the literary world, Dixon thought. Ironically, some of Dixon's works came to be regarded as representative of the very evils that he most strenuously opposed, for the words of the critic John Charles McNeill are fairly representative: "His realism is the realism of the open sore; his art the art of the billboard."[26]

In the nineteen-thirties "The Birth of a Nation" was reissued with a musical sound track by Harry Aitken, but what had been a remarkable and artistic innovation in motion picture development fifteen years earlier now appeared to be wooden and ludicrous to audiences unacquainted with the history of motion picture art. The music was but a cacophonous reminder of the once beautiful score played by the symphony orchestras that had accompanied the early picture. Part of that original score achieved a certain immortality in the theme music of the popular radio program "Amos 'n' Andy."

Dixon did not approve of the reissue of the picture, and

when it came to Raleigh, North Carolina, in Dixon's old age, he said that he cared nothing about seeing it, for it could only invite unfavorable comparison with later pictures that had had the advantages of modern techniques of production. Had the film remained on the library shelves, said Dixon, it would have stood as a classic of motion picture art. Nevertheless, "The Birth of a Nation" will always be considered the film that gave the motion picture its stature as an art form, the film that brought to the world the realization that the motion picture medium was the most powerful agency ever devised for moving men's minds. The emotional impact of "The Birth of a Nation" will always remain for those persons who saw the picture, and the twentieth century will continue to reckon with the forces and innovations set forth in it.

Dixon's relationship with "The Birth of a Nation," his experiments in film techniques, and his tireless efforts to improve the quality of motion pictures without recourse to censorship all make him an important figure in the early days of the film industry. No history of the motion picture can be complete without a portion devoted to his activities. That his work in this industry occupied only part of a very active career makes the versatility of the man even more remarkable.

IX

"*The Last of the Romans*"

If Dixon did not count his Hollywood venture a failure, at least he considered the results not so successful as he had hoped. The adulation and great popularity of the man had fallen away somewhat from the level of a few years before, but there was still much to do, and his influence was being felt in many areas. As energetic as ever, Dixon filled his time with writing and public appearances. Shortly after his return from Hollywood to New York, he planned a short trip to Raleigh to revisit scenes and friends of his earlier years. The North Carolina legislature, then in session, recalling the fact that Dixon had served a term as one of its members, directed the following resolution to his hotel:

Whereas, it has come to the attention of members of the General Assembly that Thomas Dixon, preacher, author, and playwright, and a distinguished son of North Carolina, is to be in Raleigh on Thursday of this week: Therefore, be it *Resolved by the House of Representatives, the Senate concurring*:

SECTION 1. That the Honorable Thomas Dixon be and he is hereby invited to address the members of this General Assembly in joint session in the Hall of the House of Representatives on Thursday, February seventeen, one thousand nine hundred and twenty-one, at twelve o'clock noon.[1]

As usual when Dixon spoke, the response was enthusiastic. His zest and dynamic personality were as effective as at any time in his career. He was reminded on all sides that he should have remained in politics; indeed, some of his hearers insisted that he enter the political arena again, but Dixon said that he believed himself happier in literary pursuits. In a sense Dixon had never completely left politics, for the majority of his novels, plays, and motion pictures had political implications.

On May 23, 1925, while preparing for the press a novel of modern youth entitled *The Love Complex*, Dixon was told of his brother Frank's death as a result of pneumonia incurred on a trip Frank had made from Brooklyn to Philadelphia for a speaking engagement. The unexpected death of his younger brother was a blow against which Dixon was ill prepared. Having always held a feeling of protectiveness toward Frank because of his lameness, Dixon was shaken by the news. In reviewing the career of Frank—for a number of years the president of the American Chautauqua Association—Dixon commented:

For the past twenty-two years he has been one of the foremost lecturers of America . . . one of our really great modern men of the platform. He was never a vaudeville entertainer. He always had a message that came hot from a loving heart and a beautifully poised mind. He was a brilliant and eloquent speaker. His eloquence was never cheap noise. It was the real thing. . . . He hated the maudlin. He believed that truth would make men free . . . and only the truth.[2]

One of Frank's great sorrows had been to learn that his son Frank Murray, later to become governor of Alabama, was crippled in the final drive of the Allies during the World War. The full meaning of Frank's own lameness had been brought home to Dixon as he listened to Frank tell of his son's injury, an event that Dixon later relates:

I saw his [Frank's] tears with a strange sense of awe. Never in all our intimate association of boyhood and manhood had I heard a single murmur over his own lameness. For the first time I caught a sigh from the dark hours of life through which his soul had passed. In the tremor of his voice I heard for a moment the echo of his own crutch beat through half a century of brave silent struggle and I pressed his hand with a new sympathy.[3]

The loss of Frank still lay heavily upon Dixon's spirit when, on June 14, 1925, less than three weeks after his younger brother's death, A. C. died in Baltimore. The death of both his brothers in so short a time unnerved Dixon completely. In spite of his disagreements with his older brother through the years, Dixon had always had a great respect and admiration for Clarence.

The death of A. C. prompted much editorial comment in the newspapers over the country, one of which stated:

He was one of the most aggressive leaders of the church militant. . . . He had a magnificent moral courage that nothing could appall or weaken, a splendid sincerity that even devils must have respected. As he passes from us, we stand uncovered in reverent admiration of his brave and unfaltering faith.[4]

A. C. Dixon had become internationally famous before his

death, having served outstanding pastorates in Chicago and London and in China. The author of more than a score of religious books, A. C. had been a strong advocate of the League of Nations, had favored the rigorous enforcement of the national prohibition act, and had been an outspoken critic of spiritualism and Christian Science. Having a remarkable gift of oratory second only to that of his brother Thomas, A. C. was remembered by thousands of people as a dynamic moral force. In an interview, Dixon later spoke glowingly of his elder brother:

> I have always thought he was one of the greatest preachers that the country ever produced. I also feel that he was the greatest evangelist of the day. He was my big brother, my ideal and I loved him. And naturally I am prejudiced. But when one considers the churches he held, in this country and in England, together with his great evangelistic impact upon this nation, one would naturally arrive at the conclusion that he must have been a great preacher.[5]

Dejected in spirit and oppressed by some imminent sense of death, Dixon felt that he was not able to continue his work. The roar of New York, which in other times had excited his imagination, now repelled him. He must get away, back to the hills and country scenes of his boyhood. Perhaps there he might find new heart and consolation for his recent sorrows. Early in July, with Harriet, he took the train for Asheville, hoping to get away to himself so that he could think sanely as he roamed over the hills and mountains of western North Carolina.

The Florida land boom was in full force at the time, and as Dixon climbed the peaks around Mount Mitchell, he began to visualize the area as having the potential for a great development similar to the exciting expansion of Florida.

In the following weeks, as the breezes from the mountaintops cleared the oppressiveness from his mind, Dixon became increasingly interested in the possibilities of this vast mountain section. He inquired of real estate values on every hand, discussed the matter with various friends, and wrote to contractors and architects, asking their opinion of his ideas, as yet somewhat vague and unresolved. In the midst of this new interest Dixon visited his old home town, an event recorded as follows:

> Tom Dixon, internationally famous author and playwright and last surviving male member of the renowned Dixon family, is in Shelby this week visiting boyhood scenes, talking with old friends of the Shelby that was and of the days that are gone.
>
> Stories that would make Will Rogers a continuous flow of quips and Ring Lardner humorous excerpts unending are being related down in front of the old Central Hotel and under the shade of the trees on the court house square made famous by Dixon.[6]

After visiting nearby Old Prospect Church, the burial place of his parents, Dixon turned once more to the area around Mount Mitchell. His plan, nebulous and fragmentary at first, now began to solidify in his mind. He began to visualize a great refuge for authors, musicians, actors, lecturers, and teachers—in short, a new kind of Chautauqua resort which would attract thousands of visitors annually. Great hotels, lecture halls, and dwellings would be erected to form an intellectual and cultural center such as had never before been seen in the Western World. Each succeeding day Dixon's enthusiasm for the project grew. The more he studied the matter, the grander became his overall plan. Not a man to think long without acting, he soon had interviewed a number of distinguished persons, asking their advice and requesting that they serve on an advisory board. In his first general notice to the public, Dixon described the project that had now formed in his mind:

> The Mt. Mitchell Association of Arts and Sciences was chartered to organize in this primeval forest of supreme beauty the nucleus of a refuge for creative thinkers. The Association will build on the central mountain peak of Wildacres an Auditorium in which will be established a forum for free discussion of the problems of Art, Science, Philosophy, Religion and Politics. Its ideal will be the renewal of Life through the inspiration of Nature. Its discussions will not be over the heads of the people. They will not be bound by the fetters of the narrow minded. Nor will they be allowed to degenerate into loose thinking. Around the auditorium and along the slopes of the beautiful mountain on which it will stand and across the brooks that ripple through the dense woods at its foot, the Association will build log and rustic cottages for authors, artists, scientists, educators and students.[7]

By having outstanding leaders in the various arts and sciences in residence during several weeks of the year, the Association hoped to make the area a great attraction for visitors from all over the United States. The organization, as first established, included many well-known personages with Dixon as president and Dr. Norwood G. Carroll (husband of Dixon's sister Delia) as secretary and treasurer. The advisory board included Charles Guy, justice of the Supreme Court of New York; H. W. Chase, president of the University of North Carolina; W. P. Few, president of Duke University; William Louis Poteat, president of Wake Forest College; E. C. Brooks, president of North Carolina State College; J. I. Foust, president of the North Carolina College for Women; and Dr. Delia Dixon Carroll, physician in residence at Meredith College.

In the months that followed his first conception of the project, Dixon was moving steadily forward in the great undertaking. He purchased an immense tract of virgin forest land in the Little Switzerland district near Mount Mitchell. The area, called "Wildacres," contained many ravines, hills, and valleys and three mountain ridges through which coursed several clear streams. The forests contained one hundred and thirty-six varieties of trees and nearly two hundred different species of shrubs and flowers. Rhododendron and laurel grew in great profusion throughout the area. This paradise of color and serenity, about seven miles long, was to be crisscrossed by numerous walkways and bridle paths. Wildacres, two hours' drive from Asheville and forty-five minutes from Marion, North Carolina, was soon alive with activity. Plans were laid out to construct a great hotel, install sewerage and electrical facilities, and provide tennis courts, swimming pools, stables, golf courses, and accommodations for various other sports and forms of recreation.

Constantly on hand watching the progress of the undertaking or journeying to and from New York for ideas and equipment, Dixon felt a revival of spirits from the despondency that had followed the death of his brothers. With all the enthusiasm that had made him famous, Dixon eagerly looked forward to the time when his dream would be realized. By 1928 the project had taken an impressive form. Several of the larger buildings had been completed, and Dixon announced that several hundred building lots were ready for immediate occupancy and development. Dixon, having invested nearly all of a large fortune in his plan, now saw himself as a real estate entrepreneur extraordinary. He had the conviction that here was to be a great fountainhead of culture which would be felt throughout the nation. Dixon, now sixty-four years of age, was to crown a series of brilliant careers by becoming the director of one of the most remarkable real estate ventures in the history of the country.

Then the land boom collapsed. The stock market crash of Wall Street followed soon after. Wildacres, calculated to elevate Dixon to even greater wealth and fame, now suddenly was a millstone about his neck, dragging him down to financial ruin. The land, which he had hoped to make among the most valuable areas of real estate in the United States, was now worthless. Thousands of people who had been showing great eagerness for the project suddenly lost interest. Dixon could hardly give the land away to a public suddenly frightened by the great land-boom crash in Florida and elsewhere. Dixon later recalled: "I lost every dollar and turned back to New York bewildered–wondering–what next?"[8]

No longer possessing the youth with which he had faced so many obstacles in the past, Dixon nonetheless determined that somehow he would regain all he had lost. There was still an incredible reserve of strength and determination which he counted on to see him out of the slough in which he now found himself. Like a man burning with a fever that could be abated only by constant literary effort, Dixon pushed himself unmercifully to recapture his losses. Tired of the themes that had filled his past novels, he decided to follow the streams of pure romance in his next book. Turning to account a long-time interest in South American history, he increased his knowledge of the conquest of Peru and the accounts of the Pizarro brothers by close study in the New York libraries and at his home at 867 Riverside Drive. The result, after weeks of intensive research and writing in the spring of 1929, was *The Sun Virgin*, a romantic tale about the last of the great Incas of Peru. Through the historical tapestry is woven a sentimental tale of Yma, first among the Virgins of the Sun, and her love for Alonso de Molina, one of Francisco Pizarro's lieutenants.

The book reveals Dixon's admiration for the Incas and his strong aversion to the methods of the Spanish conquistadores. The injustice of the execution of Atahualpa, the Inca ruler, is a strong indictment of the conquerors' cruelty:

> The Inca closed his eyes. The executioner circled his neck and strangled him to death while five hundred Spaniards pressed close murmuring their credos for the salvation of his soul.[9]

To Dixon the fall of the Incas was one of the most tragic developments in the establishment of European culture in the New World. The book closes on a scene of desolation:

> In Peru, a nation, whose temples once blazed with gold, lies in ashes and ruin. The jungle has devoured the great highways. The trees that once shaded them across blistering sands are dead. The aqueducts are broken and dry. Fields that waved harvests of grain and corn are barren wastes. The hanging gardens of a thousand hills stretch upward in the baking sun, a desolation of crumbling stone walls. The fruit trees that clothed valley and mountain in flaming glory have withered.
>
> The storehouses are empty. Their roofs are gone. Their walls are broken, and wild beasts whelp and stable in their great bins. Couriers no longer speed from end to end of the empire. There are no roads. There are no resthouses. The vast flocks of pensive llamas that once grazed in the rich valleys have disappeared, slain in wanton folly. Where happy villages flourished with food, shelter and clothes for millions, now stretches a desert steaming under the fierce heat of the tropic skies.[10]

Reaction among critics was varied. Some said that *The*

Sun Virgin had reached new heights of storytelling and was "no end picturesque."[11] The historical background of the novel was praised on one hand and attacked on the other. The following comment is typical of a favorable review:

> The book presents an array of historical facts, a knowledge of the topography of the country, and a picture of the manners and customs of the charming and urbane Incas which is impressive.[12]

A London critic, however, took Dixon seriously to task for borrowing too freely:

> If a schoolboy were to rewrite "The Conquest of Peru" he could scarcely fail to make it absorbing reading, so dramatic is the story of Pizarro and the last of the great Incas. The historical setting which forms the greater part of "The Sun Virgin" is derived directly from "The Conquest of Peru," and an examination of the two books shows that Mr. Dixon has taken what he wanted from Prescott, paraphrasing as he goes and occasionally rendering *oratio obliqua* into *oratio recta*; or, when he has to invent dialogue, putting modern slang into the mouth of the *conquistadores*.[13]

The review concluded, however, that in spite of obvious defects, the novel would "doubtless find many pleased readers." The general concensus of critical appraisal was that although Dixon had not written a "masterpiece," still he had not lost the ability to tell a gripping story which held the reader's interest. Public response to the book was gratifying, though it was not so great as it had been for some of Dixon's previous novels.

Dixon now occupied his time in writing articles for magazines, giving lectures, and formulating plans for future enterprises. In spite of the strong bias in his novels, he became an energetic promoter of better schools and living conditions for Negroes. He urged the creation of some kind of suburban life for the Negroes of New York:

> Here, now, is an opportunity to create a big spur in the building trades. It would be a matter of selecting a suitable suburban site and then building up a new residential town, to advance the welfare and happiness of a people who have good claim on our attention. As the Negroes advance themselves it is only proper that they should have some locality in which to enjoy greater freedom and comfort. They are a worthy people, endowed with many lovable characteristics, kindly, patient, humorous, extremely grateful for every favor extended them, and in many ways we could all benefit by taking a larger interest in them.[14]

In 1932 Dixon felt compelled to answer a book by his sister Addie [May Dixon Thacker] that dealt with the last days in the career of President Warren G. Harding. The book, *The Strange Death of President Harding,* was derived in large part from the testimony of Gaston B. Means, at the time serving a term in the federal penitentiary in Atlanta for his implication in stealing the famous Hope Diamond. Dixon, who called Means a modern Baron von Munchausen, believed that Addie had been greatly misled by Means into believing that Harding's death was mysteriously connected with a serious scandal. Himself an admirer of Harding, Dixon felt that he should try to set the record straight. In collaboration with Harry M. Daugherty, a close friend of Harding, he published *The Inside Story of the Harding Tragedy.* In keeping with his usual procedure before writing a book, he did considerable research into the background of the Harding administration and made public the following announcement in the prefatory remarks of the book:

> In the preparation of this volume I have carefully read more than two thousand autographed letters, important telegrams, documents, secret service reports, and signed affidavits.
>
> Every fact has been verified by authentic records which are now in my possession . . . .[15]

Dixon further stated that he had written the book to discredit "three scurrilous attacks" that had been previously published. The "attacks" to which he referred were *Revelry* by Samuel H. Adams, *The President's Daughter* by Nan Britton, and the book by Dixon's sister. The current interest in the Harding administration and the previous books about Harding's career caused Dixon and Daugherty's work to be widely read.

The research into the career of Harding brought Dixon's interest in political matters welling up like a geyser, and he determined to enter into politics actively again, after a period of nearly half a century. In 1932, he campaigned for Franklin D. Roosevelt, the man who, Dixon said, could lift the country out of its depression, both financial and mental. The Roosevelt influence was not new to Dixon. While still a young minister in New York, he had become a friend of Theodore Roosevelt. The men had formed a rather close attachment, and when Theodore ran for the governorship of New York, Dixon had campaigned strongly for him. He had again supported Theodore when he ran for Vice-President of the United States and when he ran for President. As long as Dixon's father lived, Dixon never told him that he had voted for a Republican, because to the elder Dixon the word "Republican" continued to be synonymous with "Reconstruction." Dixon had greatly admired Theodore Roosevelt, and when another Roosevelt, this one a Democrat, was elected to the Presidency, Dixon said that he felt as though the millennium had arrived at last. Franklin D. Roosevelt's energetic reorganization of the government caused Dixon to say that the President was staging a bloodless revolution, that the country would be able to rise above the depression under his peerless leadership.

Dixon's immediate and enthusiastic support of the new administration caused him to be invited by the National Broadcasting Company to speak to the nation over WJZ, New York, on October 2, 1933. In his address, entitled "The Moral Import of the News," Dixon urged his listeners to give wholehearted support to the Roosevelt administration, and in praising one feature of the New Deal, he said: "The NRA coal code is a Magna Charter [sic] of human rights for the sweat-smeared, begrimed, sodden dwellers of the world beneath the earth."[16]

Dixon was so successful in boosting Roosevelt's program that he decided on his own to make a widespread speaking tour in 1934 in support of the National Recovery Administration. Now seventy years of age, he was still a man of handsome and impressive appearance, his erect and commanding figure making him the cynosure of every crowd. Evidence that Dixon had lost none of his oratorical abilities from the days of the lecture circuits, twenty-five years before, was revealed in the reaction of his listeners. Colonel C. O. Sherrill, chairman of the Ohio board of the NRA and former city manager of Cincinnati, was deeply impressed by Dixon's forcefulness, saying in part:

> No man in this country is better qualified to arouse enthusiasm for the President's program of recovery than is Thomas

Dixon. I recently heard him deliver an address in Cincinnati which was one of the most moving and powerful appeals to which I ever listened.[17]

Other listeners were just as enthusiastic, their sentiments being expressed in such statements as "Thomas Dixon gave us the most stirring patriotic address we have heard in years"[18] and "For the past four months he has held thousands spellbound by his matchless eloquence, reaching new heights of power in his long career as an orator."[19]

While making his tour, Dixon had begun work upon his autobiography, with which he hoped to regain his wealth. In an interview regarding the new literary effort, Dixon said:

Yes, I think it will be my most important book. I can hardly keep my hands off it. I have been working on it for six months. I am going to make it cover the period from slavery into which I was born. Any man who has lived as long and as fully as I have should certainly be able to say something that would interest a wide range of human beings.[20]

On May 17, 1934, while working on his autobiography, Dixon received a telephone message that his sister, Dr. Delia Dixon Carroll, had been killed in an automobile accident near her home in Raleigh, North Carolina. Like her brother Thomas, Delia was a person of energetic ambition: her brilliance and perseverance in the face of much opposition because of her sex had won for her, both at medical school and in her profession, a place of respect and admiration. Her death was mourned throughout the state, and her pallbearers were such outstanding men as John C. B. Ehringhaus, governor of North Carolina; Josephus Daniels, ambassador to Mexico; Josiah Bailey, United States Senator; and Frank Page, the brother of Walter Hines

Page. Dixon, who had always maintained a close relationship with his sister, was stunned by her death. In addition, another sorrow now faced him. His wife Harriet had suffered an illness that was to make her an invalid for the rest of her life. The death of his son Jordan and then of his brothers Frank and A. C. had been reminders to Dixon that much of his life and happiness lay behind. Now the death of Delia and the illness of Harriet made it more difficult than it had been in years past to carry out his resolution for achievement.

By 1936 Dixon's political allegiance had changed. The conviction had gradually grown upon him that the government was becoming infiltrated with communistic and radical elements. He thought that the complexity of the governmental agencies had made it impossible for Roosevelt to know how serious the infiltration was. Though no particular New Deal act had caused him to turn from Roosevelt, Dixon indicated that he had sensed a tendency toward radicalism that finally determined him to denounce the New Deal. Later, in an interview, he bitterly attacked the Roosevelt administration:

> Communists control the Federal Theatre. If you are American and think as an American, you can't stay in it. The writers all bow to Lenin and Stalin and the Russian view of government.
>
> The increasing influence of Communistic advisers around him has steered Roosevelt more and more into radical channels. I have no use for them—the devil take them! Roosevelt may not be aware of the trend.[21]

Dixon had early recognized the dangers of Communism to America. In his books of nonfiction, in his novels, and in his public addresses, he had consistently lamented the apathy of the American people toward Soviet doctrines which, he said, might engulf the whole life of the nation. Even before the days of the communistic order, Dixon had been distrustful of Russian political inclinations, as stated in one of his sermons:

Politically, Russia is an unthinkable quantity to the American mind. Her government is the contradiction of every principle for which our fathers fought and for which we live. She maintains with stubborn and fatal reactionery [sic] brutality, the most crushing and absolute tyranny outside of Turkey, Spain and hell.[22]

Coupled with Dixon's dissatisfaction with the government was his conviction that a new world war was imminent. He said in 1935 that while the government was growing weaker from within, Americans in general had no concept of the dangers confronting them, and he added:

In the meantime we rapidly approach the next World War. The idea is inconceivable and yet it is coming. The leaders of Europe take it for granted, and eagerly discuss its details, preparing for it with feverish haste in spite of conferences to limit armaments, in spite of their membership in the League of Nations. Russia, loudly professing her desire for peace, supports the greatest standing army of the world and dares her foes to strike.[23]

In the pre-election months of 1936, Dixon campaigned vigorously against the re-election of Roosevelt. Earlier in the year Dixon had attended the National Convention in Cleveland, Ohio, as a Democrat representing the first district of North Carolina. The month before the Presidential election he delivered a ringing speech in Raleigh, where he had served as a legislator fifty years before. "Full of fire and pizen,"[24] he told his audience how he was becoming more and more alarmed at the trends in Washington. Judge I. M. Meekins, a Republican and long-time friend, the following year appointed Dixon clerk of the federal court for the eastern district of North Carolina.

The appointment came at a seasonable time for Dixon, for his wealth of former years was gone. He had lost his home on Riverside Drive in New York, which he had occupied for twenty-five years. In spite of continued literary efforts, his books no longer became the best sellers they had been in the first two decades of the century. He was now spinning out ideas in the afterglow of his fame. Many of the issues that had been so vital through the period of World War I now faded before the depression of the early nineteen-thirties. The school of Southern chivalry and romance to which Dixon had belonged was largely eclipsed by the novels of the naturalistic writers.

Dixon took the oath of office on May 1, 1937, in Raleigh, where exactly fifty years previously he had preached his first sermon at the Second Baptist Church. Before assuming the duties of office, he said in an interview:

> Your courts will open to me new fields for the study of human nature which I will cultivate in a series of novels on which I am at work now. And as Nathaniel Hawthorne found inspiration in the old Customs House of Salem so I hope to enrich my mind in your courts.[25]

Dixon's return to his native state occasioned considerable comment in newspaper editorials, one of which praised him for being "as fine a figure of a man as ever in American life graced pulpit or platform or stage" and further added:

> Past 70 years of age, time has whitened his hair and thickened his girth, but has not bent his shoulder or broken his spirit.
>
> As erect as in youth, he speaks; and still that matchless voice

and commanding presence, backed by a tremendous capacity to think and feel, provokes prickles along the spine and sets toes tingling.

Moreover, old he faces life with the adventurous outlook of youth, but with the added poise that comes in the serene knowledge that the years have all but done their worst. Happy to be alive and feel the great world spinning into new and dizzier grooves of change, he loses a fortune without loss of equanimity and sets his face to win another; but thumbs his nose at fate with the suggestion that if he fails, what life proposes to do to him here it must do quickly.

He is the product of an age that with the coming of radio and talking pictures man shall see no more. We shall hardly look upon his like again. He is the last of the Romans.[26]

The loss of wealth could mean no lasting injury to a man who had many times endured the vagaries of fortune. Dixon affirmed that he had never had any consciousness of riches and that he could have walked away from his house and its furnishings and would not have missed them. Only boats, in which he expressed his personality, seemed his own. In reference to his great wealth of previous years, he wrote:

In the banner years of money and success the only sense of possession I felt was that I had more money than I could possibly spend. An illusion that was dispelled in time.

In my relation to material property there has always been a screw loose in my make-up. I've always been able to make money but never tried to hold it. When times got hard I've always been able to say to myself: "Cheer up, old boy, you'll soon be dead."[27]

With his new position as a backlog of security for his remaining years, Dixon envisioned literary work in a large library with rough-hewn beams across the ceiling and a fireplace four feet wide. In such a home, which he intended to build for himself and Harriet, Dixon hoped to put on paper "the indescribable obsession and idealism that makes a Southerner."[28] In addition to performing his duties as clerk of the court, he energetically worked on his autobiography and on a major novel entitled *The Flaming Sword.* The story was to be an account of communistic infiltration throughout the United States, with the Negro population as the dupes of the Red menace. In studying many sources as background for the novel, Dixon was assisted by Miss Madelyn Donovan, who years before had played the feminine lead in Dixon's motion picture "The Mark of the Beast." Miss Donovan came to Raleigh when she had completed reading the galley proofs.

Dixon's optimistic plans for the future were short-lived, for on December 29, 1937, Harriet died, ending a long illness. A little more than a year later, on February 26, 1939, in his suite at the Sir Walter Hotel, Dixon himself was stricken by a cerebral hemorrhage. His condition remained so critical that his doctors advised that he not be moved from the hotel to a hospital. For weeks he lay in his room, unable to raise himself from his bed. Miss Donovan, seeing him now in a helpless state and realizing that close care would be essential, married him at his bedside. The ceremony was performed on March 20, 1939, in Dixon's suite in the Sir Walter Hotel.

After many weeks Dixon partially recovered from his attack and attempted sporadically to direct his clerkship. In addition, with his wife's help, he had by summer completed *The Flaming Sword.* Simultaneously with its publication came the announcement that the Monarch Publishing Company of Atlanta, which was issuing the novel, had recently been organized to publish a new series of books by Dixon and to accomplish for the South what Houghton Mifflin had done for New England. In addition, the announcement indicated that a Southern monthly periodical would soon appear following the lines of the *Atlantic Monthly*.

The title of Dixon's novel was taken from a sentence in W. E. B. Du Bois' book *Black Reconstruction in America*, which Dixon characterized as "a blazing manifesto of Communism."[29] *The Flaming Sword*, Dixon stated, was a sequel to "The Birth of a Nation" and brought the history of the conflict of color to the present. In giving the full picture, Dixon said he realized that he would be subject to attack, and in a note "To the Reader" he wrote:

> I have been compelled to use living men and women as important characters. If I have been unfair in treatment they have their remedy under the law of libel. I hold myself responsible.[30]

The interracial conflict is introduced early in the novel as Dr. Cameron, the father of Ben Cameron, who was the hero of *The Clansman* and of "The Birth of a Nation," makes a speech denouncing Du Bois, the Negro educator. The racial problem is intensified as Angela Cameron Henry loses her baby son, her husband, and her young sister through the violence of a Negro rapist. In order to drive the horrible picture of their murder from her mind, she secretly joins a Rosicrucian order in California. An old friend, Phil Stevens, finds her at last and persuades her to come to New York.

Through a young female friend Angela is introduced to a group of Communists and enters wholeheartedly into the study of their principles. As she begins to see Communism from the inside, she becomes disillusioned and opposes the system as strenuously as she had defended it previously.

The Negro appears to Angela to be the easiest bait for communistic doctrine. Toward the end of the story the Negro Communists, under the name of the Nat Turner Legion, take over the country by force. Unlike most of Dixon's novels, *The Flaming Sword* concludes without a happy ending. The novelist takes leave of his story with the government of the Soviet Republic of the United States in supreme authority.

Though Dixon was highly ambitious for the novel, sending handsome, leather-bound, autographed copies to influential persons, it was a failure. Critical appraisal generally ranged from disinterest to amused scorn, one writer stating that the publication of the book invited "news treatment rather than literary criticism,"[31] while another wrote that the reader would regard the novel as a "nightmare melodrama" and "the expression of a panic fear."[32] The readers who had once eagerly sought Dixon's books now seemed uninterested. In spite of several printings during June and July, the copies of *The Flaming Sword* soon lay gathering dust, a symbol of the changing moods and tastes of a people.

What was Dixon now to do? Old and nearly destitute, he had come to the faint afterglow of an amazing and colorful career. As he lay ill in his apartment in Raleigh, often wracked by pain and tormented by the fact that his energies, which once had served him so well, were now spent, he thought of the storms of controversy, the failures and successes, of former years. To a man always restless for new experiences, new achievements, the hours spent lying abed were almost intolerable. At times he would beseech his wife Madelyn to help him reconcile himself to these hours of vacant inactivity. Occasionally the pain brought cries of agony as it ebbed and flowed. Finally, it was thought best that Dixon be moved from his apartment to an address at 1507 Hillsboro Street. The house, set back among the trees, provided more privacy for Dixon and his wife during the periods when he was in greatest pain.

From time to time Dixon rallied somewhat and reminisced of the days that were past. He saw himself in the unfortunate position of a man who has outlived his fame. He had seen social issues and literary tastes come and go. His novels, which once had aroused so much controversy, now lay unused on the library shelves of the nation. No longer were the royalties coming in. The wealth that Dixon had spent so freely was now gone. In his trunks lay piles of stocks that once had paid large dividends; now they were worthless. But as one who had always maintained a casual attitude toward material wealth, the eighty-two-year-old man counted himself fortunate in the devotion of his wife and a few close friends.

Toward the end, Dixon became weaker and took less interest in his surroundings. For days he subsisted on nothing more than egg white stirred into orange juice. Once, at night, he rallied and asked for solid food. At last, on the morning of April 3, 1946, he seemed to lose touch with reality. Before another day, with his thoughts wandering amid the clouded intangibles of a colorful lifetime, Thomas Dixon was dead.

In death, as in life, Dixon was a controversial figure. Hard upon his burial on April 4 in Sunset Cemetery at Shelby came commentaries from many quarters, their appraisals of Dixon's career varying as widely as did those during his most active years. One obituary notice, in recalling Dixon's stories of the early Ku Klux Klan, remarked that "he capitalized on race prejudice, harped loud & long on white ('Aryan') supremacy."[33] Another writer, in discussing the quality of Dixon's novels, said that he wove through them "a pattern of violence which at its best was spine tingling and which at its worst was reminiscent of the hack western."[34] In the obituaries, some persons condemned the novels of Dixon as being too inflammatory and conducive to sectional prejudice, but one writer thought that "in stimulating the mind of the Nation to think seriously upon the issues he raised in his books and in the great film whose script he wrote, Thomas Dixon indubitably contributed much to American social progress."[35]

The day after Dixon's death, R. Gregg Cherry, Governor of North Carolina, recounted the career of Dixon with high praise. Cherry recalled that Dixon had introduced into the state legislature the first bill in the South to pension Confederate veterans, and added in summary:

> North Carolina has lost a distinguished son. Through his long list of popular and worthwhile novels, his activities on the lecture platform and in the pulpit, Thomas Dixon has made a distinctive contribution to North Carolina and to the nation.[36]

One of the most appreciative evaluations of Dixon's careers was an editorial that said in part:

> A great spirit has "passed over the river." Thomas Dixon is dead. He was a great Southerner who had the power of platform and pen to a magnificent degree. Through his long 82 years he was a legislator, lecturer, feature writer, author, preacher, and political officeholder. To all of these he took a culture that was innate, and to the wide circle who called him friend he gave something intangible and invaluable.
>
> His name belongs to the immortals of our state and nation.[37]

As to the nature of this man, who can finally say? Handsome, sensitive, proud, and passionately devoted to the tragic and heroic in life, he had an inimitable flair for capturing the imagination and emotions of a people. That he has left his imprint upon American society cannot be doubted. His uncompromising stand in some areas, his vivid imagination, and his compelling desire to succeed in personal endeavors and in influence over others make one mindful of the great potential for good and evil that reposed in his forceful personality. A paradox of bias and tolerance, he antagonized many people by his views and won others to unswerving loyalty. Though he was, as he admitted, sometimes "full of fire and pizen,"[38] on other occasions he displayed a charm that was irresistible. At times misunderstood in his motives, he was grouped with factions with which he had no sympathy. And if he was harsh to those persons he opposed, to those who knew him intimately he was a generous friend and a loving husband and father. His conflicting nature was summarized by a relative who said that he was "a dynamic personality, fiery, impetuous, and yet so gentle in the presence of those he loved."[39] Thomas Dixon remains as one of the most versatile, remarkable men of his time, and he speaks to our own with a voice that is disturbing, challenging, and prophetic.

Notes

Chapter I

1. Quoted in Mamie Jones, "Life in Cleveland County's Early Days," *Cleveland Star* (Shelby, N.C.), July 9, 1934.

2. Helen C. A. Dixon, *A. C. Dixon: A Romance of Preaching* (New York: G. P. Putnam's Sons, 1931), pp. 13 and 20. LeRoy McAfee Dixon, 1853, lived only five months; Eliza Jane Dixon, 1857, lived two years; and LeRoy Dixon, 1861, who was named after the first child, "died a few months after the arrival at Little Rock." A. C. (Clarence) Dixon was born on July 6, 1854.

Chapter II

1. For an extended treatment of the economic conditions in the South following the War Between the States, see E. Merton Coulter, *The South During Reconstruction, 1865–1877* (*A History of the South*, Vol. VIII [Baton Rouge, La.: Louisiana State University Press, 1947]), *passim.*

2. Quoted in Helen C. A. Dixon, *A. C. Dixon: A Romance of Preaching* (New York: G. P. Putnam's Sons, 1931), pp. 26–27.

3. Thomas Dixon, "Southern Horizons: An Autobiography" (MS unfinished), p. 22.

4. Sources, even in the Dixon family, spell Colonel McAfee's given name variously as "Lee Roy," "LeRoy," and "Leroy." Since he is referred to occasionally as Colonel Lee McAfee, it is likely that the first spelling given is the correct one.

5. "Southern Horizons," p. 26.

6. *Ibid.*, p. 113.

7. *Ibid.*, p. 40.

8. *Ibid.*, pp. 50–51.

9. *Ibid.*, p. 26.

10. *Ibid.*, p. 47.

11. *Ibid.*, p. 91. In a communication from Thomas Dixon in the private papers of Clara Dixon Richardson, his niece, he states, "In 1870, little Frank, while playing on the porch of the old house on the square in Shelby, fell to the ground and dislocated his hip."

12. *Ibid.*, p. 176.

13. *Ibid.*, p. 41.

14. *Ibid.*, p. 204.

15. *Ibid.*, p. 153.

16. *Ibid.*, pp. 156–57.

17. *Ibid.*, pp. 161–62.

18. The private papers of Clara Dixon Richardson.

19. "Southern Horizons," p. 89.

20. *Ibid.*, pp. 146–47.

21. *Ibid.*, p. 173.

22. *Ibid.*, p. 174.

23. *Ibid.*

24. In a letter to his daughter Louise, dated September 8, 1923, Dixon gives Suzannah Hambright Dixon's age at death as one hundred and six. In Helen C. A. Dixon, *op. cit.*, p. 80, the age at death is given as one hundred and four.

25. "Southern Horizons," p. 109.

26. *Ibid.*, p. 215.

Chapter III

1. Wake Forest College was moved in 1956 from its old site to a new campus at Winston-Salem, North Carolina.

2. "Southern Horizons: An Autobiography" (MS unfinished), p. 225.

3. E. M. Poteat, "Thomas Dixon, Junior," *The Wake Forest Student*, XXVIII (January, 1909), 382.
4. Private papers of Clara Dixon Richardson.
5. *Ibid.*
6. "Southern Horizons," p. 231.
7. *Ibid.*, p. 235.
8. Thomas Dixon, *Living Problems in Religion and Social Science* (New York: C. T. Dillingham, 1889), pp. 60–61.
9. "Southern Horizons," p. 240.
10. Quoted in Helen C. A. Dixon, *A. C. Dixon: A Romance of Preaching* (New York: G. P. Putnam's Sons, 1931), p. 94.
11. "Chronicle and Comment," *Bookman*, XX (February, 1905), 499.
12. Quoted in "Southern Horizons," p. 205.
13. *Ibid.*, p. 247.
14. *Ibid.*, p. 248.
15. Letter postmarked Wednesday, 23 [May?], 1884. From the private papers of Clara Dixon Richardson.
16. Quoted in "Southern Horizons," p. 253.
17. United States Senator Clyde R. Hoey, from Cleveland County, shared with Dixon the distinction of having been elected to the House of Representatives before his twenty-first birthday.
18. "The Watauga Club," *North Carolina Historical Review*, XVI (1939), 280.
19. "Southern Horizons," p. 271.
20. *Ibid.*, p. 269.
21. *Ibid.*, p. 275.
22. *Ibid.*, p. 272.
23. *Ibid.*, p. 277.
24. *Ibid.*, p. 272.
25. *Ibid.*, p. 279.
26. *Ibid.*, pp. 279–80.

Chapter IV

1. *Charlotte* (N.C.) *Observer*, November 28, 1926, Sec. 5, p. 1.
2. "Southern Horizons: An Autobiography" (MS unfinished), p. 283.
3. Thomas Dixon, *The Failure of Protestantism in New York and its Causes* (New York: V. O. A. Strauss, 1896), p. 14.
4. From the private papers of Clara Dixon Richardson.
5. "Southern Horizons," p. 289. This "prophecy" of Wilson's career is especially interesting in that Dixon anticipated several other

matters of national importance. See his novels on socialism and communism and his work in the motion picture industry.

6. *Wilmington* (N.C.) *Morning Star*, April 4, 1946.
7. *The Failure of Protestantism in New York and its Causes*, p. 16.
8. *Ibid.*, p. 8.
9. *Ibid.*, p. 17.
10. "Southern Horizons," p. 297.
11. *New York Times*, April 4, 1946, p. 25.
12. "Southern Horizons," p. 306.
13. *The Failure of Protestantism in New York and its Causes*, p. 61.
14. Thomas Dixon, *Living Problems in Religion and Social Science* (New York: C. T. Dillingham, 1889), p. 50.
15. *Ibid.*, p. 98.
16. Nym Crinkle [pseud. of A. C. Wheeler], "Biographical and Critical Sketch," in Thomas Dixon, *Dixon on Ingersoll: Ten Discourses Delivered in Association Hall, New York* (New York: J. B. Alden, 1892), p. 12.
17. *Ibid.*, p. 20.
18. "Southern Horizons," p. 300.
19. *Ibid.*, p. 303.
20. *Living Problems in Religion and Social Science*, p. 27.
21. Letter dated July 6, 1891, private papers of Clara Dixon Richardson.
22. Private papers of Clara Dixon Richardson.
23. New York: John B. Alden, 1892.
24. See *Evening Telegram* (New York), January 4 and 5, 1892.
25. Private papers of Clara Dixon Richardson.
26. Quoted in Helen C. A. Dixon, *A. C. Dixon: A Romance of Preaching* (New York: G. P. Putnam's Sons, 1931), p. 130.
27. Thomas Dixon, *The Life Worth Living: A Personal Experience* (New York: Doubleday, Page & Co., 1914), p. 6.
28. "Southern Horizons," p. 344.
29. *New York Times*, March 11, 1895, p. 8.
30. *Ibid.*
31. *Ibid.*
32. *Ibid.*, September 7, 1896, p. 8.
33. Some sources indicate the home had thirty-seven rooms, others thirty-two. An apparently authoritative source gives the number of rooms as thirty-five, the number used here. See Mildred Lewis Rutherford, *The South in History and Literature* (Atlanta: The Franklin-Turner Co., 1906), pp. 605–11. Perhaps the difference in room count was brought about by the variant definitions of what actually constitutes a room.

34. "Southern Horizons," p. 469.
35. *New York Times*, January 16, 1899, p. 10.
36. *Rotary Reminder* (Cleveland, Ohio, n.d.), p. 4.
37. "Southern Horizons," p. 376.

Chapter V

1. Quoted in Thomas Dixon, "Southern Horizons: An Autobiography" (MS unfinished), p. 378. Page was here referring to Thomas Nelson Page's stories of the South which dealt sentimentally with the Negro, during both slavery days and Reconstruction.
2. *Ibid.*, p. 381.
3. *Ibid.*
4. From a circular describing the novel.
5. "The Leopard's Spots," CLXXIV (April 12, 1902), 15.
6. Quoted from an advertising folder printed by Dixon's publishers.
7. Dated June 10, 1902, Paris, France.
8. M. B. Wharton, *Atlanta Journal*, April 20, 1902, p. 9.
9. Kelly Miller, *As to the Leopard's Spots: An Open Letter to Thomas Dixon, Jr.*, (Washington, D.C.: Kelly Miller, 1905), p. 20.
10. *Ibid.*, p. 19.
11. Hugh M. Gloster, *Negro Voices in American Fiction* (Chapel Hill, N.C.: University of North Carolina Press, 1948), p. 11.
12. *The Hindered Hand; or, The Reign of the Repressionist* (3d ed., rev.; Nashville, Tenn.: The Orion Publishing Co., 1905), pp. 332–33.
13. Edwin L. Shuman, "In the Realm of Books," *Chicago Record-Herald*, March 15, 1902, p. 6.
14. Mansfield Allan, "Thomas Dixon's 'The Leopard's Spots,'" *Bookman*, XV (July, 1902), 472.
15. *Charlotte* (N.C.) *Daily Observer*, September 7, 1902, p. 16.
16. Letter dated May 10, 1902, private papers of Clara Dixon Richardson.
17. *Ibid.*
18. *Ibid.*
19. "An Author's Answer to His Critics," *New York Times*, August 9, 1902, p. 538.
20. *Ibid.*
21. Quoted in *Boston Herald*, April 14, 1889.
22. *The Failure of Protestantism in New York and its Causes* (New York: V. O. A. Strauss, 1896), pp. 58–59.
23. "Booker T. Washington and the Negro," *Saturday Evening Post*, CLXXVIII (August 19, 1905), 1.

24. *Ibid.*, p. 2. In rejecting Dixon's solution of the race problem, Kelly Miller, *op. cit.*, pp. 18–19, stated that Liberia's "area of 48,000 square miles, and a population of 1,500,000, natives and immigrants," would be altogether insufficient to handle the great numbers of Negroes from America, plus the present natives.

25. *Ibid.*, p. 1.

26. *The One Woman: A Story of Modern Utopia* (New York: Doubleday, Page & Co., 1903), p. 36.

27. *Ibid.*

28. *Ibid.*, p. 37.

29. Dixon never publicly divulged the young woman's identity. Could she have been Lilian Bell, a popular writer who praised *The Leopard's Spots* highly and who, in one of her stories, modeled the hero Camden, a heroic minister, upon Dixon? See E. F. Harkins, *Little Pilgrimages Among the Men Who Have Written Famous Books* (2d ser.; Boston: L. C. Page & Co., 1903), pp. 127–28; and Lilian Bell, "Girl in Love," *Harper's Bazaar*, XXXV (November, 1901), 603–8.

30. Quoted in *The National Cyclopaedia of American Biography* (New York: James T. White & Co., 1906), XIII, 189.

31. Edward Clark Marsh, "Thomas Dixon's 'The One Woman,'" *Bookman*, XVIII (October, 1903), 161.

32. *Public Ledger* (Philadelphia), August 16, 1903.

33. "Mr. Dixon Makes Answer," *Charlotte* (N.C.) *Daily Observer*, May 7, 1905, p. 12.

34. A full discussion of this matter may be found in Frances Oakes, "Whitman and Dixon: A Strange Case of Borrowing," *Georgia Review*, XI (Fall, 1957), 333–40.

35. (New York: Doubleday, Page & Co., 1905), p. 4.

36. "Contemptuous Feeling," in *Specimen Days*, from *Complete Prose Works of Walt Whitman* (New York: D. Appleton & Co., 1908), p. 17.

37. Pages 39–40.

38. Page 9.

39. Oakes, *op. cit.*, p. 340.

40. *The Life Worth Living: A Personal Experience* (New York: Doubleday, Page & Co., 1914), p. 135.

Chapter VI

1. *The Life Worth Living: A Personal Experience* (New York: Doubleday, Page & Co., 1914), pp. 135–36.

2. "Southern Horizons: An Autobiography" (MS unfinished), p. 401.

3. "The Clansman: An American Drama in Four Acts," 1905. At least two typescript copies are available, one in the Harvard Library and the other in the Rare Books Collection of the Library of Congress. Henceforth, plays and motion pictures bearing the same titles as Dixon's novels, unless they are published separately in book form, will be indicated in quotation marks in order to distinguish them from the novels.

4. "Southern Horizons," p. 401.

5. This reference and subsequent ones dealing with the plot are from the typescript of the play.

6. "Southern Horizons," p. 408.

7. *Virginian-Pilot* (Norfolk), September 23, 1905. Occasionally page numbers and dates are not cited because of the fact that several of the newspaper clippings providing reviews of "The Clansman" do not have these references included. For many details of the public's reaction to the play, I am indebted to "The Greatest Play of the South," *Tennessee Studies in Literature*, II (1957), 15–24, a paper read by Professor Durant da Ponte at the annual meeting of the South Atlantic Modern Language Association, Chattanooga, Tennessee, November 29, 1957.

8. *Ibid.*

9. *Ibid.*

10. September 26, 1905, p. 1.

11. *Ibid.*

12. Reprinted in *News and Observer* (Raleigh, N.C.), October 1, 1905, p. 1.

13. *Ibid.*

14. *Ibid.*, October 3, 1905, p. 1.

15. *Ibid.*, October 5, 1905, p. 5.

16. *Ibid.*

17. Quoted in *Montgomery Advertiser*, October 29, 1905, p. 1.

18. Quoted in *News and Courier* (Charleston), October 18, 1905, p. 3.

19. *Ibid.*, October 19, 1905, p. 7.

20. Quoted in *Knoxville Journal and Tribune*, October 20, 1905, p. 4.

21. *Ibid.*, October 21, 1905.

22. *Atlanta Constitution*, October 31, 1905, p. 2.

23. Quoted in *Knoxville Journal and Tribune*, November 9, 1905, p. 4.

24. *Montgomery Advertiser,* November 5, 1905.
25. *Ibid.*
26. *Ibid.*
27. *Knoxville Journal and Tribune,* November 14, 1905, p. 4.
28. *Ibid.*, October 20, 1905, p. 4.
29. *Ibid.*, October 31, 1905, p. 4.
30. November 18, 1905, p. 13.
31. *Times Democrat* (New Orleans), December 15, 1905, p. 9.
32. *Ibid.*, December 17, 1905, p. 10.
33. Charles Somerville, "Pulpit Denounces 'Clansman'—Dixon Defends It," December 22, 1905.
34. *New York Tribune,* January 18, 1906, p. 7.
35. *New York Tribune,* January 9, 1906, p. 12.
36. *New York Dramatic Mirror,* CV (January 20, 1906), 3.
37. *New York Press,* January 29, 1906.
38. *Scranton* (Pa.) *Truth,* April 10, 1906.
39. Da Ponte, *op. cit.*, p. 23.
40. March 13, 1906, p. 12.
41. Quoted in "Southern Horizons," p. 411.
42. *Ibid.*, p. 417.
43. *Ibid.*
44. *Ibid.*
45. *Ibid.*
46. *J. Johnson; or, "The Unknown Man": An Answer to Mr. Thos. Dixon's "Sins of the Fathers"* [sic] (De Land, Fla.: The E. O. Painter Printing Co., 1915).
47. Saint Louis: The Saint Louis Argus Publishing Co.
48. "Southern Horizons," p. 450.
49. "American Backgrounds for Fiction," *Bookman,* XXXVIII (January, 1914), 514.
50. *Evening Sun* (Baltimore), April 4, 1946.

Chapter VII

1. A portion of this chapter appeared as an article in the *North Carolina Historical Review,* October, 1962.
2. Iris Barry, *D. W. Griffith, American Film Master* (New York: Museum of Modern Art, 1940), p. 21.
3. Lewis Jacobs, *The Rise of the American Film: A Critical History* (New York: Harcourt, Brace & Co., 1939), p. 174.
4. "Southern Horizons: An Autobiography" (MS unfinished), p. 423.

5. *Ibid.*, p. 425.
6. *Ibid.*, p. 426.
7. Milton MacKaye, "The Birth of a Nation," *Scribner's Magazine*, CII (November, 1937), 69.
8. "Southern Horizons," pp. 431–32.
9. *Ibid.*, p. 432.
10. *Ibid.*, p. 433.
11. *Ibid.*
12. *Ibid.*, p. 434.
13. *Ibid.*, p. 436.
14. *Ibid.*, p. 441.
15. Francis Hackett, "Brotherly Love," *New Republic*, II (March 20, 1915), 185.
16. *New York Times*, March 31, 1915, p. 9.
17. *Ibid.*, April 15, 1915, p. 1.
18. Quoted in Frank Veale, "Did 'The Birth of a Nation' Top 'Gone With the Wind' in Profits?" *Atlanta Times*, January 9, 1964.
19. Quoted in " 'The Birth of a Nation' is Filmed by Griffith," *Life*, VIII (January 15, 1940), 41.
20. "Southern Horizons," p. 449.
21. *Ibid.*
22. *Ibid.*, pp. 456–57.
23. MacKaye, *op. cit.*, p. 42.
24. *Ibid.*
25. *Ibid.*
26. There is considerable difference of opinion as to whether "Gone With the Wind," "The Birth of a Nation," or "The Sound of Music" has earned the highest profits in the film industry. The later history of "The Birth of a Nation" is uncertain, but its foreign receipts may have made it gross more than did "Gone With the Wind" or "The Sound of Music." For discussions of this matter, see "*Quo Vadis*, Pardner?" *Time*, LXI (March 16, 1953), 108; Bosley Crowther, "Earnings of Movie at Issue," *Winston-Salem* (N.C.) *Journal*, January 4, 1965, p. 1; Frank Veale, *loc. cit.*; Charles Moore, "Biggest Money-Maker of All?" *Atlanta Constitution*, January 7, 1965, p. 20; and Sam F. Lucchese, " 'Gone With the Wind' Top Money Maker," *Atlanta Journal*, January 18, 1965, p. 12.
27. Quoted in MacKaye, *op. cit.*, p. 69.

Chapter VIII

1. "Southern Horizons: An Autobiography" (MS unfinished), p. 449.
2. Quoted in Ray Stannard Baker, *Woodrow Wilson—Life and*

Letters (Garden City, N.Y.: Doubleday, Doran & Co., Inc., 1937), VI, 14.

3. May 3, 1916, p. 11.

4. *New York Times,* June 7, 1916, p. 11.

5. *Boston Transcript,* June 14, 1916, p. 4. See also *New York Times,* June 18, 1916, Sec. 6, p. 253.

6. "Southern Horizons," p. 450.

7. The drama "Sins of the Father" has been previously discussed. "The Almighty Dollar," a play on the evils of avarice, was copyrighted April 23, 1912; and "Old Black Joe," the story of a slave, was first presented in New York City, February 17, 1912.

8. *The One Woman* (New York: Doubleday, Page & Co., 1903), p. 38.

9. Quoted in *New York Times,* September 26, 1922.

10. *Ibid.*

11. *A Man Called White* (New York: The Viking Press, 1948), p. 8.

12. *New York Times,* January 23, 1923, p. 23. See also August 5, 1924, p. 18.

13. One of Dixon's scenarios which did not reach the screen deserves notice because it appears to have been well suited for presentation. "The Torch: A Story of the Paranoiac Who Caused a Great War" is a rather detailed account of John Brown's campaign and his subsequent seizure of Harper's Ferry. Brown appears as a fanatic, a madman, who makes the most of his martyrdom before his execution at Charlestown, Virginia. Dixon places most of the blame on Brown for having touched off the "powder keg" that caused the Civil War. "The Torch," which was "written directly for the screen," might have made a popular motion picture, for later treatments of John Brown's career in literature and on the screen attest to the public's interest in the man.

14. "Southern Horizons," p. 377.

15. "To the Reader," in *The Flaming Sword* (Atlanta: Monarch Publishing Co., 1939), p. viii.

16. *Dixon on Ingersoll: Ten Discourses Delivered in Association Hall, New York* (New York: J. B. Alden, 1892), p. 31.

17. *New York Times,* May 15, 1924, p. 21.

18. "Southern Horizons," p. 462.

19. *Ibid.,* p. 463.

20. Quoted in *New York Times,* December 31, 1894, p. 9.

21. *Living Problems in Religion and Social Science* (New York: C. T. Dillingham, 1889), p. 98.

22. Quoted in Charles H. Dickey, "Thomas Dixon Born in Small

N.C. Farm House," *Charlotte* (N.C.) *Observer,* May 6, 1934, Sec. 3, p. 4.

23. "Southern Horizons," p. 464.

24. *Ibid.*, p. 460.

25. *Ibid.*, pp. 450–51. Written in 1935.

26. Quoted in *Library of Southern Literature* (Atlanta: The Martin & Hoyt Co., 1909), IV, 1407.

Chapter IX

1. *State of North Carolina Public Laws and Resolutions, Session of 1921* (Raleigh, N.C.: Mitchell Printing Co., 1921), p. 554.

2. "Frank Dixon: A Sketch by His Brother," a clipping from a North Carolina newspaper, no title, n.d.

3. *Ibid.*

4. George W. McCoy, "A. C. Dixon, Noted Minister, Served Baptist Church Here," *Asheville* (N.C.) *Citizen-Times,* January 7, 1951, Sec. B, p. 5. Quoted from an obituary of A. C. Dixon in the Baltimore *Evening Sun,* n.d.

5. Charles H. Dickey, "Thomas Dixon Born in Small N.C. Farm House," *Charlotte* (N.C.) *Observer,* May 6, 1934, Sec. 3, p. 4.

6. *News and Observer* (Raleigh, N.C.), July 18, 1925.

7. *Wildacres: In the Land of the Sky* (Little Switzerland, N.C.: The Mount Mitchell Association of Arts and Sciences, 1926), pp. 25, 28.

8. "Southern Horizons: An Autobiography" (MS unfinished), p. 468.

9. (New York, Horace Liveright), p. 288.

10. *Ibid.*, pp. 305–6.

11. *New York Herald Tribune Books,* IX (June 9, 1929), 14.

12. *New York Times,* October 13, 1929, p. 27.

13. "The Sun Virgin," *Times Literary Supplement* (London), November 7, 1929, p. 900.

14. Quoted in *New York Times,* April 30, 1932, p. 14.

15. New York: The Churchill Co., 1932.

16. From a typescript of the speech.

17. Quoted in "This Country of Ours," a pamphlet advertising Dixon's tour, n.d.

18. *Ibid.*, as quoted from "Rotary Rays," Cincinnati.

19. *Ibid.*

20. Dickey, *loc. cit.* Dixon at first thought of entitling the autobiography "The Story of a Minister's Son, dedicated to the black sheep of the flock, by one of them." The unpublished manuscript,

left at his death, finally received the title "Southern Horizons: An Autobiography."

21. *News and Observer* (Raleigh, N.C.), May 2, 1937, p. 1.

22. *Dixon's Sermons, Delivered in the Grand Opera House, 1898–1899* (New York: F. L. Bussey & Co., 1899), p. 9. This sermon was delivered on Sunday, May 15, 1898.

23. "Southern Horizons," p. 453.

24. *News and Observer* (Raleigh, N.C.), October 13, 1936, p. 2.

25. *Ibid.*, May 2, 1937, p. 2.

26. Herbert Peele, "The Last of the Romans," *Daily Advance* (Elizabeth City, N.C.), n.d.

27. "Southern Horizons," pp. 465–66.

28. Quoted in *News and Observer* (Raleigh, N.C.), May 2, 1937, p. 1.

29. *Ibid.*, October 22, 1937, p. 8.

30. *The Flaming Sword* (Atlanta: Monarch Publishing Co., 1939).

31. Frank Smethurst, "America in Black, White and Red," *News and Observer* (Raleigh, N.C.), August 6, 1939, p. 5.

32. *New York Times*, August 20, 1939, p. 18.

33. *Time*, XLVII (April 15, 1946), 74.

34. *Fayetteville* (N.C.) *Observer*, April 4, 1946.

35. *Winston-Salem* (N.C.) *Journal*, April 4, 1946, p. 6. For some other interesting obituaries, see *Evening Sun* (Baltimore), April 4, 1946; *New York Times*, April 4, 1946, p. 25; *Newsweek*, XXVII (April 15, 1946), 58; *News and Observer* (Raleigh, N.C.), April 4, 1946; "Thomas Dixon: Obituary," *Wilson Library Bulletin*, XX (June, 1946), 696.

36. Quoted in the *Durham* (N.C.) *Morning Herald*, April 4, 1946.

37. *Ibid.*

38. *News and Observer* (Raleigh, N.C.), October 13, 1936.

39. A communication from Clara Dixon Richardson, October 5, 1953.

Bibliography

ADAMS, HERBERT B. "Bibliography of Thomas Dixon." Unpublished bibliography, Johns Hopkins University Library, 1902.

ADAMS, JAMES TRUSLOW. *The Epic of America.* New York: Triangle Books, 1941.

Addresses, Letters and Papers of Clyde Roark Hoey, Governor of North Carolina 1937–1941, ed. David Leroy Corbitt. Raleigh: Council of State, State of North Carolina, 1944.

ALLAN, MANSFIELD. "Thomas Dixon's 'The Leopard's Spots,'" *Bookman,* XV (July, 1902), 472–74.

ALLEN, JAMES STEWART. *Reconstruction: The Battle for Democracy.* New York: International Publishers, 1937.

"Arrival of a New Stage in the Art of the Movies," *Current Opinion,* LVIII (April, 1915), 251.

ASHBY, WILLIAM M. *Redder Blood.* New York: The Cosmopolitan Press, 1915.

Asheville (N.C.) *Citizen-Times,* October 12, 1952.

Atlanta Constitution, October 16, 1905.

Atlanta Constitution, October 31, 1905.

Atlanta Constitution, January 1, 1954.

Atlanta Journal, April 20, 1902.

BAKER, RAY STANNARD. *Woodrow Wilson—Life and Letters.* 8 vols. Garden City, N.Y.: Doubleday, Doran & Co., Inc., 1937.

BALDWIN, C. C. *Men Who Make Our Novels.* New York: Moffat, Yard & Co., 1919.

Baltimore Baptist, November 10, 1887.

Baltimore Baptist, November 17, 1887.

BARDÈCHE, MAURICE, and BRASILLACH, ROBERT. *The History of Motion Pictures.* Translated and edited by Iris Barry. New York: W. W. Norton Co. and The Museum of Modern Art, 1938.

BARRY, IRIS. *D. W. Griffith, American Film Master.* New York: The Museum of Modern Art, 1940.

BEALE, HOWARD K. *The Critical Year: A Study of Andrew Johnson and Reconstruction.* New York: Harcourt, Brace & Co., 1930.

———. "On Rewriting Reconstruction History," *American Historical Review*, XLV (July, 1940), 807–27.

BELL, LILIAN LIDA. "A Collarless Novelist," *Saturday Evening Post*, CLXXIV (May 3, 1902), 17.

———. "Girl in Love," *Harper's Bazaar*, XXXV (November, 1901), 603–8.

———. "The Leopard's Spots," *Saturday Evening Post*, CLXXIV (April 12, 1902), 15.

"Birth of a Nation," *Outlook*, CLVII (January 7, 1931), 32.

" 'The Birth of a Nation' is Filmed by Griffith," *Life*, VIII (January 15, 1940), 40–41, 43.

BLACK, MRS. ERNEST D. An interview, September 28, 1951.

———. A personal communication, October 15, 1951.

"The Black Hood," *Boston Transcript*, June 25, 1924.

"The Black Hood," *Literary Review*, July 5, 1924, p. 867.

"The Black Hood," *New York World*, June 15, 1924.

"The Black Hood," *Times Literary Supplement* (London), August 14, 1924, p. 500.

Book Buyer, XXIV (April, 1902), 195.

The Booker T. Washington Collection. Library of Congress, Washington, D.C.

Bookman, LXVI (October, 1927), 192.

Boston Herald, April 14, 1889.

Boston Journal, June 17, 1902.

Boston Transcript, June 14, 1916.

Boston Transcript, May 11, 1929.

BOWERS, CLAUDE G. *The Tragic Era: The Revolution after Lincoln.* Cambridge, Mass.: Houghton Mifflin Co., 1929.

BOYD, MRS. DOUGLAS. Interviews, December 16, 1951; April 26, 1952.

BRAGG, F. C. A personal communication, August 20, 1953.

———. An interview, August 23, 1953.

BRAWLEY, BENJAMIN. "The Negro Literary Renaissance," *Southern Workman,* LVI (April, 1927), 177–84.

———. *A Short History of the American Negro.* New York: Macmillan Co., 1950.

———. *A Social History of the American Negro.* New York: Macmillan Co., 1921.

Charlotte (N.C.) *Daily Observer,* September 7, 1902.

Charlotte (N.C.) *Daily Observer,* May 7, 1905.

Charlotte (N.C.) *Observer,* November 28, 1926.

Charlotte (N.C.) *Observer,* October 2, 1938.

CHESNUTT, CHARLES W. "Post-Bellum–Pre-Harlem," *Breaking Into Print,* ed. Elmer Adler. New York: Simon & Schuster, 1937.

"Chronicle and Comment." *Bookman,* XX (February, 1905), 498–500.

Cincinnati Enquirer, January 28, 1906.

"Civil War in Film." *Literary Digest,* L (March 20, 1915), 608–9.

"The Clansman." New York: The American News Co., 1905.

"The Clansman" in "Old Books," a review by Clifford Dowdey, *Georgia Review,* IX (Fall, 1955), 341–43.

Cleveland Star (Shelby, N.C.), June 2, 1936.

Complete Prose Works of Walt Whitman. New York: D. Appleton & Co., 1908.

COOK, RAYMOND A. "The Literary Principles of Thomas Dixon," *The Georgia Review,* XIII (Spring, 1959), 97–102.

———. "The Man Behind 'The Birth of a Nation,' " *The North Carolina Historical Review,* XXXIX (October, 1962), 519–40.

———. "The Versatile Career of Thomas Dixon," *Emory University Quarterly,* XI (June, 1955), 103–12.

COULTER, E. MERTON. *The South During Reconstruction 1865–1877.* (*A History of the South,* Vol. VIII.) Baton Rouge, La.: Louisiana State University Press, 1947.

COZART, W. FORREST. *The Chosen People.* Boston: The Christopher Publishing House, 1924.

CROWTHER, BOSLEY. "Earnings of Movie at Issue," *Winston-Salem* (N.C.) *Journal,* January 4, 1965.

CUPPY, WILL. "The Love Complex," *New York Times,* July 5, 1925, p. 12.

Current Biography, ed. Anna Rothe *et al.* New York: The H. W. Wilson Co., 1909.

Current History, IL (September, 1938), 45, 47.

DA PONTE, DURANT. "The Greatest Play of the South," *Tennessee Studies in Literature* (Knoxville: University of Tennessee), II (1957), 15–24.

DAVIS, CHESTER. "Thomas Dixon, Jr.: A Genius at Both Success and Failure," *Journal and Sentinel* (Winston-Salem, N.C.), December 6, 1964.

DICKEY, CHARLES H. "Thomas Dixon Born in Small N.C. Farm House," *Charlotte* (N.C.) *Observer*, May 6, 1934.

DIXON, AMZI CLARENCE. *Evangelism Old and New: God's Search for Man in All Ages.* New York: American Tract Society, 1905.

——. "Lights and Shadows of American Life," *New York Times*, November 5, 1898.

——. *Sidney Lanier, the Johns Hopkins Poet: An Appreciation.* Baltimore, Md.: 1925.

——. "Morals and Methods of Robert G. Ingersoll," *New York Times*, April 23, 1894.

——. "The Story of a Worthy Life," *Biblical Recorder* (June 9, 1909), pp. 1–5.

DIXON, HELEN C. A. *A. C. Dixon: A Romance of Preaching.* New York: G. P. Putnam's Sons, 1931.

DIXON, MADELYN DONOVAN. Interviews, November 14, 1951; December 16, 1952; June 14, 1953; June 8–9, 1966.

——. Personal communications, November 9, 1951; May 14, 1952; December 13, 1952; March 9, 1953; August 31, 1953; September 2, 1953; November 27, 1953; February 15, 1954; May 2, 1964.

DIXON, THOMAS. "The Almighty Dollar," a play, 1912.

——. "American Backgrounds for Fiction," *Bookman*, XXXVIII (January, 1914), 511–14.

——. "The Birth of a Nation," scenario for the motion picture, 1915.

——. *The Black Hood.* New York: Grosset & Dunlap, 1924.

——. "Booker T. Washington and the Negro," *Saturday Evening Post*, CLXXVIII (August 19, 1905), 1–2.

——. Letters to Henry Cathcart, October 29, 1901; October 30, 1902; July 17, 1903; February 20, 1905.

——. "The Clansman: An American Drama in Four Acts," typescript copy, 1905.

——. *The Clansman: An Historical Romance of the Ku Klux Klan.* New York: Doubleday, Page & Co., 1905.

———. *Companions.* New York: Otis Publishing Corp., 1931.
———. "Comrades," a motion picture, first entitled "Bolshevism on Trial," 1919.
———. *Comrades: A Story of Social Adventure in California.* New York: Doubleday, Page & Co., 1909.
———. "Dangers of the Reform Administration," *New York Times,* January 21, 1895.
———. A letter to Louise Dixon, postmarked September 8, n.d.
———. *Dixon on Ingersoll: Ten Discourses Delivered in Association Hall, New York.* New York: J. B. Alden, 1892.
———. *Dixon's Sermons, Delivered in the Grand Opera House, 1898–1899.* New York: F. L. Bussey & Co., 1899.
———. *A Dreamer in Portugal: The Story of Bernarr Macfadden's Mission to Continental Europe.* New York: Covici, Friede, 1934.
———. "The Drift Toward Anarchy," *New York Times,* October 5, 1896, p. 5.
———. *The Failure of Protestantism in New York and its Causes.* New York: V. O. A. Strauss, 1896.
———. "The Fall of a Nation," a motion picture, 1917.
———. *The Fall of a Nation: A Sequel to The Birth of a Nation.* New York: D. Appleton & Co., 1916.
———. *The Flaming Sword.* Atlanta: Monarch Publishing Co., 1939.
———. *The Foolish Virgin: A Romance of Today.* New York: D. Appleton & Co., 1915.
———. "Frank Dixon: A Sketch by His Brother," a clipping from a North Carolina newspaper, n.p., n.d.
———. "From the Horrors of City Life," *World's Work,* IV (October, 1902), 2603–11.
———. *The Hope of the World: A Story of the Coming War.* New York: The author, 1925.
———. *The Leopard's Spots: A Romance of the White Man's Burden —1865–1900.* New York: Doubleday, Page & Co., 1903.
———. *The Life Worth Living: A Personal Experience.* New York: Doubleday, Page & Co., 1914.
———. *Living Problems in Religion and Social Science.* New York: C. T. Dillingham, 1889.
———. *The Love Complex.* New York: Boni & Liveright, 1925.
———. *The Man in Gray: A Romance of North and South.* New York: D. Appleton & Co., 1921.
———. *A Man of the People: A Drama of Abraham Lincoln.* New York: D. Appleton & Co., 1920.
———. "The Mark of the Beast," a motion picture, 1923.

——. Communications to Harry F. Moore, dated April 24, 1938; October (–), 1941.

——. "The Moral Import of the News," a radio broadcast over station WJZ, New York, by invitation of the National Broadcasting Company, October 2, 1933.

——. "The Negro and the South," *Christian Union,* XLIII (May 22, 1890), 39.

——. "Old Black Joe," a play, 1912.

——. "The One Woman," *Independent,* LVII (November 7, 1904), 1149.

——. *The One Woman: A Drama.* New York: Munn & Co., 1906.

——. "The One Woman," a motion picture, 1918.

——. *The One Woman: A Story of Modern Utopia.* New York: Doubleday, Page & Co., 1903.

——. *Political Equality.* New York: The author, n.d.

——. "The Red Dawn: A Drama of Revolution," typescript copy, 1919.

——. "A Reply to [Howard] Scott's Speech on Technocracy," a speech delivered before the Kappa Alpha Fraternity at the Hotel Shelton, New York City, January 19, 1933, in celebration of the birthday of Robert E. Lee.

——. *The Root of Evil: A Novel.* Garden City, N.Y.: Doubleday, Page & Co., 1911.

——. "Sins of the Father: A Drama," 1910.

——. *The Sins of the Father: A Romance of the South.* New York: D. Appleton & Co., 1912.

——. *The Southerner: A Romance of the Real Lincoln.* New York: Grosset & Dunlap, 1913.

——. "Southern Horizons: An Autobiography." Unpublished manuscript, unfinished.

——. *The Sun Virgin.* New York: Horace Liveright, 1929.

——. "The Torch: A Story of the Paranoiac Who Caused a Great War," a motion picture scenario. New York: The author, 1927.

——. "The Traitor," a play, 1908.

——. *The Traitor: A Story of the Fall of the Invisible Empire.* New York: Doubleday, Page & Co,. 1907.

——. *The Victim: A Romance of the Real Jefferson Davis.* New York: Grosset & Dunlap, 1914.

——. *The Way of a Man: A Story of the New Woman.* New York: D. Appleton & Co., 1919.

——. *What is Religion? An Outline of Vital Ritualism.* New York: The Scott Publishing Co., 1891.

———. *Wildacres: In the Land of the Sky*. Little Switzerland, N.C.: The Mount Mitchell Association of Arts and Sciences, 1926.

———. "Young Men of New York," *Harper's Weekly*, XXXV (August 29, 1891), 652.

DIXON, THOMAS, and DAUGHERTY, HARRY M. *The Inside Story of the Harding Tragedy*. New York: The Churchill Co., 1932.

DIXON, THOMAS, and POLLOCK, CHANNING. A contract for collaborating in the writing of a drama based upon Thomas Dixon's novel *The Traitor*, November 18, 1902.

DIXON, THOMAS, and SCHENCK, JOSEPH M. A contract to sell the motion picture rights of Thomas Dixon's novel *The Way of a Man*, September 12, 1919.

DREER, HERMAN. *The Immediate Jewel of His Soul*. Saint Louis: The Saint Louis Argus Publishing Co., 1919.

DU BOIS, W. E. BURGHARDT. *Black Reconstruction*. New York: Harcourt, Brace & Co., 1935.

———. *The Quest of the Silver Fleece*. Chicago: A. C. McClurg & Co., 1911.

———. *The Souls of Black Folk*. Chicago: A. C. McClurg & Co., 1918.

Durham (N.C.) *Morning Herald*, April 4, 1946.

EDGAR, PELHAM. *The Art of the Novel*. New York: The Macmillan Co., 1933.

Evening Mail (New York), January 23, 1906.

Evening Post (New York), June 20, 1905.

Evening Sun (Baltimore), April 4, 1946.

Evening Telegram (New York), January 4, 1892.

Evening Telegram (New York), January 5, 1892.

Evening Telegram (New York), January 22, 1906.

Examiner (New York), 1889, n.d.

Examiner (New York), January 21, 1889.

Experiment in the Film, ed. Roger Manvell. London: The Grey Walls Press Ltd., 1949.

"The Fall of a Nation," *Review of Reviews*, LIV (July, 1916), 125.

Fayetteville (N.C.) *Observer*, April 4, 1946.

"Films and Births and Censorship," *Survey*, XXXIV (April 3, 1915), 4–5.

FLEMING, SARAH LEE BROWN. *Hope's Highway*. New York: The Neale Publishing Co., 1918.

FORD, CHARLES E., and BRENNAN, GEORGE H. A contract to consolidate the Kinemacolor Company and the Southern Amusement Company for the purpose of producing Thomas Dixon's *The Clansman* in color, n.d.

GLADDEN, G. "The One Woman," *Current Literature*, XXXVI (April, 1903), 562–63.

"A Glance at the New Novels," *American Monthly Review of Reviews*, XXVIII (November, 1903), 634.

GLOSTER, HUGH M. *Negro Voices in American Fiction*. Chapel Hill, N.C.: University of North Carolina Press, 1948.

GRANT, J. W. *Out of the Darkness; or, Diabolism and Destiny*. Nashville, Tenn.: National Baptist Publishing Board, 1909.

GRIGGS, SUTTON E. *The Hindered Hand; or, The Reign of the Repressionist*. 3d ed., rev. Nashville, Tenn.: The Orion Publishing Co., 1905.

HACKETT, FRANCIS. "Brotherly Love," *New Republic*, II (March 20, 1915), 185.

HALSEY, FRANCIS W. "Some Books to Read this Summer," *Review of Reviews*, XXV (June, 1902), 700–7.

HAMILTON, J. S. "Putting a New Move in the Movies," *Everybody's*, XXXII (June, 1915), 677–82.

"Hamlet in a Greatcoat," *Time*, LXI (March 2, 1953), 94–96.

HAMRICK, FOREST. "Thomas Dixon, Jr.," *University of North Carolina Magazine*, LII (February, 1922), 22–23.

HARKINS, E. F. *Little Pilgrimages Among the Men Who Have Written Famous Books*. 2d ser. Boston: L. C. Page & Co., 1903.

HARRIS, MAX FRANK. "The Ideas of Thomas Dixon on Race Relations." Unpublished master's thesis, University of North Carolina, 1948.

HART, JAMES D. *The Popular Book: A History of America's Literary Taste*. New York: Oxford University Press, 1950.

HENRY, ROBERT SELPH. *The Story of Reconstruction*. New York: The Bobbs-Merrill Co., 1938.

HORN, STANLEY F. *Invisible Empire: The Story of the Ku Klux Klan, 1866–1871*. Boston: Houghton Mifflin Co., 1939.

JACOBS, LEWIS. *The Rise of the American Film: A Critical History*. New York: Harcourt, Brace & Co., 1939.

JOHNSON, JAMES WELDON. "The Dilemma of the Negro Author," *American Mercury*, XV (December, 1928), 477–81.

JOHNSON, W. H. "The Leopard's Spots," *Dial*, XXXIV (May 1, 1903), 301–2.

JONES, MAMIE. "Life in Cleveland County's Early Days," *Cleveland Star* (Shelby, N.C.), July 9, 1934.

JONES, YORKE. *The Climbers: A Story of Sun-Kissed Sweethearts*. Chicago: Glad Tidings Publishing Co., 1912.

Knoxville Journal and Tribune, October 20, 1905.

Knoxville Journal and Tribune, October 21, 1905.
Knoxville Journal and Tribune, October 31, 1905.
Knoxville Journal and Tribune, November 5, 1905.
Knoxville Journal and Tribune, November 9, 1905.
Knoxville Journal and Tribune, November 14, 1905.
LANDIS, CHARLES ISRAEL. *Thaddeus Stevens, A Letter Written to the Daily New Era.* Lancaster, Pa.: The New Era Printing Co., 1916.
"Last Dissolve," *Time,* LIII (August 2, 1948), 72.
LEISY, ERNEST E. *The American Historical Novel.* Norman, Okla.: University of Oklahoma Press, 1950.
"The Leopard's Spots," *Dial,* XXXII (June 1, 1902), 389.
"The Leopard's Spots," *Independent,* LIV (June, 1902), 1548–49.
Library of Southern Literature, ed. Edwin Anderson Alderman and Joel Chandler Harris, 15 vols. Atlanta: The Martin & Hoyt Co., 1909.
Literary Review, August 15, 1925.
Los Angeles Evening Herald and Express, January 22, 1947.
"The Love Complex," *Boston Transcript,* July 8, 1925.
"The Love Complex," *Literary Digest International Book Review,* August, 1925, p. 617.
"The Love Complex," *New York Tribune,* July 26, 1905.
"The Love Complex," *Saturday Review of Literature,* II (August 29, 1925), 90.
LUCCHESE, SAM F. " 'Gone With the Wind' Top Money Maker," *Atlanta Journal,* January 18, 1965.
LUCCOCK, HALFORD E. *Contemporary American Literature and Religion.* Chicago: Willett, Clark & Co., 1934.
LUTZ, SISTER M. ANGELITA. "Thomas Dixon's Contribution to American Literature, with Special Reference to the Original Manuscript of *The Root of Evil.*" Unpublished master's thesis, Saint Bonaventure College, 1948.
MCCOY, GEORGE W. "A. C. Dixon, Noted Minister, Served Baptist Church Here," *Asheville* (N.C.) *Citizen-Times,* January 7, 1951.
MCGUIRE, W. D., JR. "Censoring Motion Pictures," *New Republic,* II (April 10, 1915), 262–63.
MCNEILL, JOHN CHARLES. "Thomas Dixon, Jr.," in Samuel A'Court Ashe, *Biographical History of North Carolina.* Vol. VII. Greensboro, N.C.: Charles L. Van Noppen, 1917.
MACKAYE, MILTON. "The Birth of a Nation," *Scribner's Magazine,* CII (November, 1937), 40–46, 69.
MARSH, EDWARD CLARK. "Thomas Dixon's 'The One Woman,' " *Bookman,* XVIII (October, 1903), 161–62.

MAURICE, ARTHUR B. "Makers of Modern American Fiction," *Mentor,* VI (September 1, 1918), 1–11.

MICHEAUX, OSCAR. *The Conquest: A Story of a Negro Pioneer.* Lincoln, Neb.: The Woodruff Press, 1913.

MILLER, KELLY. *As to the Leopard's Spots: An Open Letter to Thomas Dixon, Jr.* Washington, D.C.: Kelly Miller, 1905.

MILTON, GEORGE FORT. *The Age of Hate.* New York: Coward-McCann, Inc., 1930.

Montgomery Advertiser, October 29, 1905.

Montgomery Advertiser, November 4, 1905.

Montgomery Advertiser, November 5, 1905.

MOORE, CHARLES. "Biggest Money-Maker of All?" *Atlanta Constitution,* January 7, 1965.

MOORE, HARRY F. A personal communication, October 16, 1967.

MOTT, FRANK LUTHER. *Golden Multitudes: The Story of Best Sellers in the United States.* New York: The Macmillan Co., 1947.

NANNES, CASPAR HAROLD. *Politics in the American Drama as Revealed on the New York Stage, 1890–1945.* Philadelphia: University of Pennsylvania Press, 1950.

Nashville Banner, November 18, 1905.

The National Cyclopaedia of American Biography, edited by distinguished biographers. 37 vols. with supplement. New York: James T. White & Co., 1906.

"Negroes Protest Against 'The Clansman,' " *Oakland* (Calif.) *Tribune,* January 6, 1906.

NELSON, JOHN HERBERT. *The Negro Character in American Literature.* Lawrence, Kan.: Department of Journalism Press, 1926.

New York Daily News, December 31, 1905.

New York Dramatic Mirror, CV (January 20, 1906), 3.

New York Evening Journal, December 21, 1905.

New York Herald Tribune Books, IX (June 9, 1929), 14.

New York Herald Tribune Books, XI (June 14, 1931), 19.

New York Herald Tribune Books, May 12, 1939.

New York Herald Tribune Books, September 17, 1939.

New York Press, January 29, 1906.

New York Times, December 31, 1894.

New York Times, February 25, 1895.

New York Times, March 4, 1895.

New York Times, March 11, 1895.

New York Times, March 18, 1895.

New York Times, April 15, 1895.

New York Times, July 15, 1895.

New York Times, October 29, 1895.

New York Times, September 7, 1896.
New York Times, September 21, 1896.
New York Times, December 6, 1897.
New York Times, January 16, 1899.
New York Times, August 9, 1902.
New York Times, June 9, 1903.
New York Times, August 29, 1903.
New York Times, January 9, 1906.
New York Times, March 4, 1915.
New York Times, March 7, 1915.
New York Times, March 21, 1915.
New York Times, March 31, 1915.
New York Times, April 2, 1915.
New York Times, April 15, 1915.
New York Times, April 18, 1915.
New York Times, June 6, 1915.
New York Times, August 15, 1915.
New York Times, September 1, 1915.
New York Times, September 28, 1915.
New York Times, January 29, 1916.
New York Times, May 3, 1916.
New York Times, June 7, 1916.
New York Times, June 18, 1916.
New York Times, September 26, 1916.
New York Times, September 28, 1916.
New York Times, September 30, 1916.
New York Times, April 25, 1921.
New York Times, May 8, 1921.
New York Times, February 22, 1922.
New York Times, September 22, 1922.
New York Times, January 23, 1923.
New York Times, February 5, 1923.
New York Times, June 2, 1923.
New York Times, May 15, 1924.
New York Times, June 22, 1924.
New York Times, August 5, 1924.
New York Times, February 25, 1928.
New York Times, July 16, 1928.
New York Times, October 13, 1929.
New York Times, February 11, 1931.
New York Times, January 1, 1932.
New York Times, January 28, 1932.
New York Times, April 30, 1932.

New York Times, January 20, 1933.
New York Times, November 13, 1933.
New York Times, April 17, 1934.
New York Times, August 2, 1934.
New York Times, January 30, 1936.
New York Times, February 2, 1936.
New York Times, September 9, 1936.
New York Times, May 2, 1937.
New York Times, August 20, 1939.
New York Times, November 13, 1939.
New York Times, April 4, 1946.
New York Tribune, January 9, 1906.
New York Tribune, January 18, 1906.
New York Tribune, June 29, 1924.
New York Tribune, July 26, 1925.
New York World, June 8, 1924.
News and Courier (Charleston, S.C.), October 18, 1905.
News and Courier (Charleston, S.C.), October 19, 1905.
News and Observer (Raleigh, N.C.), October 1, 1905.
News and Observer (Raleigh, N.C.), October 3, 1905.
News and Observer (Raleigh, N.C.), October 5, 1905.
News and Observer (Raleigh, N.C.), July 18, 1925.
News and Observer (Raleigh, N.C.), October 5, 1936.
News and Observer (Raleigh, N.C.), October 13, 1936.
News and Observer (Raleigh, N.C.), May 2, 1937.
News and Observer (Raleigh, N.C.), October 22, 1937.
News and Observer (Raleigh, N.C.), March 21, 1939.
News and Observer (Raleigh, N.C.), May 31, 1940.
News and Observer (Raleigh, N.C.), July 3, 1943.
News and Observer (Raleigh, N.C.), April 4, 1946.
Newsweek, XXVII (April 15, 1946), 58.
NORDAU, MAX. A letter to Thomas Dixon, dated June 10, 1902, Paris, France.
NORRIS, FRANK. *The Responsibilities of the Novelist*. New York: Doubleday, Page & Co., 1903.
OAKES, FRANCES. "Whitman and Dixon: A Strange Case of Borrowing," *Georgia Review*, XI (Fall, 1957), 333–40.
O'NEIL, EUGENE. Communications to Harry F. Moore, July 14, 1943; August 22, 1944.
PAGE, THOMAS NELSON. *Red Rock*. New York: Charles Scribner's Sons, 1898.
"Paris Suppresses an American Film," *Literary Digest*, LXXVIII (September 29, 1923), 28–29.

PATTEE, FRED. *A History of American Literature Since 1870*. New York: The Century Co., 1915.

PEELE, HERBERT. "The Last of the Romans," *Daily Advance* (Elizabeth City, N.C.), n.d.

PEIRCE, PAUL SKEELS. *The Freedmen's Bureau; A Chapter in the History of Reconstruction*. Iowa City, Iowa: The University, 1904.

The Person and Ministry of the Holy Spirit, ed. Amzi Clarence Dixon. Baltimore, Md.: Wharton, Barron & Co., 1890.

PETERS, T. K. An interview, December 14, 1956.

POTEAT, E. M. "Thomas Dixon, Junior," *The Wake Forest Student*, XXVIII (January, 1909), 382.

"Progressive Protest Against Anti-Negro Film," *Survey*, XXXIV (June 5, 1915), 209–10.

Public Ledger (Philadelphia), August 16, 1903.

QUINN, ARTHUR HOBSON. *American Fiction: An Historical and Critical Survey*. New York: D. Appleton-Century Co., 1936.

"*Quo Vadis*, Pardner?" *Time*, LXI (March 16, 1953), 108.

RICHARDSON, CLARA DIXON. The private papers of the A. C. Dixon family collection. Personal communications October 5, 1953; October 23, 1953; November 12, 1953; November 23, 1953; December 18, 1953; June 9, 1954; July 6, 1954; January 18, 1955; April 27, 1955.

ROE, E. P. *Barriers Burned Away*. New York: Dodd, Mead & Co., 1872.

———. *Opening a Chestnut Burr*. New York: Dodd, Mead & Co., 1874.

"Rotary Rays" (Cincinnati, Ohio), n.d.

Rotary Reminder (Cleveland, Ohio), n.d.

RUMBOLD, CHARLOTTE. "Against 'The Birth of a Nation,'" *New Republic*, III (June 5, 1915), 125.

RUTHERFORD, MILDRED LEWIS. *The South in History and Literature*. Atlanta: The Franklin-Turner Co., 1906.

Scranton (Pa.) *Truth*, April 10, 1906.

SELDES, GILBERT. *The Movies Come from America*. New York: Charles Scribner's Sons, 1937.

SHUMAN, EDWIN L. "In the Realm of Books," *Chicago Record-Herald*, March 15, 1902.

SMETHURST, FRANK. "America in Black, White and Red," *News and Observer* (Raleigh, N.C.), August 6, 1939.

SOMERVILLE, CHARLES. "Pulpit Denounces 'Clansman'—Dixon Defends It," *New York Evening Journal*, December 22, 1905.

Southern Amusement Company. A lease to Thomas Dixon to produce "The Traitor," June 27, 1913.

Springfield (Mass.) *Republican*, August 2, 1925.

Springfield (Mass.) *Republican,* May 26, 1929.

State of North Carolina Public Laws and Resolutions, Session of 1921. Raleigh, N.C.: Mitchell Printing Co., 1921, p. 554.

Sun (Baltimore), March 13, 1906.

"The Sun Virgin," *Times Literary Supplement* (London), November 7, 1929.

TAYLOR, CHARLES E. "Amzi Clarence Dixon," *The Wake Forest Student,* XXVIII (January, 1909), 389.

TAYLOR, DEEMS, *et al. A Pictorial History of the Movies.* New York: Simon & Schuster, 1943.

THACKER, MAY DIXON. A personal communication, February 14, 1953.

———. *The Strange Death of President Harding.* New York: Guild Publishing Corp., 1930.

"This Country of Ours," a bulletin advertising Dixon's speaking tour for the National Recovery Administration, n.d.

"Thomas Dixon," *Bookman,* XV (April, 1902), 114.

"Thomas Dixon: Obituary," *Wilson Library Bulletin,* XX (June, 1946), 696.

"Thomas Dixon," *Review of Reviews,* XXV (June, 1902), 702.

"Thomas Dixon Again Rides His Hobby," *Denver Daily News,* August 26, 1905.

"Thomas Dixon, Jr., Is Taken to Task," *Minneapolis Journal,* April 15, 1906.

THORP, MARGARET (FARRAND). *America at the Movies.* New Haven: Yale University Press, 1939.

Time, XLVII (April 15, 1946), 74.

Times Democrat (New Orleans), December 15, 1905.

Times Democrat (New Orleans), December 17, 1905.

Times-Dispatch (Richmond), September 23, 1905.

Times-Dispatch (Richmond), September 26, 1905.

Times-Dispatch (Richmond), March 13, 1906.

"To Answer Dixon in White Pulpit," *Morning Telegraph* (New York), February, 1906.

VALLEE, RUDY. A communication to Thomas Dixon, July 15, 1942.

VAN DOREN, CARL. *The American Novel 1789–1939.* New York: The Macmillan Co., 1940.

VEALE, FRANK. "Did 'The Birth of a Nation' Top 'Gone With the Wind' in Profits?" *Atlanta Times,* January 9, 1964.

VILLARD, OSWALD GARRISON. "The Race Problem," *Nation,* XCIX (December 24, 1914), 738–40.

Virginian-Pilot (Norfolk), September 23, 1905.

Virginian-Pilot (Norfolk), November 14, 1905.

WAGENKNECHT, EDWARD. *Cavalcade of the American Novel.* New York: Henry Holt & Co., 1952.

WALKER, THOMAS H. B. *J. Johnson; or, "The Unknown Man"; An Answer to Mr. Thos. Dixon's "Sins of the Fathers"* [sic]. De Land, Fla.: The E. O. Painter Printing Co., 1915.

WARING, ROBERT L. *As We See It.* Washington, D.C.: Press of C. F. Sudwarth, 1910.

WASHINGTON, BOOKER T. *Up from Slavery.* New York: Doubleday, Page & Co., 1901.

"The Watauga Club," *North Carolina Historical Review,* XVI (1939), 280–82.

WATSON, THOMAS E. "Is the Black Man Superior to the White?" *Augusta* (Ga.) *Herald,* June 18, 1905.

WEATHERS, LEE B. *Thomas Dixon: North Carolina's Most Colorful Character of His Generation; Lawyer—Minister—Author—Orator—Playwright—Actor.* Shelby, N.C.: The author, 1949.

Weiss und Schwarz. Ein Roman aus der Geschichte der Vereinigten Staaten von Nord-Amerika (1865–1900) *von Thomas Dixon.* Übertragen von Oscar H. Trenkner. München: F. Rothbarth, 1904.

WHINERY, CHARLES C. "The Clansman," *Current Literature,* XXXVIII (February, 1905), 153–60.

WHITE, WALTER. *A Man Called White.* New York: The Viking Press, 1948.

Wilmington (N.C.) *Morning Star,* August 7, 1907.

Wilmington (N.C.) *Morning Star,* April 4, 1946.

Winston-Salem (N.C.) *Journal,* April 4, 1946.

WOMBLE, W. T., *et al.* A letter to Thomas Dixon, postmarked April 10, 1887.

WRIGHT, HAROLD BELL. *The Shepherd of the Hills.* Chicago: Book Supply Co., 1907.